THE UNPUBLISHED POETRY OF
CHARLES WESLEY

Volume II

HYMNS AND POEMS ON HOLY SCRIPTURE

THE UNPUBLISHED POETRY OF
CHARLES WESLEY

Volume II

HYMNS AND POEMS ON HOLY SCRIPTURE

Edited by

S T Kimbrough, Jr.
and
Oliver A. Beckerlegge

KINGSWOOD BOOKS
An Imprint of Abingdon Press
Nashville, Tennessee

THE UNPUBLISHED POETRY OF CHARLES WESLEY

VOLUME II

HYMNS AND POEMS ON HOLY SCRIPTURE

Copyright © 1990 by Abingdon Press

Library of Congress Cataloging-in-Publication Data

WESLEY, CHARLES, 1707–1788.
    The unpublished poetry of Charles Wesley / edited by S T Kimbrough, Jr.,
and Oliver A. Beckerlegge.
        p.   cm.
    Vol. 2 has also special title: Hymns and poems on Holy Scripture.
    Includes bibliographical references and indexes.
    (pbk. : v. 1 : alk. paper)
    1. Christian poetry, English. I. Kimbrough, S T, Jr., 1936 –
II. Beckerlegge, Oliver A., 1913 – . III. Title.
PR3763.W4A6   1988   821'.6   88-19165

ISBN 0-687-43311-8

Printed in the United States of America
on acid-free paper

TABLE OF CONTENTS

PREFACE

From the earliest period of Charles Wesley's poetical publication (*Hymns and Sacred Poems*, 1739) he developed a style of writing lyrics based upon biblical passages. Sometimes his verse is expositional and exegetical in nature. At other times it reflects upon one or more themes or facets of a passage. Often his poems are filled with language, imagery, metaphors, similes, names of places and people, phrases, and concepts taken directly from scripture. There are instances also where a biblical passage gives birth to an idea and he writes a lyric which may have little or no direct relationship to the passage cited. Unquestionably there are multiple examples where his artistic "turn of a phrase" gets to the heart of what the biblical text is saying without any of the advantages of text critical methods or hermeneutical approaches developed after his death. Of course, his knowledge of Hebrew, Greek, and Latin served his interpretative lyricism superbly.[1]

Charles Wesley's largest single collection of biblical poetry was published without the editorial assistance of his brother John in 1762 under the title, *Short Hymns on Select Passages of the Holy Scriptures* (two volumes). This work contains 2,349 hymns and poems based on passages from every book of the Bible. Perhaps a dozen or so of these lyrics have made their way into hymn books with a sustained presence up to the present, e.g. "A charge to keep I have," "Captain of Israel's Host," and "O Thou who camest from above."

The poems in volume II of *The Unpublished Poetry of Charles Wesley* are taken from manuscripts based on the four gospels, the Book of Acts, MS Scriptural Hymns, and a few other manuscript sources.[2] Most of the material postdates the two volumes of 1762. Fourteen of the MS poems published here appeared in Frank Baker's *Representative Verse of Charles Wesley* (1962) and are indicated in the footnotes. Also included are Wesley poems based on biblical passages which were published in the *Arminian Magazine* but did not appear in Osborn's collection.[3]

---

1. See S T Kimbrough, Jr., "Charles Wesley as a Biblical Interpreter," *Methodist History* XXVI (1988) pp. 139–53.
2. See the Table of Manuscript Sources, p. 13.
3. See volume I of *The Unpublished Poetry of Charles Wesley* (Nashville: Abingdon, 1988), "Foreword," p. 12, and "Preface," pp. 17–18, 21) for a full explanation of the selection process for the poetry in all three volumes of this series.

One sees clearly in the poems of this volume how Wesley continued to appropriate and rework poetry he had written earlier or already published. The poem on John 11:43 (p.247) is an expansion of an earlier one in *Short Hymns* on the same biblical passage. One finds also the use of four lines from a poem published in *Hymns and Sacred Poems* (1742).[4] Occasionally he also used phrases from earlier poems, as in the case of the verses on John 19:26–7 (p.274) and John 19:28 (p. 275).

In one instance a poem based on John 19:30 (p. 275), "'Tis finished, the Messiah dies" is found only in part in *Short Hymns* and in part in MS John. It appears in its fullest form of ten verses only in MS Thirty, which includes verses found neither in MS John nor in *Short Hymns*. All ten verses appear here together for the first time.

George Osborn's publication in volumes IX–XIII of *The Poetical Works of John and Charles Wesley* (1868–72) of the poetry found in *Short Hymns* along with many hitherto in his lifetime unpublished poems from Charles Wesley manuscripts which are also the basis for this volume has been both helpful and confusing: helpful in that he made some unpublished material accessible for the first time, but confusing because he apparently had no developed method for the selection of material. He randomly published portions of poems, e.g. two verses of a six verse poem, with no explanation. He combined verses of one poem with those of another in like metre.[5] The greatest disadvantages of his editorial style are that he did not explain his method and did not cite in detail the sources from which he selected unpublished material.

Manuscript poems of which Osborn published only portions and/or in conglomerate forms are published here for the first time in the fullest form as recorded by Wesley in the manuscripts. The footnotes provide a documentation of any portions of poems which appeared in Osborn. The contents of the present volume are found on page 5; volumes I and III are concerned with different types of poetry.

VOLUME I

The American War and other poems on patriotism
Epistles
Courtship and marriage
Family hymns and poems
John Wesley's marriage

4. See footnote 58 on p. 271: John 19:1.
5. For example, instead of printing the two-verse poem on Mark 15:47 (p. 70) as Wesley wrote it, he published only one verse by combining the first four lines of each verse and gave no indication whatsoever as to what he had done or why.

VOLUME III

Hymns for preachers
Hymns for ordination
Hymns for festivals
Devotional hymns
Intercessory hymns
Hymns for malefactors
Epitaphs
Epigrams
Miscellaneous hymns and poems
Fragments
Poems of doubtful authorship
Index of first lines to all poems in volumes I–III

TECHNICAL MATTERS

In general the technical matters outlined in volume I on pages 13–15 are applicable to volume II. There are some additional comments, however, which pertain to volume II.

(1) Charles Wesley usually capitalized the words "thee" and "thou" as forms of address for God, but he is not always consistent. The text printed here follows the manuscripts regardless of the capitalization or non-capitalization of these words. When the word "thine" refers to God and is not an adjective, it too may be capitalized.

(2) The few instances of "ye" as an equivalent for the definite article have been changed to "the."

(3) Wesley's use of quotation marks is varied but correct and seems to depend upon his habit of writing at the time. Sometimes he employed them at the beginning of each line, when a series of successive lines comprised a quotation.[6] At other times, even for successive lines of a quotation, he placed quotation marks only at the beginning and end of the quotation.[7] There are other instances where he used no quotation marks, when a quotation is clearly intended.[8]

(4) The abbreviations for biblical books are printed here as used by Wesley in the manuscripts. Where biblical references and/or texts have been omitted, they are supplied within brackets. Often he did not write out in full the biblical text upon which a poem was based and added

6. See the last eight lines of the poem on Luke 18:11–12, p. 169.
7. See verses 1 and 2 of the poem on Luke 14:17, p. 150.
8. For example: Myriads hosanna cry. See the poem on Luke 19:36, pp. 178–179.

either "etc." or "&c." after the quoted portion. His style of recording texts is reproduced here as it appears in the manuscripts.

At times Wesley joined the main parts of biblical verses which were essential to his intention. He often indicated resulting omissions only by a comma. Where necessary for clarity, these textual omissions are indicated as follows: [. . .]. Incorrect biblical references, which are infrequent, have been rectified and the footnotes indicate errors Wesley made in the manuscripts.

(5) In a few cases words peculiar to eighteenth century English language usage or earlier have been explained in the footnotes, e.g. intend'ring,[9] salutiferous.[10]

(6) In general the biblical quotations used by Wesley before each poem in the manuscripts and published in this volume are from the Authorized Version. However, sometimes he used his brother John's translations in full or in part from *Explanatory Notes upon the New Testament* (1755), and in some instances Charles made his own translation from the Greek. In general, variants from the Authorized Version are cited in the footnotes. In those instances in which Wesley cited scriptural references only, the editors have supplied the textual quotations. Occasionally Wesley recorded a biblical reference incorrectly. The few occurrences are corrected in the body of the text and the errors are indicated in the footnotes.

(7) In Sections I–V the page numbers in parentheses at the end of each poem specify the respective pages in the MS cited at the beginning of each section. Sections I–V include poems from lengthy homogenous MS sources designated MS Matthew, MS Mark, MS Luke, MS John, and MS Acts. These are arranged in chronological order according to the chapters of the biblical books, a method which was Wesley's own in the MSS. Occasionally unpublished poems based on passages from these same biblical books, yet coming from other Charles Wesley sources, have been included at the proper place in the chapter chronology of the biblical books. Such occurrences and the MS sources are included in the footnotes.

(8) Whenever page breaks divide a verse of poetry and no verse number appears to the left of the first line of the verse, the divided lines comprise a single-verse poem. The structure of verses divided by page breaks within multiple-verse poems will be obvious from the other verses.

(9) Whenever Wesley wrote alternative readings in the margins of the MSS, or above or below lines in the body of a poem, and did not

---

9. See line five of the poem on John 19:26–7, p. 276.
10. See line three of verse 4 of the poem on Luke 17:12–13, p. 163.

cross out one reading in preference to another, these readings have been indicated in the footnotes. Occasionally an italicized word represents a word underlined in the MSS because there is an alternative suggested.

(10) Editorial footnotes, which include documentation and comments, appear within square brackets, as do all editorial elaborations of and additions to the manuscript texts. Footnotes without brackets are Wesley's own. Occasionally he inadvertently dropped a consonant in his handscript, e.g. vesel. The few instances thereof have been bracketed and are indicated by adding the missing letter within brackets, e.g. ves[s]el. Roman numerals within square brackets indicate unnumbered poems or parts of poems

Once again deep appreciation is expressed to the Center of Theological Inquiry, its late founder and Chancellor, Dr. James I. McCord, Trustees, and Advisory Board for funding the editorial process of this series during Dr. Kimbrough's tenure there and to the Center staff: Gloria B. Kramer, Kate Le Van, and Patricia Grier for technical assistance. Gratitude is also extended to The Rev. Dr. S. H. Mayor, Director of the Cheshunt Foundation, Cambridge, for permission to make use of MS Cheshunt, and to Alison Peacock, the Methodist Archivist at the John Rylands Library, University of Manchester.

Editors:

S T Kimbrough, Jr.,
Center of Theological Inquiry
Princeton, New Jersey

Oliver A. Beckerlegge,
York, England

MANUSCRIPT SOURCES AND ABBREVIATIONS

TABLE OF MANUSCRIPT SOURCES*

MS Matthew: Charles Wesley, Box II.C.23
MS Mark: Charles Wesley, Box II.C.18
MS Luke: Charles Wesley, Box II.C.19
MS John: Charles Wesley, Box II.C.20
MS Acts: Charles Wesley, Box II.C.21
MS Psalms: Charles Wesley, Box I.C.49
MS Thirty: Charles Wesley, Box I.C.30
MS Scriptural Hymns: Charles Wesley, Box II.C.25
MS Clarke: Charles Wesley, Box I.C.45
MS Misc. Hymns: Charles Wesley, Box I.C.26
MS CW III(a): Case 3, Charles Wesley, Box V
MS CW IV: Charles Wesley, Box V
MS Cheshunt (Westminster College, Cambridge)
MS Richmond

ABBREVIATIONS

Poet. Works = George Osborn, *The Poetical Works of John and Charles Wesley*, 13 vols. (London: 1868–72). Citations from these volumes will be made by the volume and page number, e.g. *Poet. Works*, XI, pp. 302–3.

Rep. Verse = Frank Baker, *Representative Verse of Charles Wesley* (Nashville: Abingdon, 1962). Poems from this volume will be cited by their number followed by the page number, e.g. *Rep. Verse*, No. 245, pp. 272–4.

* See Frank Baker, *Representative Verse of Charles Wesley* (Nashville: Abingdon, 1962), pp. 387–94, for a description of the manuscript sources of Charles Wesley's poetry. The box numbers following the titles of the manuscripts indicate the designations of the Finding List of the Methodist Archives of The John Rylands Library of the University of Manchester, England.

Notes = John Wesley, *Explanatory Notes upon the New Testament* (London: Bowyer, 1755). Citations of this work will be made where Charles Wesley has followed his brother's translation of a New Testament passage instead of the Authorized Version.

Short Hymns = Charles Wesley, *Short Hymns on Select Passages of the Holy Scriptures*, 2 vols. (Bristol: Farley, 1762). Citations from these volumes will be made by the volume and page number, e.g. *Short Hymns*, II, p. 219.

AV = the Authorized Version of the Bible (1611).

SECTION I

THE GOSPEL OF MATTHEW

THE GOSPEL OF MATTHEW
(MS Matthew)

Mt. 1:21, *Thou shalt call his name Jesus, for he shall save his people from their sins.*

   1.   Jesus *from*, not *in*, our sins
          Doth still his people save:
     Him our Advocate and Prince,
          Our Priest and King, we have;
     Strength in him with righteousness,
  With pardon purity, we gain,
     Priests his praying Spirit possess,
          And kings forever reign.

   2.   Sav'd from sin thro' faith we found
          Ourselves by grace forgiven:
     Jesus' grace doth more abound,
          And makes us meet for heaven:
     The full virtue of his name
  Our hallow'd souls at last shall prove,
     To the utmost sav'd proclaim
          His pure almighty love. (p. 4)[1]

Mt. 2:3, *Lo, the star which they saw in the east went before them, till it came and stood over where the young child was.*

   1. No more I rashly turn aside,
     Or quit my true celestial Guide,
         T'inquire of foolish man;
     Directed by his word alone,
     I seek the infant-God unknown,
         And cannot seek in vain.

---

1. [Verse 1 appears in *Poet. Works*, X, p. 141.]

2. Or if my Light itself withdraw,
     With simple faith and humble awe
         I urge my dreary way,
     Till Jesus' star again appear,
     And pointing to the Saviour near
         Its gladning beams display. (p. 6)

Mt. 4:3, *When the tempter came to him, he said, If Thou be the Son*
    of God, etc.

[II]

1. When God declares me reconcil'd,
     His pardon'd, dear, adopted child,
     Allur'd into the wilderness
     He lets the tempter prove my grace:
     Satan impels me to despair,
     Or doubt my heavenly Father's care,
     To question if I am his son,
     And not to trust my God alone.

2. By hunger in this desert tried,
     I will not in myself confide,
     But trust my Father's love to feed
     My soul with immaterial bread:
     When, as He will, the manna given,
     The living Bread sent down from heaven
     I shall with simple faith receive,
     And by the Word & Spirit live. (p. 16)[2]

Mt. 4:10, *Thou shalt worship the Lord thy God, and him only shalt*
    thou serve.

I shall, if thou bestow the power
    Of living faith divine,
In spirit and in truth adore
    Thy Father, Lord, and mine;

2. [In MS Matthew there is another poem on this text numbered I, which appears in *Poet.*
Works, X, p. 151.]

If Thou my hallow'd soul inspire,
    I shall obedient prove,
And burn, like that celestial quire,
    With flames of purest love. (p. 22)

Mt. 4:16, *The people which sat in darkness saw great light, and to*
them which sat in the region and shadow of death, light is
sprung up.

1.   In our unregenerate state,
    Strangers to ourselves and God,
We in grossest darkness sat,
    In the shades of death abode,
Confines of that hellish night;
    When we saw the gospel-grace,
Saw the great eternal Light
    Beaming from Immanuel's face.

2.   Suddenly the Light sprung up,
    Rose the Day-star in our hearts:
Earnest of our heavenly hope,
    Jesus still himself imparts;
Grows the pure, celestial ray
    More & more with faith's increase,
Makes at last the perfect day,
    Opens into endless bliss. (p. 23)

Mt. 5:42, *Give to him that asketh, &c.*

The reasoning selfishness of man
Can it the word of God explain?
Or shall I trust the learn'd, employ'd
By pride to make the precept void?
With faith's unfeign'd simplicity,
Jesus, I turn from man to Thee;
Thy own Interpreter Thou art,
Write thy own meaning on my heart. (p. 41)

Mt. 6:3, *Let not thy left hand know what thy right hand doeth.*

1. The good thou dost for Jesus' sake
    Ev'n from thy bosom-friend conceal,
    Nor let remembrance bring it back,
    Or fondly on the action dwell,
    But shun the soul-insnaring sight,
    And find in God thy whole delight.

2. Thy alms and works of righteousness
    The closest secresy require:
    Thy God and not thyself to please,
    Be this thy humble heart's desire,
    And leave whate'er for Him is done
    Hid from thyself in God alone. (p. 45)

Mt. 8:4, *Jesus saith unto him, See thou tell no man.*

> The pastor good and humbly wise
> The pomp of shining actions flies
>   Which God thro' him hath done,
> Forbids the heal'd to spread *his* fame,
> Gives all the praise to Jesus' name
>   Neglectful of his own. (p. 83)

Mt. 8:4, *See thou tell no man, but go, . . . shew thyself to the priest.*

1. Whene'er Thou dost the grace bestow,
    Lest proudly I the blessing show,
        A second gift impart,
    "Tell it to none" — with vain delight,
    "Tell it to none" — in mercy write
        Upon my broken heart.

2. If cleans'd by Thee ev'n now I am,
    Let my obedience first proclaim
        My great Physician's praise;
    Before my lips to others tell,
    Thou bidst me to the priest reveal
        The wonders of thy grace.

3. Order'd by Thee, O Lord, I go,
   And to the priest myself I show
   Heal'd by a touch of thine,
   That when the priest thy witness sees,
   Convinc'd, he may himself confess
   My Healer is Divine. (p. 83)[3]

Mt. 8:7, *Jesus saith unto him, I will come and heal him.*

O how gracious is my Lord,
   Hearkning to a sinner's cry,
Listning for a sigh, or word,
   O how ready to reply!
Scarce He gives me time to pray,
   "Jesus, come, my sickness heal,"
Knowing what I meant to say,
   Jesus answers me, "I will." (p. 84)[4]

Mt. 9:1, *They brought to him a man sick of the palsy.*

Jesus, a soul afflicted see,
Brought by the power of faith to Thee
   And plac'd beneath thine eye:
Thy love, thine all-redeeming love
His sin and sickness can remove,
   And freely justify. (p. 95)

Mt. 9:5, *Whether is easier to say, Thy sins be forgiven thee, or to say, Arise, and walk?*

Saviour, Thou with equal ease
   Soul and body canst restore,
Me from all my sins release,
   Purge the guilt, and break the power:

3. [Verses 1 and 3 appear in *Poet. Works*, X, p. 219, but with variant readings. *Poet. Works*, copies *Short Hymns*, II, p. 151. We reproduce Charles Wesley's final preference here and elsewhere.]
4. [This verse appears in *Short Hymns*, II, pp. 151–2, and in *Poet. Works*, X, p. 211, in a six-lined form.]

Nothing can thy will withstand,
Thy benign, almighty will:
Speak, and let the kind command
Me, ev'n me this moment heal. (p. 96)

Mt. 9:6, *But that ye may know that the Son of man hath power upon earth to forgive sins, &c.*

Lord, I dare not ask a sign:
But Thou canst my body save,
Lift me up by power divine
From the margin of the grave,
By the outward wonder show
What thy grace hath wrought within,
Thus constraining me to know
Thou hast sav'd my soul from sin. (p. 96)

Mt. 9:13, *Go ye and learn what that meaneth, I will have mercy, and not sacrifice.*

1. To whom should thy disciples go,
Of whom should they be taught, but Thee?
Thy Spirit doth thy meaning show:
O might He shew it now to me,
And give my heart to understand
The new, the old, supreme command.

2. Blessings Thou dost to sinners give,
Not sacrifice from us require,
Thou wil'st that we should still receive,
Should after all thy mind aspire.
And moulded in thine image prove
Thy first, great attribute is Love. (p. 100)[5]

---

5. [*Rep. Verse*, No. 164B, p. 213, as here. The first four lines of verse 1 and the first two lines of verse 2 appear in *Short Hymns*, II, p. 154, and in *Poet. Works*, X, p. 223, with two additional lines as one verse of eight lines.]

Mt. 9:15, *The days will come when the Bridegroom will be taken from them, and then shall they fast.*

> The fasting days are these:
> We for his absence mourn,
> Our eye no more the Bridegroom sees,
> But weeps for his return:
> We thus thro' life abstain,
> Lament, and daily die,
> Till we behold our Lord again,
> And clasp him in the sky. (p. 101)

Mt. 9:17, *Neither do men put new wine into old bottles; else the bottles break, and the wine runneth out, and the bottles perish.*

1. We run before the grace divine,
    If, while their hearts are unrenew'd,
   Hard tasks we rig'rously injoin,
    And yokes impose on converts rude:
   To men of an unconquer'd will
    Who doctrines premature explain,
   Old bottles with new wine we fill,
    With truths they cannot yet contain.

2. While warm with undiscerning zeal,
    We urge the novice on too fast,
   To scale at once the holiest hill,
    As his first labour were his last:
   He swells as wholly sanctified,
    As perfect in a moment's space,
   He bursts with self-important pride,
    And loses all his real grace.

3. Eager that all should upward press,
    Should see the summit with *his* eyes,
   Impatient for his own success,
    Be perfect now, the preacher cries!
   The work of grace so well begun
    He ruins by his headlong haste:
   The wheat is choak'd, with tares or'erun,
    And Satan lays the vineyard waste.

4. Our only wisdom is, to trace
        The path whereby the Spirit leads,
    The usual course of saving grace,
        Which step by step in souls proceeds,
    Instructs them more and more to grow,
        A people for their Father born,
    Till all his mind at last they know.
        And ripe for God to God return.

5. To us, most wise, most gracious Lord,
        The Spirit of thy conduct give,
    That duely ministring the word,
        Sinners we may, like Thee, receive;
    May never mar thy work begun,
        Or lose one drop of grace sincere,
    But gently lead thy followers on
        Till perfect all in heaven appear. (pp. 101–2)

Mt. 10:4, *And Judas Iscariot who also betrayed him.*

1. The wisdom of our Lord would chuse
        A traitor by the fiend possest,
    That none the guiltless may accuse,
        Or stumbling at a wicked priest,
    Deny the Ministerial call,
    And dare for one to censure all.

2. Whate'er the messenger he sends,
        He gives the efficacious grace:
    The word and sacrament depends
        On Christ for its assur'd success,
    Whate'er of good on earth is done
    Christ doth it all, and Christ alone. (p. 112)[6]

6. [*Rep. Verse*, No. 165, p. 213.]

Mt. 10:5, *Go not into the way of the Gentiles.*

Not as his inclination leads,
But by the order of his Lord,
The minister of Christ proceeds,
And propagates the gospel-word,
And spreads the power of reigning love,
Which lifts our souls to thrones above. (pp. 112–13)

Mt. 10:20, *It is not ye that speak, but the Spirit of your Father which speaketh in you.*

Tho' poor, and ignorant, and weak,
Our Lord is with us to the end,
The Head doth in the members speak,
And God doth his own cause defend:
The Spirit of our Father lives
In all whom one with Christ He owns;
Resistless power and wisdom gives,
And gives their names to thunder's sons. (p. 119)

Mt. 10:21, *The brother shall deliver up the brother to death, and the father the child, &c.*

When Jesus comes, in this our day
We see the word accomplish'd still,
The father doth the son betray,
The children would their parent kill;
Abhorring their own flesh and blood,
They burst thro' nature's closest ties:
And thus the world adore *their* god,
Well-pleas'd with human sacrifice. (p. 119)

Mt. 10:34, *Think not that I am come to send peace on, &c.*

1. Not to indulge our sloth and ease,
   Not to confirm our worldly peace,
   Didst Thou on earth appear,
   But that we might thy kingdom know,
   And find, cut off from all below,
   The Lord our portion here.

2. Thou kindly cam'st to stand between,
   To separate us from sinful men,
   Us from ourselves to part,
   That rescued by Thy Spirit's power
   Thy saints may cleave to earth no more,
   But give Thee all their heart.

3. Now, Lord, apply thy powerful word,
   Use upon us thy Spirit's sword
   Who dare abide thy day;
   Thy people from the world divide,
   Cut off our selfishness and pride,
   Our sins forever slay. (p. 123)[7]

Mt. 10:41, *He that receiveth a prophet in the name of a prophet,
shall receive a prophet's reward.*

All are not prophets of the Lord,
   Yet every faithful soul may share
A prophet's infinite reward,
   Who doth for Jesus' servants care:
The man that speaks in Jesus' name,
   I pray my God his toil to crown,
And thus his promis'd wages claim
   Who make by faith his work my own. (p. 127)

7. [Verses 1 and 2 appear in *Poet. Works*, X, p. 240.]

Mt. 11:4, *Go, and shew John again those things which ye do hear and see.*

Jesus himself to works appeals;
　　Him by his works he bids us prove,
Yet what the warm enthusiast tells
　　Of dreams, and visits from above,
He wills his hearers to receive,
And simply on his word believe. (p. 129)

Mt. 11:29, *Take my yoke upon you, and learn of me, for I am meek and lowly in heart: and ye shall, etc.*

1.　　O how shall I attain
　　　　The meek tranquillity,
　　　The gentleness humane,
　　　　Divine, which was in Thee,
　　The quiet of a lowly heart,
　　The rest which never can depart!

2.　　Rest to my weary mind,
　　　　My burthen'd spirit's ease,
　　　By faith in Thee I find:
　　　　But gasp in perfect peace
　　To live of holiness possest,
　　To die into eternal rest. (p. 139)

Mt. 12:16, *He charged them that they should not make him known.*

1.　The purport of thy strange command,
　　　Saviour, if I understand,
　　　　Allow me my request,
　　Beyond the reach of praise and pride,
　　Jealous for thy own glory, hide
　　　　A sinner in thy breast.

2. O were my soul shut up in Thee,
     Safe in thy obscurity,
       Forgotten and unknown,
    My good from human eye conceal'd,
    Or not till that great day reveal'd
       Which shows Thee on thy throne! (p. 145)

Mt. 13:25, *While men slept, his enemy sowed tares.*

While gospel-husbandmen repose,
    And dream of crowns without the cross,
His tares the adversary sows,
    Unmark'd, and unobserv'd withdraws:
The tares produce a sudden crop,
    The tares above the wheat increase;
Now, now! we see them *now* spring up,
    Five hundred perfect witnesses! (pp. 161–2)[8]

Mt. 13:31, *The kingdom of heaven is like to a grain of mustard-seed.*

1. The kingdom rises from a grain
     Into a tree by just degrees,
    Our hasty nature to restrain,
     To check our blindfold forwardness,
    Which teaches God the when and how,
    Which urges man, *Be perfect now!*

2. Our darkest ignorance of pride,
     Our unbelief, O Lord, remove,
    Which sets thine oracles aside,
     Thy words audacious to improve,
    And spread *at once* the hallowing leaven,
    And preach a shorter way to heaven.

8. [There are two poems on this text; the first appears in *Short Hymns*, II, p. 166, and *Poet. Works*, X, p. 273.]

3. O may I never teach my Lord,
   Wise above what is written be!
   Me by the method of thy word
   Bring on to full maturity,
   Save on, when Thou hast purg'd my guilt,
   But save me when, and as Thou wilt. (p. 163)

Mt. 13:44, *The kingdom of heaven is like unto treasure hid in a field: which when a man hath found, etc.*

1. He did not proclaim To all that pass'd by,
   "How happy I am, How sanctified I!"
   But finding a measure Of heavenly power,
   Conceal'd the rich treasure, And labour'd for more.

2. The gift who receives, And hastens to tell
   He calls on the thieves His treasure to steal:
   Who vainly refuses, Or lingers to hide,
   His riches he loses Thro' folly and pride.

3. The grace I have found, O Jesus, with Thee,
   I hide in the ground For no man to see:
   The grace I confide in, The treasure Thou art,
   Who lov'st to reside in A penitent heart.

4. Of pardon possest, My God I adore:
   Yet can I not rest, Impatient for more;
   A greater salvation I languish to prove,
   A deeper foundation, A solider love.

5. The grace to insure, The treasure conceal'd,
   A mendicant poor I purchase the field,
   Sell all to obtain it, And seek till I find,
   And ask, till I gain it In Jesus his mind. (p. 165)

Mt. 14:30, *Beginning to sink, he cried . . . Lord, save me.*

1. Still in every trial new
   My want of grace I feel,
   Pray for fresh supplies to do
   And suffer all thy will;

> Need of thy supporting word,
> Continual need of prayer I have;
> Save me this, most mighty Lord,
> And every moment save.

2. Let me cry for help to Thee,
> The instant I begin
> Sinking in the troubled sea,
> Yielding to my own sin:
> Then, in answer to my prayer,
> Thou wilt extend thy mercy's hand,
> High above the billows bear,
> And bring me safe to land. (p. 176)[9]

Mt. 15:31, *The multitude wondered when they saw the dumb to speak, the maimed to be whole, etc.*

1. All glory to Thee Our ancestors' God,
> Whose wonders we see On sinners renew'd!
> Our best adoration Thy benefits claim,
> Thy grace and salvation Forever the same.

2. The spiritual blind Their Saviour behold,
> Inlighten'd they find Their way to the fold:
> The lame we see walking, The maim'd are restor'd,
> The dumb are all talking In praise of their Lord.

3. Thy work is begun: But O, let it be
> With power carried on In them and in me;
> Who own our condition, Afflicted and poor,
> And trust the Physician To perfect our cure. (p. 187)

Mt. 16:16, *Thou art the Son of the living God.*

> Son of the living God from heaven
> Is Christ for our salvation given:
> But sprung from Jesus on the tree
> Sons of a dying God are we! (p. 195)

---

9. [Verse 1 appears in *Poet. Works*, X, pp. 285–6 and verse 2 in *Short Hymns*, II, p. 169. In the latter verse the metre is quite different.]

Mt. 18:1, *The disciples came unto Jesus, saying, Who is greatest in the kingdom of heaven?*

> Pride in the church! (how can it be?)
> The kingdom of humility!
> Spiritual, self-exalting pride,
> Which sits as by Jehovah's side!
> Ambition to be counted best,
> To soar, and shine above the rest!
> What words that Lucifer can paint,
> Who calls himself a *perfect saint*! (p. 210)

Mt. 18:2, *Jesus called a little child unto him, and set him in the midst of them.*

> But let the holy Child Divine
>   Himself my Pattern be:
> No innocence, O Lord, like thine
>   Can teach humility:
> Free from the faults and blemishes
>   Which Adam's offspring stain,
> Thee, only Thee will I confess
>   A sinless child of man. (p. 210)

Mt. 18:6, *These little ones which believe in me.*

> Whom Jesus for his followers owns
> He calls, and keeps his little ones:
> Others above themselves they prize,
> Less than the least in their own eyes;
> They never boast their grace, or dare
> Their own perfection to declare,
> But still their littleness maintain,
> Till great in heaven with Christ they reign. (p. 212)

THE UNPUBLISHED POETRY OF CHARLES WESLEY

Mt. 19:2, *Great multitudes followed him, and he healed them there.*[10]

1. We cannot follow Christ in vain,
      Whose word to all that seek is sure,
    But following on we must obtain
      The healthful mind, the perfect cure:
    He never lingers or delays
      His promis'd benefits to give;
    Yet waits, before he grants the grace,
      Till man is ready to receive.

2. Sinners of old, for ease, or food,
      Pursued the Saviour of mankind:
    The spiritual, eternal good,
      We come with faith in Him to find:
    Drawn by the odour of his name
      The sweetness of his grace and love,
    We hope to see that heavenly Lamb,
      And share his marriage-feast above. (pp. 220–1)

Mt. 20:9, *And when they were come that were hired about the eleventh hour, etc.*

1. Who held on earth the lowest place,
      Yet faithful to their little power,
    Their measure small of feeble grace,
      Labour'd for one important hour;
    They find the same reward above,
      To weak and strong by Jesus given,
    And triumph (if as much they love)
      As much as the first saints in heaven.

2. Heaven is for all alike prepar'd,
      And one short moment may suffice
    To win the infinite reward,
      T'insure the never-fading prize:

10. [See *The Unpublished Poetry of Charles Wesley*, Volume III, Section IX for a shorthand poem based on Mt. 19:11–12. It is included there with other poems from MS Shorthand.]

But let not the presumptuous fool
    Repentance to the last defer;
Nor let a poor departing soul
    Of mercy ev'n in death despair. (p. 233)[11]

Mt. 20:23, *To sit on my right hand, and on my left, is not mine to give, unless to those for whom, etc.*

1. The first superlative reward,
        Saviour, it is not thine to give
    To all, but only those prepar'd
        Such weight of glory to receive;
    Who drink thy passion's deepest cup,
        Abide temptation's fiercest fire,
    And soonest take thy burthen up,
        And latest on thy cross expire.

2. Elected by thy Father's grace
        For these He hath reserv'd above
    A mightier bliss, an higher place,
        And larger draughts of heavenly love:
    And perfected thro' sufferings here,
        They here superior grace obtain,
    Who least in their own eyes appear,
        And in thy patient kingdom reign.

3. They live the outcasts of mankind,
        Entreated like their Lord below,
    With Him in sharpest sufferings join'd,
        The closest fellowship they know;
    In daily death his life they live,
        Till, call'd to lay their bodies down,
    The conquerors from his hands receive
        A fairer palm, a brighter crown. (p. 238)

11. [Verse 2 appears in *Poet. Works*, X, p. 332.]

Mt. 21:1, *And when they drew nigh unto Jerusalem, then sent Jesus two disciples, &c.*

He comes his people to redeem,
Enters his own Jerusalem,
To buy us with his mortal pain,
And glorious in his church to reign!
And lo, the triumph of an hour,
The short, anticipated power
Prepares him for his gainful loss,
And paves the passage to his cross! (p. 240)

Mt. 22:2, *The kingdom of heaven is like, &c.*

Great the nuptial mystery
    Which heaven and earth unites,
Christ allies himself to me,
    And God in man delights:
Christ I for my Lord receive,
Who left for me his throne above,
    To the heavenly Bridegroom cleave
        By humble faith and love. (p. 257)

Mt. 22:3, *[And sent forth his servants to call them that were bidden to the wedding: and they would not come.]*

1.   Here in truth and righteousness
        Betroth'd to Christ I am,
    (Christ, the smiling Prince of peace)
        And call'd after his name:
    Truly my consent I gave,
        Heart to heart, and will to will,
    Yielded that his love should save:
        And lo, he saves me still.

34

2.   Now I live to Jesus join'd,
      My Husband's flesh and bone,
    One with Him in heart and mind,
      In soul and spirit one:
    He is mine, and I am his,
    Till Him I in his glory meet;
    Then consummated in bliss
    The marriage is compleat. (p. 257)[12]

Mt. 22:4, [*Again, he sent forth other servants, saying, Tell them which are bidden, Behold, I have prepared my dinner: my oxen and my fatlings are killed, and all things are ready: come unto the marriage.*]

1.   Oft repuls'd by sinful men,
      Yet will not Christ depart,
    Still he comes, and sues again,
      And cries, Give me thy heart!
    Yet Thou knowst, so strangely kind,
    That when I give my heart to Thee,
    Nothing there thy love can find
    But sin and misery.

2.   Wisdom I in Thee possess,
      When thine I truly prove,
    Wealth, and power, and holiness,
      And beatific love;
    Perfect love, whose depth and height
    The saints alone can comprehend,
    Full, ineffable delight,
    And joys that ne'er shall end.

3.   Husband of thy church below,
      The feast itself Thou art,
    Thee the bread, the life we know
      Of every faithful heart,
    Banquet with and on our God,
    The Paschal Lamb for sinners slain,
    Eat thy flesh, and drink thy blood,
    And life eternal gain. (p. 258)

12. [The two verses are in slightly different metres.]

Mt. 22:5, [*But they made light of it, and went their ways, one to his farm, another to his merchandise.*]

> Wretched world! the call who slight
> To real happiness,
> Seek in wealth their vain delight,
> In soft, voluptuous ease,
> Sunk in sloth, or lost in care,
> Who Jesus' proffer'd grace refuse,
> Both implung'd in late despair
> Their souls forever lose. (pp. 258–9)

Mt. 22:6, [*And the remnant took his servants, and entreated them spitefully, and slew them.*]

> Wretched far above the rest
> Who shamefully entreat
> Those that bid them to the feast,
> And tread beneath their feet:
> They their hated brethren slay
> Who daily thirst to shed their blood,
> Murtherers of the servants they,
> And murtherers of their God. (p. 259)

Mt. 22:7, [*But when the king heard thereof, he was wroth: and he sent forth his armies, and destroyed those murderers, and burned up their city.*]

> Thus they fill their measure up
> Who hate the messengers:
> What can their damnation stop,
> When the great King appears?
> Jesus in the flaming skies
> With his Angelic hosts shall come,
> Fire their earthly paradise,
> And all his foes consume. (p. 259)

Mt. 22:8, [*Then saith he to his servants, The wedding is ready, but they which were bidden were not worthy.*]

Justly is his case deplor'd
Who, bidden to the feast,
Scorns the kind inviting word,
And will not be his guest:
Most deplorable the man,
Who, tasting once the heavenly food,
To his vomit turns again,
And loaths the feast of God. (p. 259)

Mt. 22:10, [*So those servants went out into the highways, and gathered together all as many as they found, both bad and good: and the wedding was furnished with guests.*]

1.   God his grace on them bestows
Whom he vouchsafes to call,
No respect of persons knows,
But offers Christ to all:
In the wedding-garment clad
(The faith which God will not reprove)
Poor and rich, and good and bad
May banquet on his love.

2.   Many a bold, presumptuous guest,
Unholy and unfit,
Share the sacramental feast,
And at his table sit;
Sinners who to sin turn back,
Strangers to their Saviour's love,
Souls that never shall partake
The marriage-feast above. (p. 260)[13]

13. [The two verses are in slightly different metres.]

Mt. 23:7, *They love to be called of men, Rabbi, Rabbi.*

> *Our* Scribes and Pharisees we see
> Proud of their rank and dignity,
> Puff'd up when honours they receive,
> Provok'd, when men refuse to give:
> Honours they haughtily require,
> Possess with fondness of desire,
> Eager defend with angry heat,
> And lose them with the last regret. (p. 268)

Mt. 23:15, *Woe unto you, Scribes and Pharisees, hypocrites; for ye compass sea and land to make one proselyte, and when he is made, ye make him two-fold more the child of hell than yourselves.*

> The proselyte ye make
>   Is still unchang'd in heart,
> Tho' for a new opinion's sake
>   He take the Church's part:
> By your devotion fir'd
>   He breathes your spirit too,
> And fights with double rage inspir'd
>   Against the truth, like you. (p. 272)

Mt. 23:16–22, *Woe unto you, ye blind guides, which say, Whosoever shall swear by the temple, etc.*

> 1. Your superstition vain
>   Its own conviction brings,
>   Who interdict the use profane
>   Of consecrated things:
>   But Him that gives their use
>   And sacred character,
>   Ye for your hallowing God refuse,
>   And quite cast off his fear.

2.　　The temple ye despise,
　　　Like Pharisees of old,
　The gift above the altar prize,
　　　And idolize the gold:
　　　The offering ye prefer
　　　To Mary's better part,
　And thus the ignorance declare
　　　And blindness of your heart.

3.　　Foolish and blindfold guides,
　　　Ye have no eyes to see
　The Temple true where God resides
　　　In all his majesty;
　　　The Spring of holiness
　　　To things & persons given,
　On earth the Consecrating Place,
　　　The only Shrine in heaven.

4.　　That Altar in the skies,
　　　Alas, ye will not lift
　Your hearts to Him, who sanctifies
　　　The offerer and the gift:
　　　Whate'er a sinner gives
　　　To God thro' Christ alone
　The Father graciously receives
　　　As offer'd by his Son. (pp. 273–4)

Mt. 23:23, *Woe unto you, Scribes and Pharisees, hypocrites; for ye pay tithe of mint, and anise, & cummin, and have neglected the weightier matters of the law, &c.*

1.　　Your strict and only care
　　　In matters small is show'd,
　While gros[s]ly negligent ye are
　　　In the great things of God,
　　　Th'essential righteousness
　　　Imparted from above,
　The spirit pure of gospel-grace,
　　　The life of faith and love.

2.   In ceremonies nice,
        Who will not break the least,
     Ambition, pride, and avarice
        Your conscience can digest;
        Who at a triffle strain,
        Ye teach the multitude
     To keep, like you, the rules of men,
        And break the laws of God. (p. 274)

Mt. 23:25, *Woe unto you, Scribes and Pharisees, hypocrites; for ye make clean the outside of the cup, etc.*

     Ye make the outside clean,
        Nor fear that God should see
     Your inmost souls defil'd with sin,
        And all impurity:
        Corrupt, and full your hearts
        Of rapine and excess,
     Your conscience and your inward parts
        Are very wickedness. (pp. 274–5)

Mt. 23:26, *Thou blind Pharisee, cleanse first that which is within the cup and platter, etc.*

     Thou teacher blind, and proud
        Of outward righteousness,
     Thy heart must first be wash'd in blood,
        And purified by grace;
        Thine actions then would show
        Thine heart and conscience clean,
     And all thy conversation flow
        From the pure love within. (p. 275)

Mt. 23:27–28, *Woe unto you, Scribes and Pharisees, hypocrites; for ye are like unto whited sepulchres, etc.*

1.   The sepulchre ye white,
        As righteous men appear,
     And outwardly expose to sight
        A reverend character:

Whate'er ye seem to be,
The Lord thro' all your art
Perceives your deep hypocrisy,
Your rottenness of heart.

2. Ye stand with all your deeds
Before his eyes confest,
Who every dreadful secret reads
In your polluted breast:
That hideous, ghastly place
Your heart shall soon be seen,
While Jesus spreads it to the gaze
Of angels and of men. (pp. 275–6)

Mt. 23:32–33, *Fill ye up then the measure of your fathers. Ye serpents, &c.*

[I]

Fill then your measure up,
Ye serpents' murtherous brood:
No mercy at your hands we hope,
Who hate th'incarnate God:
Who hate the righteous poor,
Your *edict mild* repeal,
And for your wretched souls insure
The hottest place in hell.

2. When God permits, revive
Your sanguinary laws:
Resisting unto blood, we strive
In our Redeemer's cause:
Throw down our legal fence
(We know your devilish aims),
Oppress our blacken'd innocence
And vote us to the flames! (pp. 276–7)[14]

14. [Reference to the poems on Matthew 22:29–31 in *Poet. Works*, X, p. 363, shows that Wesley referred here to Rome's persecutions.]

Mt. 23:32–33.

II

Jesus, the God of love,
The Infinite in grace,
Cannot command, cannot approve
A sinner's wickedness:
But when the day is past,
He may his grace deny,
And justly let the soul at last
Fill up its sin, and die. (p. 277)

Mt. 23:34, *Behold, I send unto you prophets, and wise men and*
scribes; and some of them ye shall kill and crucify, etc.

1. Happy the age and place
    Where God's peculiar love
Vouchsafes his witnesses to raise,
    And openly approve;
    Where full of faith divine
    As in the gap they stand,
With fervent zeal and wisdom shine,
    And guard a sinful land.

2. But O', what endless woes
    Are treasur'd up for them
Who Jesus' messengers oppose,
    And spitefully condemn;
    Who scourge them with their tongues,
    Who buffet with their lies,
And loading with repeated wrongs
    At last to murther rise!

3. Thro' pride and malice blind,
    The proffer'd grace ye scorn,
The blessings for your soul design'd
    Ye into curses turn:

42

Salvation long refus'd
Your sinful measure fills,
And Christ with all his saints abus'd
Your just damnation seals. (pp. 277–8)

Mt. 25:1, *Then shall the kingdom of heaven be likened unto ten virgins, which took their lamps, etc.*

Jesus, all thy subjects here
Are call'd to holiness,
They the virgin-character
Of purity profess:
Loving Thee with chaste desire,
All baptiz'd into thy name
Should thro' life to heaven aspire,
That marriage of the Lamb. (p. 299)

Mt. 25:5, *While the Bridegroom tarried, they all slumbred and slept.*

1.   While the Bridegroom seems to stay,
         By sinful sleep opprest
     Sinners quite forget the day,
         And saints in safety rest:
     Sinners in their sins lie down,
     In worldly quietness and ease:
         Saints injoy the peace unknown,
         The true substantial peace.

2.   God the world in mercy spares
         When ripe for punishment,
     Still the dreadful day defers,
         That sinners may repent:
     Good and bad their eyelids close,
     Before they hear the trumpet's call,
         All their breathless limbs repose,
         And death o'rewhelms them all. (p. 300)

Mt. 25:10, *They that were ready, went in with him to the marriage,*
& the door was shut.

> Ready for their full reward,
> In holiness compleat,
> Saints with their exalted Lord
> In heavenly places sit:
> All on their Beloved lean,
> Admitted to the nuptial feast,
> Rest eternally shut in,
> In Jesus' arms they rest. (pp. 302–3)

Mt. 25:11, *Afterwards came also the other virgins, saying, Lord,*
Lord, open to us.

> Fools with repetition vain
> Their lingring prayer present,
> Nothing doth for them remain
> But hellish punishment:
> Nothing can reverse their fate,
> Who wake, alas, to sleep no more,
> Knock and call (but all too late)
> When death hath shut the door. (p. 303)

Mt. 25:22, *He also that had received two talents came, and said,*
Lord, thou deliveredst unto me, etc.

> Who saves his own and neighbour's soul
> Doubles the talent he receives,
> Having done all, refers the whole
> To Christ, when his account he gives:
> Before his Saviour in the skies
> He stands, demanding no reward:
> He serv'd on earth (let that suffice)
> A great, and good, and faithful Lord. (p. 307)

Mt. 25:23, *Well done, good and faithful servant.*

My goodness now I cannot boast,
My faithfulness I cannot see:
What in mine inmost soul Thou dost,
While doing, is unknown to me:
The way, and measure of thy grace
Still be it, Lord, to me unknown,
So Thou at last thy servant praise
For work which Thou thyself hast done. (p. 308)[15]

Mt. 25:26, *His Lord answered . . . Thou wicked & slothful servant,*
thou knewest that I reap, &c.

1. The harmless, inoffensive man
   Is cast before the bar of God,
   Cast by his own excuses vain
   For not performing what he coud:
   And, burying that preventing grace,
   Who justly perish unforgiven,
   Shall mixt with fiends in groans confess
   They might have sung with saints in heaven.

2. With shame and sorrow I confess
   The vilest wickedness is mine;
   Sloth is the vilest wickedness;
   If idle in the work divine
   I stand, and hide my talent still,
   Till all my gracious day is past,
   For doing neither good nor ill
   I must be justly damn'd at last. (pp. 309–10)[16]

15. [A variant of this verse in a different metre appears in *Poet. Works*, X, p. 388.]
16. [Verse 1 appears in *Poet. Works*, X, p. 390, and verse 2 appears as a separate poem in a different metre.]

Mt. 26:10, *She hath wrought a good work upon me.*

> Jesus justifies expence,
>   Toward himself profusely shew'd,
> Works of *such* magnificence
>   Praises as sincerely good:
> Offerings of a willing heart
>   Small or great he deigns t'approve,
> Stamps them with his own desert,
>   Loves whate'er proceeds from love. (pp. 318–19)

Mt. 26:11, *Ye have the poor always with you.*

> Yes; the poor supply thy place,
>   Still deputed, Lord, by Thee,
> Daily exercise our grace,
>   Prove our growing charity;
> What to them with right intent
>   Truly, faithfully is given,
> We have to our Saviour lent,
>   Laid up for ourselves in heaven. (p. 319)[17]

Mt. 26:37, *He took with him Peter, and the two sons of Zebedee, and began to be sorrowful and very heavy.*

1. Jesus to those he most approves
   And as his choicest fav'rites loves,
   Doth more abundantly impart
   His grief and heaviness of heart:
   And all who thankfully embrace
   The marks of his distinguish'd grace,
   Shall nearest him above sit down,
   With brighter jewels in their crown.

2. Lord, in my contrite heart reveal
   What Thou wert pleas'd for me to feel:
   That deep, mysterious grief unknown
   Thou shalt not bear it all alone:

17. [This poem appears in both *Short Hymns,* II, p. 189, and in *Poet. Works,* X, p. 398, as a verse of six lines in a different metre.]

My sins, the cause of thy distress,
My sins I mournfully confess,
Thy cup partake, thy sorrow share,
And to my grave thy burthen bear. (p. 325)

Mt. 26:38, *My soul is exceeding sorrowful.*

1.   The Man of sorrows now
        Thou dost indeed appear,
    Beneath my guilty burthen bow,
        And tremble with my fear:
        Thy pain is my relief,
        And doth my load remove,
    For O, if all thy soul is grief,
        Yet all thy heart is love!

2.   Conform my heart to thine,
        And gladly I partake
    The sorrow and the love Divine,
        A sufferer for thy sake:
        With Thee I tarry here,
        (For such my Lord's desire)
    And watch, and pray, and persevere,
        Till pain with life expire. (p. 326)[18]

Mt. 27:43, *He trusted in God; let him deliver him now, if he will*
have him; for he said, I am the Son of God.

"God never can his own reprove,
"Or bruise the objects of his love:"
'Tis thus the foolish world blaspheme,
And mock our confidence in Him:
But chasten'd by Paternal grace
Our God more closely we embrace,
Assur'd we in his love abide;
For all his sons are crucified. (p. 354)[19]

18. [Verse 1 appears in *Short Hymns*, II, p. 191, and *Poet. Works*, X, p. 403.]
19. [After this poem at the end of the MS in Charles Wesley's shorthand is written: "Finished March 8, 1766."]

THE GOSPEL OF MARK

THE GOSPEL OF MARK
(MS Mark)[1]

Mk. 1:3, *The voice of one crying in the wilderness.*

1.   The preacher of thy gospel-word,
     The sure forerunner of his Lord,
     Sent to prepare the way for Thee,
     A voice and nothing else should be,
     Sequester'd from the ways of men
     Be always heard, and never seen.

2.   The world he must not seek to please,
     A man out of the wilderness,
     Friendless, from earth detach'd, unknown,
     Saviour, he speaks for Thee alone,
     Incessant in thy name he cries,
     Thy herald, till for Thee he dies. (pp. 1–2)

Mk. 2:19–20, *Can the children of the bride chamber fast, etc.*

[I]

1.   Long as he did reside
           On earth to chear his bride,
     With the Bridegroom's presence blest,
           Could the friends of Jesus mourn,
     Fasting at a nuptial feast,
           Triumph into sadness turn?

2.   But soon from earth remov'd
           They wail'd their Best-belov'd,
     Oft in fasts his loss deplor'd:
           Thus they our ensamples rise,
     Thus we languish for our Lord,
           Pine to meet him in the skies. (pp. 18–19)

1. [At the top of p. 1 in Wesley's shorthand is written: "Began March 8, 1766."]

51

Mk. 2:19–20.

II

1.   When Jesus first appears,
And wipes away our tears,
When from us our sins he takes,
Joy unspeakable we prove;
That th'espousing time he makes,
Time of pure delight and love.

2.   Hearing the Bridegroom's voice,
We only can rejoice:
Fear at his appearing flies,
Grief, and penitential pain,
Trouble, and temptation dies;
Kings we in his presence reign.

3.   No abstinence severe
Can be, while Christ is here:
High on eagles' wings we soar,
Safe in heavenly places dwell;
War and strife we reckon o're,
Suffering is impossible.

4.   But soon or late we moan
Our joyous Bridegroom gone,
Miss that sensible delight,
Extasy of infant grace,
Lose the Beatific Sight,
See no more his heavenly face.

5.   His face unless he hide,
We never can be tried:
Wherefore not in wrath, but love
Jesus partially withdraws,
Leaves his own, our faith to prove,
Leaves us bleeding on his cross.

6.   Then a long fast we keep,
    And for his absence weep:
Nothing can our souls relieve,
    Nothing can our loss supply;
Comfortless for Christ we grieve,
    Truly fast, and daily die.

7.   Throughout our mournful days
    Our misery we confess,
With the Man of sorrows droop,
    Share his consecrated pain,
Drink his passion's deepest cup,
    Till he shews himself again.

8.   Come Thou, our living Head,
    Our true, immortal Bread,
Enter every soul forlorn,
    Speak the latest conflict o're,
Into joy our sorrow turn,
    Come, and never leave us more. (pp. 19–20)

Mk. 2:23, *As he went through the cornfields, etc.*

While Jesus lets his followers eat,
    He suffers hunger still,
That pastors may themselves forget,
    And more for others feel:
By miracle the croud he fed,
    Not his own wants supplied,
He hungred in the people's stead,
    Thirsted for them, and died! (p. 20)

Mk. 3:7, *A great multitude followed him.*

[I]

Jesus whom the world forsake,
Pious souls their refuge make,
While their persecuted Lord
By the multitude ador'd,
Kindly all who come receives,
Life to all his followers gives. (p. 26)

Mk. 3:7.

II

One in Jesus' work employed
Gains by losing for his God:
If on some he lose his pains,
Listning multitudes he gains,
Strengthen'd by their fervent zeal,
Triumphs that they run so well. (p. 26)

Mk. 3:8, *A great multitude, when they had heard what great, etc.*

1. Saviour, by the world unknown,
   We have heard what Thou hast done,
   Thou hast in our gospel-days
   Wrought thine ancient works of grace,
   Hast thy pard'ning love reveal'd,
   Crouds of sinsick spirits heal'd.

2. Wherefore now on Thee we press,
   Plagued with sin's severe disease:
   Thee if we can touch, we know
   Power into our souls shall flow,
   Make our peace and pardon sure,
   Bless us with a perfect cure. (p. 27)

Mk. 3:19, *He ordained Judas.*

1.   Jesus a traitor chose
       Into the ministry,
    To shew us, his perfidious foes
       His officers may be:
       And who their Lord betray
       We for his sake esteem,
    But Christ's authority obey,
       But truly honour Him.

2.   The vilest minister
     Outward respect may claim:
And dignities we still revere;
     For Jesus did the same:
     Whom earth and heaven adore
     He stoop'd to man's commands,
He bow'd himself to lawful Power,
     Tho' lodg'd in wicked hands. (p. 29)

Mk. 4:29, *When the fruit is brought forth, immediately he putteth in the sickle.*

When a saint is quite mature,
     And fully sav'd by grace,
Pure in heart as God is pure,
     His God no longer stays:
He who sow'd the harvest reaps,
Removes the fruit to paradise,
     There the perfect spirits keeps,
     Till all to judgment rise. (p. 41)

Mk. 4:31–2, *It is like a grain of mustard seed, which, etc.*

[I]

The principle of grace divine
Sown in this earthly heart of mine,
Is humble joy, and heavenly peace,
And true, implanted righteousness:
Though scarce discernible the grain,
It doth the tree of life contain,
The purity of saints above,
And all the powers of perfect love.

II

When Jesus hath his kingdom sown,
It imperceptibly grows on;
No mention of "a work between,
Hearts instantaneously made clean,

The root of sin at once destroy'd,
The new, imaginary void,"
The Spirit bound by fancied rules,
The church o'rerun with frantic fools!

III

Lord, when thy love begins to reign,
The kingdom seems the smallest grain,
Deeper into the heart descends,
Appears, and gradually extends,
Arrives at full maturity,
A seed, a plant, a shrub, a tree;
And when ten thousand storms are past,
Subsists the same from first to last. (pp. 42–3)

Mk. 5:20, *He began to publish how great things Jesus, etc.*

1.   I publish abroad
The great mercy of God
On me, and on multitudes more:
Our souls He hath heal'd
And the devils expel'd,
That all may admire and adore.

2.   O that all would apply
To our Saviour, and try
What a freedom his Spirit imparts!
He would cast out their sin
By his own coming in,
And eternally reign in their hearts. (pp. 52–3)

Mk. 5:23–5, *One of the rulers besought him greatly, etc.*

Jesus *his* times and moments knows,
When least he seems our prayers to hear,
The mercy which to none he owes
His gracious will doth oft defer;
That following on with patient haste
We all may to his wisdom leave,
And heal'd at first, or heal'd at last,
The fulness of his life receive. (p. 53)

Mk. 6:51, *He went up unto them into the ship, etc.*

1. Jesus present to the heart
Bids our fears and sins depart,
Present with his church He is,
Bids our persecutions cease:
When delusion's flood runs high,
Let but Jesus speak, 'Tis I,
Error shall to truth give place,
False to real holiness.

2. Sinking now into the deep
Enter, Lord, the shatter'd ship;
Tost about with every wind,
Rest and Thee we long to find:
Let this storm of error cease,
Let thy church retrieve her peace,
Rescued by thy gracious power
Love, and wonder, and adore. (p. 72)

Mk. 6:54–5, *They knew him, and ran throughout that, &c.*

1. We cannot rest, who Jesus know,
Till others know Him too,
Till Christ on them his gifts bestow,
On them his wonders show:
Sinners we bring to Christ where'er
Distemper'd souls we find,
And wish that all with us may share
The Saviour of mankind.

2. We spread the odour of his name,
His name divinely sweet,
The helpless, sick, and blind, and lame
We cast at Jesus' feet;

We publish the whole land around
  The world's Physician near:
He now in England's church is found;
  Come all, and meet him here. (pp. 72–3)[2]

Mk. 7:27, *Jesus said unto her, It is not meet to take, etc.*

Those whom most the Saviour loves
  To succour he delays,
Long their faith and patience proves,
  And tries their utmost grace,
Seems to disregard their prayers,
  Treats with rigorousness extreme;
Thus his favourites he prepares
  For all that is in Him. (p. 78)

Mk. 8:26, *He sent him away to his house, saying, Neither, etc.*

1. A sinner blind, to sight restor'd,
      Should first into himself retreat,
    Maintain communion with his Lord,
      And muse, and wonder at his feet,
    In silent love on Jesus gaze,
    And ask a deeper root of grace.

2. A soul that hath the truth receiv'd
      Far from himself forbears to roam,
    Keeps close to Him he hath believ'd,
      And taught of God, he dwells at home,
    Before he publishes his cure,
    Or testifies his pardon sure.

2. [Verse 1 appears in *Poet. Works*, X, p. 502.]

3. *Tell it to none*, is Christ's advice,
    But wait till Christ the time declare:
   Tell it to all, our nature cries,
    And lo, we push into the snare,
   Bereft of all our boasted power,
   And tenfold blinder than before.

4. Lord, if thou hast my blindness heal'd,
    My soul inlighten'd by thy grace,
   Instruct me when to rest conceal'd,
    And when thy goodness to confess,
   With humble thankfulness to own
   The work, the praise, is all thine own. (pp. 90–1)

Mk. 8:30, *He charged them that they should tell no man of him.*

[I]

Jesus would be declar'd to none
    Before th'appointed day,
But we impatient to be known,
    Vainly ourselves display:
The season due to testify
    Our nature cannot find:
But who on Jesus' grace rely
    Shall know his time and mind.

II

Himself must first at Pilate's bar
    His Godhead testify,
And bold in death the truth declare
    Which all his foes deny:
He thus for us obtains the power
    Our Saviour to proclaim,
And publish in the chosen hour
    Th'Almighty Jesus' name. (pp. 91–2)

Mk. 9:10, *They kept that saying with themselves, questioning, etc.*

> The preachers should forbear to speak
> Of truths and mysteries unknown,
> Till whom in fervent prayer they seek
> They find the Comforter sent down,
> To teach their hearts th'unfolded word,
> And witness of their living Lord. (p. 98)

Mk. 10:14, *Forbid them not.*

> Partisans of a narrow sect,
> Your cruelty confess,
> Nor still inhumanly reject
> Whom Jesus would embrace:
> Your little ones preclude them not
> From the baptismal flood,
> But let them now to Christ be brought,
> And join the church of God. (p. 105)

Mk. 10:20, *All these have I observed from my youth.*

> Innocence in youth, how rare
> Th'inestimable grace!
> Yet how few alas, there are
> Who God their strength confess!
> Outward sin who never knew
> He knows not whence his virtue flows,
> Steals the praise to Jesus due,
> And on himself bestows. (p. 108)

Mk. 10:21, *Then Jesus beholding him, loved him.*

> 1.   Not for sin or splendid vice
> The harmless youth He lov'd:
> Innocence in Jesus' eyes
> Will always be approv'd:

Goodness negative, sincere
He his own gift with pleasure sees,
Smiles to mark our servile fear,
And legal righteousness.

2.   What in us is lacking still
Thy mercy, Lord, shall show,
Gently bind our yielding will
Our goodness to forego:
Then we shall our own deny,
Thy perfect righteousness to prove,
Joyfully sell all, and buy
The jewel of thy love. (p. 108)

Mk. 10:22, *He was sad at that saying, and went away grieved; etc.*

Th'advantages of riches see,
And envy them who will!
They steal the heart, O Lord, from Thee,
With care and sorrow fill:
A stranger to himself and God
Whoe'er on wealth relies,
Will never find the narrow road
Which leads us to the skies. (p. 109)

Mk. 10:35, *Master, we would that thou shouldst do for us, etc.*

Should vile, unworthy sinners dare
Prescribe what God to man shall give,
Or tell him, in presumptuous prayer,
We would the kingdom *now* receive!
We would impatiently rush on,
The summit in an instant gain,
Evade the cross, yet take the crown,
And *now* in full Perfection reign! (p. 112)

61

Mk. 12:1, *A certain man planted a vineyard . . . and let it, &c.*

1. Man's soul, the vineyard of the Lord,
   Planted by his creating word,
   Inclos'd, and hedg'd about it was,
   And fenc'd with all his righteous laws:
   To water him with sacred blood
   The sacramental winepress stood,
   To screen from every adverse power
   The church arose, his brasen tower.

2. God let his vineyard out to man,
   His rent of glory to obtain,
   Told him his soul was not his own,
   But made to serve his Lord alone;
   He bade him feed, increase, improve
   His grain of faith, his seed of love,
   And stock'd him with sufficient grace
   To bear the fruits of righteousness. (p. 128)[3]

Mk. 13:21, *If any man say to you, Lo, here is Christ, etc.*

From the old deceiver's snare
   Keep me, Lord, in life's decline,
Bid mine inmost soul beware
   Lest I take his voice for thine,
Fall into delusion's maze,
   Wandring stars at last approve,
Saints thro' instantaneous grace,
   Boasters of their perfect love. (p. 145)

Mk. 13:27, *Then shall he send his angels, and shall, etc.*

1. Thrice happy day that shall reveal
   The bearers of election's seal,
   The saints indeed, the heavenborn race,
   The vessels pure of spotless grace.

---

3. [Verse 2 appears in *Poet. Works*, XI, p. 49.]

2. We then shall each with each agree,
   The long expected union see,
   The church compleat, in spirit one,
   Assembled round that azure throne.

3. The Lord shall soon his angels send
   For all who his return attend,
   Throughout the universe dispread,
   And gather in the chosen seed.

4. Us in their hands ev'n now they bear,
   Guardians of every royal heir;
   But let them spread their golden wings,
   And waft us to the King of kings! (p. 148)

Mk. 14:12, *Where wilt thou that we go and prepare, etc.*

> Tho' crouds may uncommission'd run
>   T'usurp the priestly character,
> Th'Apostles' successors alone
>   The Christian passover prepare:
> But *we* thro' grace our sins remove,
>   Purge out the old unleaven'd bread,
> And then by humble faith and love
>   On Jesus in our hearts we feed. (p. 154)

Mk. 14:13, *There shall meet you a man bearing a pitcher of water, etc.*

> The water pure must go before,
>   And cleans'd in the baptismal flood
> We our redeeming Lord adore:
>   The mystery of his sprinkled blood,
> Commemorating the slaughter'd Lamb,
>   With Him we sing, with Him we feast,
> Thro' whom we out of Egypt came,
>   Thro' whom we gain that heavenly rest. (p. 155)

Mk. 14:34, *My soul is exceeding sorrowful unto death, etc.*

1. A Christian should with Christ remain,
Contemplate that mysterious pain
    Which we could never know,
If Christ did not in love reveal,
And give the tempted soul to feel
    A portion of his woe.

2. The drop Thou didst to me bequeath
I taste; thy sorrow unto death,
    It breaks my mournful heart:
But let me breathe my soul like Thee,
And with resign'd tranquillity
    Into thy arms depart. (pp. 161–2)

Mk. 14:35, *He fell on the ground, and prayed, that if it were possible, etc.*

1. By grief and sin's enormous load
Opprest, I fall before my God,
    And for deliverance pray;
If justice can give place to love,
Father, the bitter cup remove,
    Or take my life away.

2. But if thou wil'st the load t'abide,
Mine anguish from thy people hide,
    My fearful agony,
Nor let them thro' my sufferings faint,
Or see their pastor die for want
    Of holiness and Thee. (p. 162)

Mk. 14:49, *The scripture must be fulfilled.*

Call'd my Master to confess,
Suffering for my faithfulness,
By th'appointment of his will
Do I not his word fulfil?

Christ's afflictions now are mine,
Now I answer God's design,
For the Head and body's sake
Jesus' cup and cross partake. (p. 165)

Mk. 14:50, *They all forsook him, and fled.*

Jesus the Lord by man forsook
The sinner's punishment hath took,
Beneath our guilt and curse he stood,
For we have all forsaken God!
And now if hold of Christ we take,
Our Father will not us forsake,
But pardon, sanctify, and heal,
And with our souls forever dwell. (pp. 165–6)

Mk. 15:13, *They cried out again, Crucify him.*

We blame the rabble who prefer'd
   A robber to God's only Son,
(That blind, ungrateful, impious herd)
   Yet we alas, the same have done,
To his preferring our own will,
Our heavenly Lord we daily kill. (p. 172)

Mk. 15:17, *They clothed him with purple, & platted a crown of
thorns, & put it about his head.*

1. Kings of earth, to Christ bow down,
   Him who wears the thorny crown;
   Monarchs, who command the globe,
   Hail him in his purple robe;
   Homage to your Sovereign pay,
   At his feet your sceptres lay.

2. See, that all beneath your power
   Serve the King whom ye adore,
   That He may exalted be,
   Use your whole authority,
   Truth and piety maintain,
   Only live, that Christ may reign. (pp. 172–3)

Mk. 15:19, *Bowing their knees, they worshipped him.*

> If worship were, to bow the knee,
> Heathens adore as well as we:
> 'Tis not the knee, but heart, that prays,
> The heart that humbly sues for grace;
> Fixing our heart on Christ above
> We worship in the truth of love:
> The body bow'd is but the sign,
> And shews the service is divine. (p. 173)

Mk. 15:20, *When they had mocked him, they led him out to crucify him.*

> The wicked still our Lord oppress,
>   Their utmost rage and malice try,
> And when from mockeries they cease,
>   Him in his saints they crucify. (p. 173)

Mk. 15:23, *They gave him to drink wine mingled with myrrh: but he received it not.*

1.   Jesus tastes the bitter cup,
            The woe that yet remains,
        Tastes, but will not drink it up
            To stupify his pains:
        Without comfort or support
    He hangs, and bears the wrath alone,
        Will not cut his sufferings short,
            Or lose a single groan.

2.   Wonderful oeconomy
            Of agonies Divine!
        With a mind so calm and free
            To suffer, Lord, is thine:
        Jesus, lavish of thy blood,
    Insatiably athirst for pain,
        Thus Thou shew'st thy zeal for God,
            And thus thy love for man! (p. 175)

Mk. 15:24, *When they had crucified him, they parted his garments, etc.*

1. Members of his Church we know
  The poor his body are:
 All the goods he had below,
  They should his garments share:
 But the greedy soldiers seize
 What should supply his people's need,
  Leave the members in distress,
  And neither clothe nor feed.

2. Venerable gamesters play,
  Right venerable men,
 Each contends the goodliest prey,
  The largest share to gain,
 Eager each the whole t'ingross,
 As churchmen never satisfied,
  First they nail Him to the cross,
  And then his spoils divide. (pp. 175–6)

Mk. 15:28, *He was numbred with the transgressors.*

 My God expiring on a cross
 Numbred with the transgressors was,
  That I may numbred be
 With all his sons and saints in light,
 And gain the Beatific Sight
  Of Him who died for me. (p. 177)

Mk. 15:30, *Save thyself, and come down from the cross.*

1. One who hangs on yonder tree,
  Bleeding by his Saviour's side,
 Loves with his Belov'd to be,
  Cleaves to Jesus crucified:
 Never will he thence come down,
 Quit the cross, to lose the crown.

2. Not content with Christ to live,
      Daily on his cross to bleed,
    Let me all his pangs receive,
      Suffer till I bow my head,
    See th'accomplish'd sacrifice,
    Die when my Redeemer dies! (pp. 177–8)

Mk. 15:34, *My God, my God, why hast thou forsaken me!*

[I]

1.   Father, regard the cry
        Of Jesus' broken heart,
      And tell my guilty conscience why
        Thou dost from Him depart:
      Answer my Saviour's prayer,
        The prayer of dying love,
      Thy righteous wrath appeas'd declare
        And all my sins remove.

2.   Thou dost forsake thy Son,
        That I my due may know,
      Forsook for all which I have done,
        And left to endless woe;
        Thou hid'st from Him thy face,
        That I may not be driven
      To find in hell my proper place,
        But strangely 'scape to heaven. (pp. 179–80)

II

1.   From Thee his fav'rite, why
        Doth God his face conceal?
      Because He would not have us die,
        The world he lov'd so well:
        Because in love with pain
        Thou dost for sinners bleed,
      Thyself abandon to be slain
        A Victim in our stead.

2.   Casting a dying look
       Thy God thou cou'dst not find,
Because thy Spirit had forsook
       Our whole apostate kind,
Nor could our fallen race
       Rise and return to God,
Or e'er retrieve thy Spirit's grace,
       But thro' thy sprinkled blood. (p. 180)[4]

Mk. 15:39, *When the centurion saw that he so cried out, and gave up the ghost, etc.*

How powerful our Redeemer's cries
       Which life in death impart,
Which open still the sinner's eyes,
       And pierce his echoing heart!
By faith I hear his speaking blood,
       His mangled form I see,
And know, This is the Son of God,
       Whose cries converted me. (p. 182)

Mk. 15:40–1, *There were women looking on [. . .] Who when he was in Galilee followed him, etc.*

1.   Happy the saints that follow'd Thee,
       By their willing ministry
          Thine outward wants supplied!
When others fled, they found the grace
To stand in solemn grief, and gaze
          On Jesus crucified.

2.   O might I thus thro' life endure,
       Serve my Saviour in the poor;
          But while thy death I see,
Conform'd to an expiring God,
I would be cover'd with thy blood,
          And groan, and die with thee. (p. 182)

4. [Verse 2 appears in *Poet. Works*, XI, p. 90.]

Mk. 15:47, *Mary Magdalene and Mary the mother of, &c.*

1. Still by the holy matrons led
        Let us our dearest Lord pursue,
    True to the Living, and the Dead,
        Nor ever lose Him from our view:
    By contrite grief and humble fear
        Our strict fidelity approve,
    And follow on, and persevere
        In stedfast faith and constant love.

2. Him in his life and death we trace,
        In every state to Jesus come,
    Our Saviour on the cross confess,
        Our Saviour in the silent tomb:
    Low in the silent tomb he lies,
        Worthy to be by all ador'd,
    He lives immortal in the skies
        Our glorious Head, our heavenly Lord! (p. 183)[5]

Mk. 16:1, *Mary Magdalene, and Mary the mother of James, had bought, etc.*

True faith with unremitting strife
Desires, and searches after life;
It seeks and finds it in the grave
Of Him, who died our souls to save. (p. 184)

Mk. 16:2, *Very early in the morning, they came unto the sepulchre.*

True love holds on its even way,
Which grief can neither damp nor stay,
A fire inkindling in the soul
Which death can neither quench nor cool. (p. 184)

5. [The first four lines of each verse are combined to form one verse in *Poet. Works*, XI, p. 91.]

Mk. 16:3, *They said among themselves, Who shall roll us away the stone, etc.*

1. Who Jesus seek with zeal sincere
   No dangers can excite my fear,
   I mark the hindrances that rise,
   But love thro' all undaunted flies:

2. Impel'd by active love, I come
   To find him in his empty tomb,
   Nor mind the obstacles I see
   Quite insurmountable by me.

3. My impotence to Him is known:
   I cannot roll away the stone,
   But humbly trust in my Belov'd,
   And mountains are by faith remov'd.

4. While at the sepulchre I stay,
   The mountain shall be roll'd away,
   And I shall see my Lord arise,
   Drawn by his Spirit to the skies. (pp. 184–5)

Mk. 16:18, *They shall lay hands on the sick, &c.*

1. For the sick of sin we plead,
   And wrestle in thy name,
   Through thy Spirit intercede,
   And life and pardon claim:
   What we ask in faith, we have,
   Thou dost the prostrate souls restore;
   Witnessing thy power to save
   They rise, and sin no more.

2.   But are outward wonders ceas'd
And seen no more below?
Shall the Babylonish priest,
Or madman answer, No?
Fly the legendary tales,
Away with wild delusion's dream!
Still the truth of God prevails,
And still we trust in Him.

3.   If the ancient faith Thou give,
Th'almighty Cause restore,
Wilt thou not the work revive
Of thy stupendous power?
Known are all thy works to Thee;
Our only prayer, O Lord, is this,
Let thy will accomplish'd be
In our eternal bliss. (p. 193)[6]

6. [Verse 1 appears in *Poet. Works*, XI, p. 99.]

THE GOSPEL OF LUKE

THE GOSPEL OF LUKE
(MS Luke)[1]

Lk. 1:24, *Elisabeth conceived, and hid herself five months.*

Miracles of uncommon grace
On chosen fav'rites shown
Humility will first suppress,
    Nor haste to make them known:
But when necessity compels,
    And Jesus gives the word,
His witness all the truth reveals,
    To magnify the Lord. (p. 5)

Lk. 1:26–27, *In the sixth month the angel Gabriel was sent from God — to a virgin, &c.*

1.   The solemn hour is come
        For God made visible,
    Fruit of a virgin's womb
        A man with men to dwell,
    The Saviour of the world t'appear
    And found his heavenly kingdom here.

2.   The sinners' Sacrifice,
        The Head of angels see
    From Jesse's stem arise,
        And grasp the Deity!
    His sacred flesh the only shrine
    That holds Immensity Divine.

1. [At the top of p. 1 "April 8" is written in Wesley's shorthand and at the bottom of p. 366, "Finished April 29, 1766."]

3. Let all mankind abase
   Their souls before the Lord,
 And humbly prostrate, praise
   The great incarnate Word,
 And welcome Jesus from above
 With joy, and gratitude, and love. (p. 6)

Lk. 1:29, *She was troubled at his saying.*

 The humble starts at danger near,
   Troubled his own praise to hear,
   As then expos'd to pride:
 He dares not call his grace his own,
 But cries, Let God be prais'd alone,
   Let God be magnified! (p. 6)

Lk. 1:35, *The Holy Ghost shall come upon thee, and the power of the Highest shall, etc.*

1. In Jehovah's incarnation
   Father, Son, and Spirit join!
 Holy Ghost, thy inspiration
   Sanctifies the Birth Divine;
 Father, thy o'reshadowing power
   Strange fertility imparts,
 Forms whom all thy hosts adore,
   Forms him still in faithful hearts.

2. Jesus who assumes our nature
   Unto us his nature gives,
 Our Omnipotent Creator
   Still in all his people lives:
 Virgin-hearts again conceiving
   Compass the celestial Man,
 Comprehend by true believing
   Whom the heavens cannot contain. (pp. 7–8)

Lk. 1:49–50, *He that is mighty hath done to me great things, etc.*

1. Let all th'Incarnate God adore,
   The mercy, holiness, and power
      Of the great One in three!
   The Father hath his power display'd,
   Th'eternal Word a creature made,
      And God begins to be.

2. The Son our mortal flesh assumes,
   Our merciful High-priest becomes,
      The Spirit of holiness
   Immeasurable grace supplies,
   His human nature sanctifies,
      And fills the hallow'd place. (p. 14)

Lk. 1:55–56, *He hath holpen his servant Israel in remembrance of his mercy, etc.*

1. The God of faithfulness and love,
   His mercy and his truth to prove,
      Hath call'd his word to mind,
   Hath succour on the Mighty laid,
   And sent in Christ his saving aid
      To us, and all mankind.

2. He hath his promises fulfil'd,
   Jesus is in our flesh reveal'd
      To every sinner given,
   And all of Abraham's lot possest
   May live emphatically blest
      With pardon, grace, and heaven. (pp. 16–7)

Lk. 1:69, *He hath raised up an horn of salvation for us, etc.*

   Our souls and bodies to redeem
        The Father rais'd our Saviour up,
   In David's house, from David's stem,
        Ordain'd a fallen world to prop,
   To save, and on his people prove
   His whole omnipotence of love. (p. 18)

Lk. 1:70–71, *As he spake by the mouth of his holy prophets, etc.*

> Accomplishing his gracious word
>   By all his holy prophets spoke,
> The Lord hath sent us Christ the Lord,
>   To bruise our foe, and burst his yoke,
> From sin and death to set us free,
> And slay our last great enemy. (p. 18)

Lk. 1:80, *The child grew, and waxed strong in spirit, etc.*

> A preacher should himself conceal,
> Sequester'd in the desart dwell,
>   Content for years to fast and pray,
> Daily in grace and knowledge grow,
> Till strong for God, the Master show
>   His messenger in open day:
> Dead to the low desires of men
> The anchorite should then be seen;
>   Yet daily still himself deny,
> Simple and bold the truth declare,
> The people for his Lord prepare,
>   And Jesus' servant live and die. (p. 21)

Lk. 2:4–5, *Joseph also went up, to be taxed with Mary his espoused wife, etc.*

> Every ordinance of man
>   With Jesus we revere,
> Honouring who on earth sustain
>   The royal character;
> Jesus doth the pattern show,
> Ador'd by the angelic race,
> From before his birth below
>   The Lord of all obeys! (p. 22)

Lk. 2:7, *She . . . laid Him in a manger; because, &c.*

1. Whom the heavens cannot contain,
   God, the great eternal God,
   Born below, refus'd by men,
   Makes with beasts his first abode:
   While He needs his creatures' aid,
   They their needful aid deny,
   Leave him in a manger laid,
   Lord of all in earth and sky.

2. See, ye blushing sons of pride,
   See your God a child become!
   When He would on earth reside,
   Earth can scarce afford him room:
   Wrapp'd himself in swaddling bands
   Who with darkness swathes the sea,
   Who the universe commands,
   Comprehends immensity!

3. Triumph we, the sons of grace,
   That our God is born so poor,
   Doth his majesty abase
   Our salvation to secure:
   Glorying in our Infant-King,
   Him we in the manger own,
   Him whom highest seraphs sing
   High on his eternal throne. (pp. 22–3)[2]

Lk. 2:12, *This shall be a sign unto you; ye shall find, etc.*

1. Is this, O Lord, the sign
   That makes thy Greatness known,
   The ornament of power Divine,
   The glory of thy throne?
   Ennobled by thy birth
   My faith the manger sees,
   And all the precious things on earth
   Are vile, compar'd to this.

2. [Verses 2 and 3 appear in *Poet. Works*, XI, pp. 115–16.]

2.   'Tis here thy mind I know,
      Thy hidden kingdom see;
  Thou com'st from heaven to reign below
      By deep humility;
    The High and Lofty One
    Thou dost our meanness bear:
  And by humility alone
      Thy royal state we share. (p. 25)

Lk. 2:13, *And suddenly there was with the angel a multitude of the heavenly host praising God.*

1.   The angel-quires their voices raise
    To hymn a new-born Infant's praise,
    Own his Divine, Almighty power,
    And harping with their harps adore.

2.   And shall the ransom'd sons of men
    God in his humbled state disdain,
    The manger, as the cross, despise,
    Or stumble at their Maker's cries?

3.   Let Jews and Greeks as folly deem
    His infancy, his death blaspheme
    (That two-fold rock of human pride,
    A Saviour born and crucified!)

4.   Who truly in our Lord believe,
    With joy and triumph we receive
    The saving grace in Christ bestow'd,
    The Wisdom and the Power of God. (p. 26)

Lk. 2:18, *And all they that heard it wondred at those things which were told them, etc.*

  Shepherds indigent and plain,
    Jesus' first apostles hear,
  Hear them who that wondrous Man
    Simply to the world declare!

O might I my Lord admire,
God himself both hear and see,
Emulate th'Angelic choir,
Gaze to all eternity! (p. 28)

Lk. 2:25, *The same man was just and devout, waiting for the* *Consolation of Israel, etc.*

1.   A righteous man who fears
The Saviour out of love,
Doth only live, till Christ appears
His servant to remove:
By Jesus' Spirit led
He on his Lord attends,
Till Israel's Comforter and Head
With all his hosts descends.

2.   He first receives Him here,
God's co-eternal Son,
The Author and the Finisher,
And knows as he is known;
Receives Him from the skies
In plenitude of grace,
By faith embraces him, and dies,
To see his Saviour's Face. (pp. 30–1)

Lk. 2:27, *He came by the Spirit into the temple.*

Drawn by the Spirit of grace
Who to the house repair
Where God vouchsafes his name to place,
Shall meet his Saviour there,
In that mysterious bread
Shall find the latent God,
And on his sacred body feed,
And drink his precious blood. (pp. 31–2)

Lk. 2:28, *Then took he Him up in his arms, &c.*

1.   When in his arms he held,
      And to his bosom press'd,
    He found him to his heart reveal'd,
      And God for Jesus bless'd;
      The power and life of God
      He felt with Jesus given;
    And when his hoary head he bow'd,
      He carried Christ to heaven.

2.   O for an end like his!
      My long-expected Lord,
    Thou knowst I cannot die in peace,
      Till Thou perform thy word:
      O could I compass Thee,
      My Saviour now embrace,
    Now in thy love salvation see,
      And glory in thy face! (p. 32)[3]

Lk. 2:29–32, *Lord, now lettest thou thy servant depart in peace, &c.*

1. Father, since Thou permittest
     A weary soul's release,
    And for thy presence fittest,
     I now depart in peace.
    With joyful consolation
     I out of life depart,
    For I have seen Salvation,
     Have felt Him in my heart.

3. [Verse 1 appears in *Poet. Works*, XI, p. 120.]

2. Thine image & thy favor
    With Jesus is restor'd,
    And shewing me my Sav[iou]r,
    Thou hast perform'd thy word,
    Hast recompens'd my patiance
    With Jesus Christ, design'd
    Thy Blessing to the nations,
    Thy Gift to all mankind.

3. Jesus thine Heir Anointed
    The common Sav[iou]r is,
    Light of the world appointed,
    And Israel's glorious bliss:
    Illumin'd by his Spirit
    I find my way to Thee,
    And die, O Lord, t'inherit
    The joys prepar'd for me. (pp. 32–3)[4]

Lk. 2:35, *Yea, a sword shall pierce through thy own soul.*

1. When Jesus languish'd on the tree,
        Full of sacred sympathy
            She shar'd the mortal smart,
    As dying with her dying Lord
    She felt the sharp prophetic sword
            That pierc'd her faithful heart.

2. Conform'd to an expiring God,
        We who feel his sprinkled blood
            The same distress abide;
    And every soul that Jesus knows
    Partakes his bitterest pangs and woes,
            Together crucified. (p. 34)

Lk. 2:40, *The child grew.*

Jesus the child by growing shews
That still He in his members grows,
His body here receives increase
In faith, and love, and holiness:

4. [*Rep. Verse*, No. 169, p. 215.]

83

No instantaneous starts we find,
But more and more of Jesus' mind,
Till our full stature we attain,
And rise into a perfect man. (p. 35)

Lk. 2:45, *When they found him not, they turned back again to Jerusalem, etc.*

Dismay'd I should not be,
Or think I seek in vain;
When Christ will not be found by me,
He bids me search again:
Not by the Romish Sect,
But real saints ador'd,
Amidst the church of his elect
I trust to find my Lord. (p. 36)

Lk. 2:46, *They found him in the temple.*

Jesus whom once I knew,
But lost out of my sight,
I come determin'd to pursue,
To seek by day and night,
I follow hard and fast,
To all his paths repair,
And look to meet my God at last
In his own house of prayer. (p. 36)

Lk. 2:46, *They found him sitting in the midst of the doctors, etc.*

What divine humility
Doth the great Prophet show!
Hearkning to thy creatures, Thee
Th'eternal God we know:
Plac'd among the doctors Thou,
That all the doctors may submit,
To their heavenly Teacher bow,
And listen at thy feet. (p. 36)

Lk. 2:48, *Why hast thou thus dealt with us?*

> Self-love cannot conceive
> The gracious mystery,
> That Thou shou'dst in affliction leave
> The souls belov'd by Thee:
> But left in grief and pain,
> Thine absence we deplore,
> And seeking on, we find again
> And never lose Thee more. (p. 37)

Lk. 3:4, *Prepare ye the way of the Lord.*

> 1. Repentance preach'd we never hear,
>   But in the lonely desert place,
>   There only we incline our ear,
>   When 'scaping to the wilderness
>   We leave an hurrying world behind,
>   And time for cool reflection find.

> 2. A ready way repentance makes
>   For God to man, and man to God,
>   The sinner who his sin forsakes
>   Shall feel applied th'atoning blood,
>   The broken heart shall take him in
>   Who comes to save the lost from sin. (p. 39)[5]

Lk. 3:5, *Every valley shall be filled, &c.*

> 1. Giver of penitence, begin
>   Thy previous work of grace in me,
>   Convinc'd, confounded at my sin,
>   Deep sunk in false humility
>   My groveling, abject spirit raise;
>   Yet all my righteous pride abase.

5. [Verse 2 appears in *Poet. Works*, XI, p. 124.]

2.   To rectify my crooked will,
    To smoothe my nature's ruggedness,
Reform'd from every outward ill
    O bid me now from sinning cease,
Thy way into my heart prepare,
And then display thy glory there. (p. 40)[6]

Lk. 3:8, *Say not within yourselves, We have Abraham to our father.*

    Our fathers' piety,
    Unless we live like them,
Will prove a vain, delusive plea,
    Will serve but to condemn;
    Unless their steps we trace,
    We our own souls o'rethrow,
And sink, a vile degenerate race,
    Into eternal woe. (p. 42)

Lk. 3:8, *God is able of these stones to raise up children unto Abraham.*

    Repentance is a grace
    Which flows from Christ alone,
We cannot change the sinful race,
    Or mollify the stone:
    But if our God ordain,
    The rebel's reconcil'd,
Turn'd into flesh the hardned man,
    The stone into a child. (p. 42)

Lk. 3:9, *Now also the axe is laid unto the root of the trees, etc.*

1.   Sinner, who dost not bear
    The penitential fruit,
The righteous Judge will not defer,
    The axe is at the root:

6. [Verse 2 appears in *Poet. Works*, XI, p. 125.]

His justice hath decreed
To cast thee into hell,
And every barren tree shall feed
The fire unquenchable.

2.   The sentence past on all
Doth no exception make,
But every graceless soul shall fall
Into the burning lake;
Who want that holiness
Our God they cannot see,
But perish, driven from his face,
To all eternity. (pp. 42–3)[7]

Lk. 3:11, *He that hath two coats let him impart to him that hath none.*

Alms cannot alone, we know,
Cannot grace from God procure,
Yet at his command we show
Mercy to the helpless poor;
When our sins we truly leave,
We our neighbour's wants supply,
Till to us the Saviour give
Food and raiment from the sky. (p. 43)

Lk. 3:21, *Now when all the people were baptized, it came to pass, etc.*

1.   The King of saints, with glory crown'd,
Among a croud of sinners found,
Our Representative he makes
Himself, and our transgressions takes,
Baptiz'd, to purge us from all sin,
To wash our lives and conscience clean.

---

7. [Verse 1 appears in *Poet. Works*, XI, p. 126.]

2. He clave the sea by his command,
And Israel led to Canaan's land:
Now by his power He parts the air,
And heaven is open'd thro' his prayer,
That all his ransom'd ones may rise,
And find a passage to the skies. (p.46)

Lk. 3:23, *Jesus . . . began to be about thirty years of age.*

1. Who came to make his Father known
For thirty years Himself conceal'd,
Nor then his ministry begun
When first to public view reveal'd;
He teaches by his long retreat,
His silence bids our hearts be still,
His toil instructs us to submit,
And serve in man's his Father's will.

2. O what an endless treasure lies,
Jesus, in thy obscurity!
What springs of heavenly blessings rise
For those whose life is hid with Thee!
Who small in their own eyes and poor
Thy meek humility approve,
And rest in thy retreat secure,
And silence like their Saviour love!

3. Self-love would imitate thy zeal,
And pride thy shining actions do,
But little ones delight to dwell
With Thee, retir'd from public view:
O might my lot be cast with these
By man neglected and unknown,
I only want my Lord to please,
To live and die for God alone.

4. Jesus, my long-sequester'd God,
The lesson of thy life I hear;
It bids me shun the noisy croud,
And Thee in solitude revere:

Important far above our thought
Was thy conceal'd humility:
Silence for thirty years it taught;
Thy other truths were taught in three. (pp. 47–8)[8]

Lk. 4:9, *He set him on a pinnacle of the temple.*

1. Ah, wretched souls, who, lifted up
By Satan to the temple's top,
 The highest, holiest place,
Look down with scorn on all below,
Your own superior virtue *show*,
 Your own consummate grace!

2. Whom God exalts, he humbles too:
But devilish pride hath blinded you
 Who your perfection boast:
The fiend hath set you up on high,
And casts you down in sin to die,
 To die forever lost.

3. While yet on ruin's verge ye stand,
Beneath Jehovah's mighty hand
 Your towering selves abase;
Cast yourselves down at Jesus' word,
Own, ye vile worms, before the Lord
 Your utter sinfulness.

4. Crawl on the earth, nor ever more
At Satan's instigation soar
 Above the clouds to sit;
Humility your whole delight,
And your ambition's utmost height
 To weep at Jesus' feet. (p. 51)[9]

8. [Verses 1 and 4 appear in *Poet. Works*, XI, on pp. 129–30, respectively.]
9. [*Rep. Verse*, No. 170, pp. 215–16.]

Lk. 4:26, *Unto none of them was Elias sent, save unto a woman that was a widow.*

> The poor I to the rich prefer,
>   If with thine eyes I see;
> To bear thy Spirit's character
>   The poor are chose by Thee:
> The poor in every age and place
>   Thou dost, O God, approve
> To mark with thy distinguish'd grace,
>   T'inrich with faith and love. (p. 56)

Lk. 4:28, *When they heard these things, they were filled with wrath.*

> We tell the proud indignant race
>   That heaven is due to none,
> The source and principle of grace
>   Is hid in God alone:
> The number of his chosen here
>   We must insist is small;
> Yet still the God of love we clear,
>   Who offers life to all. (p. 57)

Lk. 4:34,[10] *I know thee who thou art; the holy one of God.*

> Talkers of a grace unknown
>   Only imitate the fiend,
> They proclaim the Holy One,
>   They the Son of God commend:
> Devils still may Jesus praise:
>   We who hear and do his word,
> Followers after holiness,
>   We shall find it with our Lord. (p. 57)

---

10. [Wesley incorrectly wrote Lk. 4:32.]

Lk. 5:3, *He entered into one of the ships, &c.*

1.   That apostolic ship,
That church where Christ abides,
Loosed from the earth, while in the deep,
    Above the deep it rides.
    Of unity the school,
    Of truth the sacred chair!
Jesus delights to sit and rule,
    And teach his people there.

2.   He at the helm appears,
Directs by his command,
Cooperates with his ministers,
    And bids them leave the land,
    Themselves from sin secure,
    From worldly things remove,
And keep their life and conscience pure,
    And work for Him they love. (p. 63)[11]

Lk. 5:4, *Now when he had left speaking he said unto Simon, Launch out into the deep, etc.*

1.   When our Incarnate God
No longer spake to men,
His church expanded all abroad
    Thro' the wide world was seen;
    Their net th'Apostles spread,
    Where'er their Lord they brought,
And strangely took with rapid speed
    Whole nations at a draught.

2.   None hath a right to throw
The net of Jesus' word,
Till Jesus bids the preacher go
    Commission'd by his Lord:

11. [Verse 1 appears in *Poet. Works*, XI, p. 141.]

But if his Spirit move,
Into the boundless sea,
Into the world we launch, and prove
Our prosperous ministry. (pp. 63–4)[12]

Lk. 5:6, *When they had this done, they inclosed a great, &c.*

If Thou the fishers guide,
Immortal souls we win,
Casting the net on the right side
We gather thousands in:
And tho' the figure break,
The gospel-net is sure,
The word of God is never weak
But always must endure. (pp. 64–5)[13]

Lk. 5:9, *He was astonished at the draught of fishes.*

Wondring he must express
His pious, humble fear:
Miraculous is his success,
And shows that God is near:
But stranger far the draught,
And made him more aghast,
Fisher of men, when Peter caught
Three thousand at a cast. (p. 66)

Lk. 5:10, *So was also James and John, &c.*

But more amaz'd I prove
How wondrous kind Thou art,
While by thy sweet alluring love
Thou dost my soul convert,
Out of the worldly deep
Dost draw by mercy's power,
And bring me in the sacred ship
To the celestial shore. (p. 67)

12. [Verse 1 appears in *Poet. Works*, XI, p. 141.]
13. [The first half of this verse appears in *Poet. Works*, XI, p. 142.]

Lk. 5:11, *When they had brought their ships to land, they forsook all, and followed him.*

How shall I thank thy love
Which hath such wonders done?
I'll set my heart on things above,
And live to God alone:
I would be wholly thine
Who gav'st thyself for me,
My all with grateful joy resign,
And die, to follow Thee. (p. 67)

Lk. 5:17, *As he was teaching, the power of the Lord was present to heal them.*

1. Jesus replete with truth and grace,
   Today as yesterday the same
Diffuses thro' our sinsick race
   The virtues of his balmy name,
Where'er he comes, by teaching heals,
And pardon on the conscience seals.

2. The gospel is his saving power,
   As every palsied soul shall prove,
When brought by faith, and laid before
   The Son of man, the God of love,
Helpless his pitying eye they meet,
And gasp for mercy at his feet. (p. 70)

Lk. 5:18, *And behold, men brought in a bed a man which was taken with a palsy, etc.*

1. Lo, in the arms of faith and prayer,
   We that thy pardning grace have known
A desperate Paralytic bear,
   And fain would bring him to thy throne,
An impotent and prayerless soul
Who wants the will to be made whole.

2. All methods of approaching Thee,
   Jesus, in his behalf we try:
   Nothing seems hard to charity,
   To us who on our Lord rely,
   By faith determin'd to remove
   Whate'er obstructs our zealous love. (pp. 70–1)

Lk. 5:19, *When they could not find by what way they might bring him in, because of the multitude, etc.*

The multitude of worldly cares
   And hindrances we now break thro',
Burst by the violence of our prayers
   A passage to the Saviour's view,
Force thro' the formal croud our way,
And at thy feet the sinner lay. (p. 71)

Lk. 5:20, *And when he saw their faith, he said unto him, Man, thy sins are forgiven thee.*

Thou seest our faith, bestow'd by Thee;
   We trust Thou wilt his guilt remove:
Made conscious of his misery,
   Condemn'd, absolve him by thy love,
Tell him, his sins are all forgiven,
And bless him with a Taste of Heaven. (p. 71)

Lk. 5:21, *The Scribes and the Pharisees began to reason, saying, Who is this, etc.*

Let Scribes and Pharisees blaspheme,
   And charge their blasphemies on Thee,
We know Thou canst on earth redeem
   Our souls from all iniquity,
The great prerogative Divine,
The power to cancel sin is Thine. (pp. 71–2)

Lk. 5:22, *But when Jesus perceived their thoughts, he answering said unto them, etc.*

Thou seest the ground of every heart,
    Thou its most secret plague canst heal;
Physician of mankind Thou art;
    Bid the proud reasoners be still,
Pity the men thro' envy blind,
And cure the darkness of their mind. (p. 72)

Lk. 5:23, *Whether is easier to say, Thy sins be forgiven thee, or to say, etc.*

Our bodies tottering o're the grave
    Thou daily dost to health restore;
With equal ease the sinner save,
    The soul by thy forgiving power
Out of his sins command to rise,
And trace thy footsteps to the skies. (p. 72)

Lk. 5:24, *But that ye may know that the Son of man hath power upon earth to forgive sins, etc.*

Whom now we to thy grace commend
    On him thy pardning mercy show,
Heal by a word our dying friend,
    That learned infidels may know
Thy power on earth, thy right Divine
To pardon sins, — as great as mine! (p. 72)

Lk. 6:2, *The Pharisees said unto them, Why do ye that which is not lawful to do on the sabbath days?*

1.   In outward things alone
        Who their religion prove,
    And hate the good they have not known,
        The law fulfil'd in love:

They only cloke their pride,
With humble words conceal,
Beneath a tender conscience hide
The envious rage of hell.

2. A false pretended zeal
For the Divine command,
Forbids our hearts its sense to feel,
Its end to understand:
Our pride and selfishness
Profane the day of rest:
But when from our own works we cease,
We keep the Christian feast. (p. 77)[14]

Lk. 6:5, *The Son of man is Lord also of the sabbath.*

Our gracious Lord gives back the day
He for his own did chuse,
His needful blessings to convey,
And serve his creatures' use:
And shall not we with pure delight
Our gratitude approve,
And every day our God requite
By humble praise and love? (p. 77)

Lk. 6:11, *They were filled with madness, and communed one with another what they might do to Jesus.*

1. Follower of Christ, thy calling see!
Inrag'd at Him for doing good,
The world will never pardon thee,
But counsel take to shed thy blood,
With madness of Satanic zeal
The servant, as his Lord, to kill.

14. [Verse 1 appears with slight alterations in *Poet. Works,* XI, p. 150.]

2. Whoe'er thou art, resolv'd to trace
That Friend and Patron of mankind,
Expect from an ungrateful race
Thy Saviour's recompense to find,
Yet bold go on, thy life lay down,
Endure the cross, and win the crown. (p. 78)

Lk. 6:14, *Simon, whom he also named Peter.*

1. Entring into the ministry,
A man intirely chang'd should be
In nature and in name,
A stranger to the world below,
The world should now no longer know
Or reckon him the same.

2. Firm as a rock that cannot move,
His soul should neither wish nor love,
Should neither hope nor fear,
Insensible of joy and pain,
Superior to the goods of men,
And to the evils here. (pp. 78–9)

Lk. 6:17, *He came down with them — and a great multitude came to hear him, etc.*

Still our dear redeeming Lord
Stoops to bless us from above,
Publishes th'inlightning word,
Ministers the saving love:
With the croud that still draw near,
With th'untutor'd sons of pain,
Ignorant, I come to hear,
Sick of sin my cure to gain. (p. 79)

Lk. 6:29–30, *Unto him that smiteth thee on the one cheek offer also the other, etc.*

Saviour, the laws of selfish man
Thou dost not supersede,
But a more perfect way explain
Which few delight to tread:

May I among that holy few
  Be with thy counsel blest,
And meekly bear, and simply do
  What Thou accountest best. (p. 80)

Lk. 7:6, *Lord, trouble not thyself, for I am not worthy that thou shouldest enter, etc.*

O could I to my Saviour pray
  With simple faith and humble love,
Long from my soul Thou wou'dst not stay,
  But come, and all my griefs remove:
To sinners vile in their own sight
  Thou more than grantest their request,
To dwell with such Thou tak'st delight,
  Their heavenly, everlasting Guest. (pp. 93–4)

Lk. 7:8, *For I also am a man set under authority, having soldiers under me, etc.*

All things to thy command submit,
  All things are possible with Thee:
Thine ancient miracle repeat,
  Exert thine healing grace on me;
With me let thy good Spirit stay,
  Command the evil to depart,
And bid me now my Lord obey
  With all my soul, and strength, and heart. (p. 94)

Lk. 7:9, *Jesus marvelled at him, and said, I have not found so great faith, etc.*

Jesus commends the good in man,
  The gift he freely did bestow,
The pride of nature to restrain,
  Himself he doth the Author show:
He doth an Heathen's faith admire,
  His people's jealousy to raise,
That *we* the blessing may desire,
  That *we* may spread the Giver's praise. (pp. 94–5)

Lk. 7:14, *He came and touched the bier (& they that bare him stood still), etc.*

1. He comes to raise the dead again,
   He strikes him with disease or pain,
      And touches thus the bier,
   His hand upon the body lays,
   Or power into his soul conveys
      Thro' his attentive ear.

2. How great thy love, to stop and turn
   A sinner by his passion borne
      To that infernal grave!
   Buried he there woud always lie,
   But that thy quickning power is nigh
      His sinful soul to save. (p. 96)

Lk. 7:16, *There came a fear on all: and they glorified God, saying, That a great prophet, etc.*

1. Jesus, th'incarnate God, we praise,
   Proclaim his mighty works of grace
      With wonder, joy, and fear:
   God hath his people visited,
   A Prophet great in word and deed
      Doth in our land appear.

2. Dead, dead in sins and trespasses
   Us to the life of righteousness
      He hath in love restor'd,
   And rendring back what we receive
   We only think, and speak, and live
      To magnify the Lord. (p. 97)

Lk. 7:17, *This rumour of him went forth throughout all Judea, and throughout all the region, etc.*

> O that our dear Redeemer's fame,
> And all the virtues of his name
>   Throughout the earth were spread,
> That every soul with us might know
> Jesus, the Life reveal'd below,
>   The Raiser of the dead. (p. 98)

Lk. 7:21, *In that same hour he cured many of their infirmities, &c.*

> Jesus, we hear thine actions speak
>   That Thou art He, by God decreed
> To cast out fiends, to heal the sick,
>   Restore the blind, and raise the dead;
> Thy language plain we understand,
>   Perceive with joyful hearts and eyes
> The works of an Almighty Hand,
>   And greet our Saviour from the skies. (p. 99)

Lk. 7:22, *The blind see, the lame walk, &c.*

> On us, O Christ, thy mission prove,
>   Thy full authority to heal,
> The blindness of our hearts remove,
>   The lameness of our feeble will,
> Open our faith's obedient ear,
>   Our filthy, leprous nature cure,
> Call us out of the sepulchre,
>   And preach Perfection to the poor. (p. 99)[15]

15. [*Rep. Verse*, No. 172, p. 217.]

Lk. 7:34, *Ye say, A friend of publicans and sinners.*

A Friend to us, but not our sins,
We bow to Jesus' sway,
Our Saviour and exalted Prince
Who takes our sins away:
A Friend of publicans, he gives
Us power to do his will,
And humbled penitents receives
Into his kingdom still. (p. 100)

Lk. 7:35, *Wisdom is justified of all her children.*

Wisdom by all her children here
Is own'd and justified,
Christians indeed for Christ appear,
As champions on his side;
They vindicate the sinner's Friend,
His discipline approve,
And free from sin their lives commend
The liberty of love. (p. 101)

Lk. 7:39, *This man, if he were a prophet, would have known, who, and what manner of woman, etc.*

God omniscient as Thou art,
Manifested here below,
Well thou know'st a sinner's heart
Better than myself I know:
Who, and what a wretch am I,
Only thou canst comprehend,
Thou, thro' whom I now draw nigh,
Know, and touch the sinner's Friend. (p. 102)

Lk. 7:43, *Thou hast rightly judged.*

Jesus, Thou hast spoke the word,
Comfortable word for me:
Ought not I t'embrace my Lord,
Cleave with warmer love to Thee?

All my heart's desire Thou know'st:
Fain I would my zeal approve:
Let me, if forgiven most,
Most my gracious Saviour love. (p. 103)

Lk. 7:45, *This woman, since I came in, hath not ceased to kiss my feet.*

Who before the Saviour lies
Should the mourner's task repeat;
Penitents can never rise,
Never cease to kiss his feet:
Thus may I my faith approve,
Lower sinking still and lower,
Jesus in his members love,
Honour Jesus in the poor. (p. 104)

Lk. 7:46, *My head with oil thou didst not anoint; but this woman hath anointed my feet, etc.*

1. Jesus takes the sinner's part,
   Her whom Pharisees condemn,
   Searcher of his creature's heart
   Turns the charge from her to them,
   Bids their haughtiness give place,
   Thrice commends whom they reprove,
   Triumphs in his work of grace,
   Praises her superior love.

2. Know, ye zealots proud and blind,
   Ye who profligates despise,
   Profligates, when Christ they find,
   More than you, the Saviour prize:
   Precious balm on Christ they pour,
   Lavish what they most esteem,
   Glad his costliest gifts restore,
   Nothing count too dear for Him. (pp. 104–5)

Lk. 8:1, *He went throughout every city and village, preaching, and shewing, etc.*

1. Bishop of souls, where shall we see
   A bishop that resembles Thee,
   Who trav'ling hard from place to place
   Proclaims the power of reigning grace,
   And dares by copying them approve
   Thy zeal, and vigilance, and love!

2. The evangelic Spirit give,
   That they who now in honours live,
   May humbly track their humble Lord,
   May freely minister the word,
   And simply poor advance thy cause,
   And spread the kingdom of thy cross. (p. 107)

Lk. 8:13, *They on the rock are they, which, when they hear, receive the word with joy, etc.*

The word they may with joy receive,
But only for a time believe,
   And soon unfaithful prove,
In fierce temptation's hour they faint,
Wither, and fade away, who want
   The root of humble love. (pp. 108–9)

Lk. 8:14, *That which fell among thorns are they, which, when they have heard, go forth, etc.*

Worldlings the gospel hear in vain,
Go forth into the world again,
   Their lusts to gratify,
With pleasure chok'd, or wealth, or care,
No fruit they to perfection bear,
   But live in sin, and die. (p. 109)

Lk. 8:15, *They . . . bring forth fruit with patience.*

1. The word, the seed of righteousness,
   Sown in our hearts we gladly feel.
   With joy our proffer'd Lord embrace,
   With rapturous joy unspeakable
   Receive the news of sin forgiven,
   And taste in love our present heaven.

2. Yet the incorruptible seed
   Doth never in a moment rise,
   But buried deep, as lost and dead,
   Long in our earthy hearts it lies,
   Water'd, before the fruit appears,
   With showers of grace, and floods of tears.

3. Howe'er our hasty nature fret,
   Or instantaneous growth require,
   We must, we *must*, with patience wait,
   With humble languishing desire,
   And when ten thousand storms are pass'd,
   Bring forth the perfect fruit — at last.

4. Patience we need the word to keep,
   Patience in persevering prayer,
   Patience to urge our way, and weep,
   And wait the proper time to bear,
   The season due which God ordains,
   The end of all our griefs and pains.

5. Patience in doing good we need,
   Patience in meekly bearing ill,
   Patience till the immortal seed
   Victorious o're our sins we feel,
   Patience to toil, and strive, and pray,
   And fight, and suffer — to that day. (pp. 109–10)[16]

---

16. [Verses 1–3 appear in *Poet. Works*, XI, p. 170.]

Lk. 8:18, *Take heed how ye hear.*

> O how ought we to hear
> The gospel of our Lord,
> How 'scape the punishment severe,
> And gain the full reward!
> By this we stand or fall:
> This awful word shall be
> Savour of life or death to all,
> Of heaven or hell — to me. (pp. 110–11)

Lk. 8:22–3, *He entered into a ship with his disciples.*

> 1. The present life our passage is,
>   The world we must cross o're,
> As vessels tost on dangerous seas,
>   To that eternal shore:
> Temptation is the stormy wind,
>   Corruption's stream we feel,
> Which fills our feeble heart and mind,
>   Which sinks us into hell.

> 2. We sink as every moment down
>   Into the threatning deep,
> And Jesus seems to leave his own,
>   And Providence to sleep:
> Higher he lets the tempest rise,
>   He lets the floods o'reflow,
> And darkness intercepts the skies,
>   And Tophet yawns below. (pp. 111–12)

Lk. 8:30, *Jesus asked him, What is thy name? and he said, Legion: because many devils, etc.*

> The soul possest by base desires
> Satan with every lust inspires,
>   His kingdom to maintain,
> Foul thoughts, a countless multitude,
> Whole hosts of fiends and passions lewd
>   As in their palace reign. (p. 114)

Lk. 8:31, *They besought him that he would not command them to go out into the deep.*

> Struck, but with no remorse within,
> He dreads the wages of his sin,
>   He trembles to be thrust
> By wrath into th'abyss of fire,
> And rather wishes God a liar,
>   And the great Judge unjust. (p. 114)

Lk. 8:32, *They besought him that he would suffer them to enter into the swine.*

> If gratified in his request
> He, for the pleasures of a beast,
>   Would all besides resign,
> Abandon'd to his carnal will,
> With sordid husks his senses fill,
>   And wallow with the swine. (pp. 114–15)

Lk. 8:40, *When Jesus was returned, the people gladly received him, etc.*

1. Lord, we for thine absence mourn,
       When out of our sight Thou art;
   Comfort us by thy return,
       Gladden every waiting heart:
   Teach our hearts to wait aright,
       Till the brightness of thy face
   Change our darkness into light,
       Change our nature into grace.

2. Man would all the reasons know
       Why thou dost thy followers leave:
   But *we* let thy Spirit blow,
       As he lists his comforts give:
   Thou, by whom the heart's prepar'd,
       All my sloth and haste remove,
   Then come back my full reward,
       Then come in my perfect love. (p. 115)

Lk. 8:45, *The multitude throng thee and press thee, and sayest thou, Who touched me?*

Numbers for custom['s] sake
The outward signs partake,
Still the name of Christ profess,
Sharers of the gospel-word,
After him they throng and press,
Press, but never touch the Lord. (p. 117)

Lk. 8:46, *Jesus said, Somebody hath touched me: for I perceive that virtue is gone out of me.*

No good in man can be,
But what proceeds from Thee:
Jesus, full of truth and grace,
Virtue now from Thee hath flow'd;
I my Spirit's cure confess,
Glorify the pardning God. (p. 117)

Lk. 8:48, *Daughter, be of good comfort, thy faith hath made thee whole, go in peace.*

1.   When Christ himself reveals
His peace my pardon seals,
Then his Spirit he bestows,
Then the power of faith I prove,
Comfort all my heart o'reflows,
Joy, and righteousness, and love.

2.   Lord, if my sin-sick soul
Thou hast indeed made whole,
Bid me go in humble peace,
Go to that celestial prize,
Go to perfect holiness,
Go to God in paradise. (p. 118)[17]

17. [Verse 2 appears in *Poet. Works*, XI, p. 174.]

Lk. 9:2, *He sent them to preach the kingdom of God, and to heal the sick.*

> Whoe'er the heavenly kingdom preach,
>   Which always will endure,
> They still an healing doctrine teach,
>   And dying spirits cure:
> Evince their mission from above
>   By this authentic sign,
> Their gospel on believers prove,
>   The saving power Divine. (p. 123)

Lk. 9:10, *The apostles, when they were returned, told him all that they had done, etc.*

> After our ministerial toil,
> Retir'd with Christ we rest awhile,
>   For farther toil prepare,
> Our works before his flaming eyes,
> Our words, and thoughts we scrutinize
>   With shame, and praise, and prayer. (p. 124)

Lk. 9:14–16, *Make them sit down, &c.*

> 1. A bishop primitively good
>   Deals to his flock their needful food,
>   And feasts them with the word sincere;
>   Loos'd from the world, he bids them sit
>   As listning at their Saviour's feet
>   The great eternal Truth to hear;
>   He first partakes the heavenly bread,
>   And lifts his soul with manna fed
>   In humble praises to the skies;
>   By prayer he brings the blessing down
>   The evangelic feast to crown,
>   The bread of life which never dies.

2. He breaks to all the mystic bread,
    The word to each, as each hath need,
       By ministerial hands conveys;
    Pastors subordinate he sends,
    The people to their care commends
       To stewards wise of gospel-grace.
    The truth from Christ deliver'd down,
    And made thro' his apostles known
       Their genuine successors receive,
    And if our Lord his love imparts,
    We feed on Jesus in our hearts,
       And fill'd with God forever live. (p. 126)

Lk. 9:22–3, *The Son of man must suffer many things, and be rejected — and be slain, etc.*

1. In that suffering Son of man
       My true way to heaven I see:
    All who rise with Thee to reign,
       First partake the cross with Thee;
    They that let Thee die alone
    Hope in vain to reach thy throne.

2. Yes, the sufferings of our Head
       Are in us endur'd again,
    All who in thy footsteps tread
       Vilified, rejected, slain,
    Every day thy lot receive,
    Die thy death, thy life to live.

3. Daily we ourselves deny,
       Call'd to seek the things above,
    Every passion crucify,
       Worldly lust, and creature-love,
    Follow by thy Spirit led,
    Sink as free among the dead.

4. Then emerging from thy grave
   That mysterious rise we know,
   Know thy utmost power to save,
   Life of God reveal'd below,
   Token of the body's rise,
   All the life of paradise. (p. 128)

Lk. 9:24, *Whosoever will save his life, shall lose it.*

Friend to his flesh alone
His flesh who cherishes,
And in a shadow vain walks on,
And seeks himself to please,
With nature's will complies;
His own worst enemy,
He hates his real life, and dies
To all eternity. (p. 129)

Lk. 9:27, *There be some standing here which shall not taste of death,*
till they see, etc.

1. O were it in my heart made known,
   Before I lay this body down,
   That I shall surely see
   The power of thy victorious grace,
   The joy, and peace, and righteousness,
   The kingdom fixt in me.

2. How gladly then should I resign
   My soul into the hands Divine,
   To meet my Lord again,
   To see the God of boundless love
   And worship at thy throne above,
   And triumph in thy train. (pp. 130–1)

Lk. 9:29, *As he prayed, the fashion of his countenance was altered, and his raiment, etc.*

1. A faithful soul that ceaseless prays
   The prayer of God, and sees his face
       In Jesus Christ reveal'd,
   Doth in his heavenly image shine,
   Transfigur'd by the Spirit Divine,
       And with his signet seal'd.

2. The glory which all thought transcends
   Ev'n to his outward man extends,
       The wisdom from above,
   The image in his face is seen,
   His simple, meek, and modest mien,
       His innocence and love. (pp. 131–2)

Lk. 9:33, *Let us make three tabernacles; one for Thee, &c.*

1. Who tastes the truth, and Jesus sees
   In all the Scripture-mysteries
       The law and prophets' End,
   Delights to meditate and pray,
   Would gladly on the mountain stay,
       And never more descend.

2. But O, it cannot, cannot be,
   That pleasant sweet tranquillity,
       That permanence of rest:
   A follower of the Lord MUST sink,
   His Master's cup of passion drink,
       And live, like Him, distrest;

3. Must with the Man of Sorrows grieve,
   The mountain for the people leave,
       Go on to Calvary,
   Expend his life in doing good,
   Toil, till he sweats that sweat of blood,
       And dies upon that tree! (pp. 133–4)[18]

18. [Verse 1 appears in *Poet. Works*, XI, p. 184.]

Lk. 9:34, *There came a cloud, and overshadowed them, and they feared, etc.*

1. The darkness doth to light succeed,
   To rapt'rous joy the humble dread,
      (Howe'er our flesh complain,
   And still for consolations pine)
   Permitted by the will Divine
      The cloud returns again.

2. We enter then into the cloud,
   When Christ suspends the light bestow'd,
      Or sensibly withdraws,
   That, feeling all our comforts gone,
   Our souls may cleave to Him alone,
      And hang upon his cross. (p. 134)

Lk. 9:41, *O faithless generation, how long shall I be with you, and suffer you? Bring thy son hither.*

   Full of impurity
   We bring the youth to Thee:
Shall our unbelief withstand?
   Thou the Lord almighty art:
By the word of thy command
   Drive the foe out of his heart. (p. 138)

Lk. 9:42, *As he was yet a coming, &c.*

   Him if the tempter shake,
   And a last effort make,
Yet display thy saving power,
   On the sinner dispossest,
To his joyful friends restore,
   To his heavenly Father's breast. (p. 138)

Lk. 9:45, *They understood not this saying, — and feared to ask him.*

> Happy the man who ever bears
>   Thy cross upon his heart imprest,
> A burthen nature shuns, nor dares
>   Th'experience of thy death request:
> Yet, Lord, I ask Thee to explain
> The myst'ry of thy cross to me:
> And lo, I share thy mortal pain,
> Obedient unto death with Thee. (p. 139)

Lk. 9:46, *Then there arose a reasoning among them, which of them should be greatest.*

> Christ from his power diverts our mind,
>   On his humility to place:
> We leave the cross, the power to find,
>   Ourselves above the rest to raise,
> Ambitiously affect the throne,
> And love no greatness but our own. (p. 139)

Lk. 9:48, *He that is least among you all, the same shall be great.*

> 1. How are you least in your own eyes
>   Who others from yourselves remove,
>   Rank in the highest class, and prize
>   Yourselves for your superior love,
>   Too holy with the rest to join,
>   *Select* in purity divine?

> 2. Begin, ye worms, yourselves to know,
>   Who would be truly good and great,
>   Your proud preeminence forego,
>   And take with shame the lowest seat;
>   And then with open'd eyes ye see
>   No greatness but humility. (p. 140)

Lk. 9:49, *We forbad him, because he followeth not with us.*

Where is the sect or party free
From nature's jealous bigotry?
Who blame the bitter zeal of *Rome*
Their brethren to destruction doom:
Ev'n those who Christ in measure know,
The envious imperfection show,
And cool[l]y praise or loud condemn
The men that follow not with them. (pp. 140–1)

Lk. 9:50, *Forbid him not.*

II

Possessors of the Saviour's mind,
Joyful where'er the truth we find,
The truth we cordially approve,
And all the friends of Jesus love;
His servants ev'n in Babel see,
And wish them full prosperity,
Who carrying on our Lord's design
Advance the work of grace divine. (p. 141)[19]

Lk. 9:53, *They did not receive him, because his face was as though he would go, etc.*

Heav'nward when we turn our face
    Us the world will not receive,
Tell us this is not our place,
    No relief or shelter give:
Yet we no resentment feel,
    Mindful of our Master's word;
Let them hate, refuse, repel,
    Treat the servants as their Lord. (p. 142)

19. [The first poem on this text appears in *Short Hymns*, II, p. 218 and *Poet. Works*, XI, p. 188.]

Lk. 9:55, *Ye know not what manner of spirit ye are of.*

We who Jesus' Spirit know,
  Meekly share his grief and pain,
Cannot bitter anger show,
  Cannot of our foes complain,
Tho' they seek to shed our blood,
  Patient we the wrong abide,
Followers of a martyr'd God,
  Him who for his murtherers died. (p. 143)

Lk. 9:56, *The Son of man is not come to destroy men's lives, but to save them.*

Son of man, Thou didst not come
  Sinners to destroy but save:
Save my soul, reverse its doom,
  Save my body from the grave;
Hold my soul in life, I pray,
  Till in holiness renew'd
First I see the perfect day,
  Then the Blis[s]ful Face of God. (p. 143)

Lk. 9:58, *Foxes have holes, and the birds of the air have nests, but the Son of man, etc.*

1.   Saviour, how few there are
  Who thy condition share,
Few who cordially embrace,
  Love, and prize thy poverty,
Want on earth a resting-place,
  Needy and resign'd like Thee!

2.   I dare not ask thy pain
  And sorrow to sustain:
But if Thou vouchsafe me power
  Thee by want to glorify,
Blest with love I ask no more,
  Poor I live, and patient die. (p. 144)

115

Lk. 9:59–60, *He said unto another, Follow me: but he said, Lord, suffer me first, etc.*

>One would fain his follower be
>Whom Jesus doth refuse:
>One declines the ministry;
>And him He stoops to chuse;
>Shews us thus, whoe'er pretend
>The preachers at *their* bidding run,
>Preachers to appoint and send
>Belongs to Christ alone. (p. 144)

Lk. 9:60, *Let the dead bury their dead; but go thou, and preach the kingdom of God.*

>Worldly things to worldly men
>Thy servants, Lord, should leave:
>Lo, I come, if Thou ordain,
>And a poor worm receive,
>Preach the power of grace divine,
>Which may by every heart be known:
>Fix thy kingdom now in mine,
>And make me all thy own. (pp. 144–5)

Lk. 10:1, *The Lord appointed other seventy also, &c.*

>1.   Two and two, not one and one,
>   He sends His messengers,
>   Makes by them His coming known,
>   By them His way prepares:
>   What shall part whom God hath join'd,
>   Or break th'indissoluble cord?
>   Two are one in heart and mind,
>   When Jesus is the third.

>2.   Pleas'd He is, who cannot need
>   The help of feeble man,
>   Instruments to use and speed,
>   And ministers t'ordain;

Thus their need of concord shows
And makes them each with each agree,
Union on his church bestows,
And founds the Hierarchy. (p. 146)[20]

Lk. 10:2, *The labourers are few: pray ye therefore the Lord of the harvest, &c.*

Of careless pastors ye complain,
Scandalous priests who serve for gain,
Or quite neglect their flock to feed,
And send poor hirelings in their stead:
The faithful labourers are few;
But the defect we charge on you;
You by your sloth the sheep betray,
Who never once for labourers pray. (p. 146)

Lk. 10:7, *Remain, eating & drinking such things as they give you, etc.*

Who labours in the word from man
      No recompense, but bread, receives;
Accepting his successful pain
      The great reward his Master gives,
No sensible or transient good,
But all which God on Christ bestow'd. (pp. 147–8)

Lk. 10:8, *Eat such things as are set before you.*

1. A preacher should with freedom use
        The food which poor or rich prepare,
    Nothing reject, and nothing chuse,
        The better, or the meaner fare
    With equal thankfulness receive,
    Nor live to eat, but eat to live.

---

20. [Verse 1 appears in *Poet. Works*, XI, p. 190.]

2. Detatch'd from every earthly good
   The servant should on earth appear,
   Hard labouring for immortal food,
   Content with Christ, his portion here,
   Of that one needful Good possest,
   And nothing want of all the rest. (p. 148)[21]

Lk. 10:9, *Say unto them, The kingdom of God is come nigh unto you.*

1. Earth's conquerors seek with fire and sword
   Their neighbour's realms to waste and seize;
   The King of kings, the heavenly Lord
   Sends forth his messengers of peace,
   And would to all his kingdom give,
   And kindly force us to receive.

2. Whene'er the joyful sound we hear,
   Of God in Jesus pacified,
   The kingdom and the King is near,
   And comes with sinners to reside:
   And if he now his love imparts,
   We find him reigning in our hearts. (p. 148)

Lk. 10:16, *He that heareth you, heareth me.*

1. The genuine Apostolic word
   From every chosen instrument
   We hear as from their heavenly Lord,
   Honour the Sender in the sent,
   Our ear, and willing heart incline,
   And prove by faith the word Divine.

21. [Verse 1 appears with slight alterations in *Poet. Works*, XI, p. 191.]

2. But who th'Ambassadors despise,
   Their office, word, and person scorn,
   Refuse a message from the skies,
   From God and not from man they turn,
   Divine authority disown,
   Reject the Father and the Son. (p. 149)

Lk. 10:22, *All things are delivered to me of my Father, &c.*

1. All power, authority, and grace
   Deliver'd to our Head
   He uses for the chosen race,
   His true, believing seed:
   The fulness of the Godhead dwells
   In God's incarnate Son,
   And Christ to sinful men reveals,
   And makes his Father known.

2. Jesus, Thou wou'dst of all mankind
   The Friend and Saviour be,
   Thou wou'dst that every soul should find
   God reconcil'd in Thee:
   And when thy bleeding love Thou show'st,
   And dost to me impart,
   The Father, Son, and Holy Ghost
   Resides within my heart. (p. 153)

Lk. 10:28, *This do, and thou shalt live.*

Do it Thyself in me,
I then shall do thy will,
Shall live thy life, inspired by Thee,
And all thy words fulfil,
Perfect in every good,
When Thou hast perfect made,
Thy law shall then on me be show'd
In purest love obey'd. (p. 154)[22]

22. [The first half of the verse appears in *Poet. Works*, XI, p. 196.]

Lk. 10:30, *A certain man went down from Jerusalem to Jericho and fell among thieves, etc.*

1. How desperate is the state of man!
   My misery will his case explain
       Who among robbers fell:
   Pure from the hands of God I came;
   Now in the cruel hands I am
       Of sin, the world, and hell.

2. That city of the living God
   Was built to be my soul's abode;
       My soul from thence came down,
   Down to this Jericho beneath,
   This place accurst of sin and death,
       And endless pains unknown.

3. Far from the new Jerusalem,
   Deeper and deeper still I seem
       Implung'd in guilt and woe,
   Lower, and lower still I sink,
   And trembling hang as on the brink
       Of the dark gulph below.

4. The thieves have torn away my dress,
   That robe of spotless righteousness
       I did in Eden wear:
   Spoil'd of my immortality,
   Naked of God, my shame I see,
       And Satan's image bear.

5. The thieves have rob'd, and stript, and bound,
   And mangled me with many a wound,
       And bruis'd in every part:
   My putrid wounds stand open wide,
   My head is faint, and sick of pride,
       And all corrupt my heart.

6. Too long insensible I lay,
   The ruffians had secur'd their prey,
      And left my spirit dead:
   Or if one spark of life remains,
   It makes me feel my mortal pains,
      And feebly gasp for aid. (pp. 155–6)

Lk. 10:31, *And by chance there came down a certain priest that way,* etc.

1. The prophets, saints, and patriarchs old
   Could man's most helpless case behold,
      But not his fall repair;
   They saw, but pass'd the sinner by,
   They left as at the point to die
      The wounded traveller.

2. The venerable priest may see
   My wounds, but cannot succour me,
      But cannot heal his own;
   Not all the righteousness of man
   Will mitigate my grief and pain,
      Or for my sins atone. (p. 156)

Lk. 10:32, *Likewise a Levite, when he was at the place, came and looked on him,* etc.

1. The Levite stern approaches nigh,
   Observes with unrelenting eye,
      And shows my desperate case,
   Commands, but brings me no relief,
   But aggravates my sin and grief,
      And all my wounds displays.

2. The Law commands, Do this and live,
   But power and grace it cannot give,
      It cannot justify,
   It leaves the miserable man
   To bleed, and languish, and complain,
      Till in my sins I die. (pp. 156–7)

Lk. 10:33, *But a certain Samaritan, as he journeyed, came where he was, etc.*

1. But Life I see in death appear!
   The good Samaritan is near,
      From heaven to earth he comes,
   His country he for me forsakes,
   Upon himself my nature takes,
      And all my sins assumes.

2. Attach'd to earth he sees me lie,
   He marks me with a pitying eye,
      And all my wounds surveys:
   Ev'n now his yearning bowels move,
   His heart or'eflows with softest love,
      And heaven is in his face. (p. 157)

Lk. 10:34, *He went to him, and bound up his wounds, pouring in oil and wine, etc.*

1. Stranger unknown, Thou art my God!
   From me, while weltring in my blood,
      Thou canst not farther go:
   Pour in thy Spirit's wine and oil,
   Revive me by a gracious smile,
      Thy pardning mercy show.

2. Bind up my wounds by opening thine,
   Apply the balm of blood Divine
      To save a sinner poor;
   To life, and joy, and gospel-peace
   (Sure pledge of perfect holiness)
      My gasping soul restore.

3. The bitterness of death is past,
   And lo, I on thy mercy cast,
      Into thy church convey'd
   Most surely feel my cure begun;
   And still I trust thy love alone
      And hang upon thine aid. (p. 157)

Lk. 10:35, *On the morrow when he departed, he took out two pence,*
&c.

1. Thy patient in thy hands I lie,
   All helplessness, all weakness I,
      But thy almighty skill
   On sinners to the utmost shew'd,
   Shall thro' the virtue of thy blood
      My soul compleatly heal.

2. Thou didst, ascending up on high,
   Pour down thy blessings from the sky,
      And gifts on man bestow,
   Gifts to supply thy people's wants,
   Gifts for the perfecting the saints
      In thy great inn below.

3. Thou bidst the ministerial host
   Dispense thy med'cines at thy cost;
      And with thy sympathy
   My wounds he carefully attends,
   Talents, and gifts, and grace expends,
      And life itself on me.

4. Sure from his dear returning Lord
   To gain the hundred-fold reward,
      The steward of thy grace
   Laborious in the strength divine,
   Saves his own soul, in saving mine,
      And dies to see thy face. (pp. 158–9)

Lk. 10:38–9, *Martha received Him into her house.*

1.   Martha's faith in active life
         Was laudably employ'd,
      Tending Christ with zealous strife,
         She serv'd th'eternal God:
      Mary waiting at his feet
   The life contemplative express'd:
      Let the happy sisters meet,
         For join'd they both are bless'd.

2.   One who Mary's lot injoys
        Excus'd from earthly care
      Hearkens to his Saviour's voice
        In calm repose of prayer,
      Reading, musing on the word,
    In silence gathering all his powers,
      Holds communion with his Lord,
        And God in truth adores.

3.   O that I might humbly sit
        With His beloved ones,
      Happier at my Saviour's feet
        Than monarchs on their thrones!
      Who before His footstool bow
    Are sure His quickning voice to hear;
      Jesus, speak: I listen now,
        And all my soul is ear! (pp. 159–60)[23]

Lk. 10:40, *But Martha was cumbred about much serving, and came to him, etc.*

[I]

Blest the house, and doubly blest
  Which Christ a church hath made:
Martha there with toils opprest
  Calls Mary to her aid:
Wisely they their time divide
'Twixt secular and sacred care,
  All their works are sanctified
    By sacrifice and prayer. (p. 160)

Lk. 10:40.

II

Mary could not envy feel,
  Or covet Martha's place,
Chuse the height of tumult's wheel
  Before the depth of grace:

23. [Verses 1 and 3 appear in *Poet. Works*, XI, pp. 196–7.]

O might I but hear thy word
In silence and tranquillity,
Never would I leave my Lord,
Or turn my heart from Thee. (pp. 160–1)

Lk. 10:41, *Martha, Martha, thou art careful and troubled about many things.*

1.   Hurrying on with eagerness
     In works of charity,
    Warm, impatient for success,
     Thou must distracted be;
    Day and night engag'd, employ'd,
(While others all thy thoughts engross)
    Anxious how reproach t'avoid,
     And how insure applause.

2.   Calm and quiet is the zeal
     Which the good Spirit inspires,
    Yields submissive to his will,
     And nothing else desires:
    Active soul, to Jesus fly,
The grace of watchful prayer implore,
    Only wish to satisfy
     Thy God, and seek no more. (pp. 161–2)

Lk. 10:42, *One thing is needful.*

1.   Needful for the good of man
     One only thing there is,
    Here to live for God, and gain
     The everlasting bliss:
    Earth we soon shall leave behind,
Our life is as a shadow gone;
    An eternal soul should mind
     Eternity alone.

2.   What is everything beside
For which the world contend?
Baits of lust, or boasts of pride,
Which in a moment end:
After earthly happiness
I can no longer pant or rove,
Need no more, who all possess
In Jesu's heart-felt love. (p. 162)[24]

Lk. 10:42, *Mary hath chosen that good part, &c.*

1.   Martha's chosen work is good,
But Mary's better still;
Mary rests on earth employ'd
Like those on *Zion's* hill,
Antedates th'immortal joys,
Partaker with the heavenly powers,
Hears her dear Redeemer's voice,
And lost in love adores.

2.   Rest, thou favour'd spirit, rest,
Who in His presence art,
Of the needful thing possess'd,
And *Mary's* better part:
Choose who will that happy place,
He there shall unmolested sit;
Never can the Saviour chase
A sinner from His feet.

3.   Here we would thro' life remain
From all distraction free,
Closest fellowship maintain
By faith and love with Thee,
In the Spirit of humble prayer,
Of praise and sacrifice abide,
Till Thou waft us thro' the air,
And seat us at thy side. (p. 163)[25]

24. [Verse 2 appears in *Poet. Works*, XI, p. 198, and in a different metre in *Short Hymns*, II, p. 219.]
25. [Verses 1 and 2 appear in *Poet. Works*, XI, p. 198.]

Lk. 11:6, *For a friend of mine in his journey is come to me, and I have nothing, etc.*

> Trav'ling thro' the vale of woe,
> A soul is lodg'd with me,
> Nothing can it find below
> But want and poverty,
> In its journey to the skies
> I cannot furnish it with bread:
> Father, hear, in mercy rise,
> My famish'd guest to feed. (p. 168)

Lk. 11:7, *He from within shall answer and say, Trouble me not; the door, etc.*

1.
> Pleas'd with importunity,
> In heaven Thou hear'st my prayer;
> Mercy's door I open see,
> And all thy children there:
> Thine abodes of endless rest
> In succouring me Thou need'st not leave:
> Rise, and answer my request,
> And now thy Spirit give.

2.
> Still I knock & ask & seek,
> A pressing beggar I;
> Speak, the word of comfort speak,
> And grant me the supply,
> Pity a poor traveller,
> With toil fatigued, with hunger faint;
> Give, for Thou hast bread to spare,
> O give me all I want! (pp. 168–9)[26]

26. [Verse 2 appears in *Poet. Works*, XI, p. 203.]

Lk. 11:9, *Ask, and it shall be given you: Seek, &c.*

Asking for thy righteousness,
    I shall the gift receive,
Find the kingdom of thy grace,
    And by thy Spirit live;
Entring thro' the open door,
The holy God I soon shall see,
    Praise, when time shall be no more,
        The glorious One in Three. (p. 170)

Lk. 11:10, *For every one that asketh, receiveth, &c.*

Every one that asks shall have,
    And he that seeks shall find
Christ omnipotent to save
    Our whole apostate kind:
Christ the Door shall be thrown wide,
That all who knock may enter in,
    Shelter'd in his bleeding side
        Beyond the reach of sin. (p. 170)

Lk. 11:11–12, *If a son shall ask bread of any of you, &c.*

1.   Thou who know'st a father's heart,
        To thy own children good,
    Less benign than Him thou art,
        Who fills the world with food;
    Nature's love 'tis God bestows,
    A drop of that unfathom'd sea;
        Mercy all His works o'erflows,
            And now extends to Thee.

2.   God bestows on every one
        The true substantial good;
    Sinners change his bread to stone,
        To bane his wholesom food:

His most precious gift of grace
Wherewith our souls are satisfied
Oft we turn to wantonness,
And damn ourselves by pride. (pp. 170–1)[27]

Lk. 11:20, *If I by the finger of God cast out devils, no doubt the kingdom, etc.*

The reign of sin and Satan cease
By power Divine expel'd,
When Jesus' lips create my peace,
And speak my pardon seal'd:
I know thy kingdom is brought in,
Is surely fixt in me,
When fill'd with perfect hate of sin,
And love of purity. (p. 171)

Lk. 11:21, *When a strong man armed keepeth, &c.*

1. The world immerst in Satan lay,
The world by Satan was possest,
Till God assum'd our sinful clay,
T'expel the demon from our breast,
Extend the vict'ry of his grace,
And vindicate the ransom'd race.

2. Long undisturb'd the tempter keeps
His house, and rules without control;
The soul in his possession sleeps,
The careless, gay, unthinking soul
No trouble fears, no evil sees,
But rests secure in hellish peace. (pp. 171–2)[28]

27. [Verse 1 appears in *Poet. Works*, XI, p. 204.]
28. [Verse 2 appears in *Poet. Works*, XI, p. 204.]

Lk. 11:23, *He that gathereth not with me, scattereth.*

> Indifference is a crime in all,
>> But most in Jesus' minister,
> A man of God, whom God doth call
>> To serve his Master's interests here;
> Sent to collect the flock and guide,
>> To feed, and strengthen them, and keep,
> By negligence he scatters wide,
>> And leaves to wolves the wandring sheep. (p. 173)

Lk. 11:24, *When the unclean spirit is gone out, &c.*

1.
> Let saints rejoice with fear;
>> Th'ejected fiend is near:
> From thine inmost soul expel'd
>> Christ hath forc'd him to depart,
> Hath in thee his love reveal'd,
>> Purified by faith thy heart.

2.
> Yet do not rest secure
>> If now thy heart be pure:
> Thine infernal enemy
>> Arm'd with sevenfold rage will come,
> Seek his former place in thee,
>> Strive to gain his ancient home.

3.
> Driven by stronger grace
>> Out of his dwelling-place,
> All its avenues he knows,
>> Knows thy old besetting sin,
> Watches if thine eyelids close
>> Unperceiv'd to enter in. (p. 173)[29]

29. [Verses 2 and 3 appear in *Poet. Works*, XI, p. 205.]

Lk. 11:28, *Yea rather, blessed are they that hear the word of God, and keep it.*

1. Angels the virgin-mother bless,
   All ages her renown declare:
   But greater blessings we possess
   Who in our hearts the Saviour bear:
   She suckled the celestial Child;
   Fed with the milk of his own word,
   We know our Father reconcil'd,
   And feast by faith on Christ the Lord.

2. We hear the word divine and do,
   Strong in the grace which Christ bestows,
   And drink the wine forever new,
   The joy which from his Spirit flows,
   Which angel-tongues can ne'er express,
   The bliss to saints triumphant given,
   While all our happy souls confess,
   Obedient love is present heaven. (p. 174)

Lk. 11:33, *No man when he hath lighted a candle, putteth it in a secret place, etc.*

Truth divine must not be hid:
   Truth doth all to Christ invite:
Who the scripture's use forbid
   Wrong the children of the light.
O that all mankind might hear,
   Gospel-light with Jesus see!
Jesus, to the world appear,
   Shew the way to heaven in Thee. (p. 175)

131

Lk. 11:34, *When thine eye is single, thy whole body also is full of light.*

> Thee, Lord, I would in all things see;
> Mine eye be singly fixt on Thee
>   Whom still I aim to please,
> So shall my soul be fill'd with love,
> And life, and wisdom from above,
>   And perfect holiness. (p. 175)

Lk. 11:34, *But if thine eye is evil, thy body also is full of darkness.*

> But if I aim at aught beside,
> Thro' selfish vanity and pride,
>   Eclips'd and dark within
> My soul will lose the heavenly light,
> Fill'd and o'rewhelm'd with sudden night,
>   With folly, grief, and sin. (p. 176)

Lk. 11:35, *Take heed therefore, that the light which is in thee be not darkness.*

> 1. But those who most the caution need
>   Disdain to tremble or take heed,
>   Refuse themselves to prove;
>   They will not let their light be tried,
>   Or search, if that be perfect pride
>   Which they call — perfect love.

> 2. Then if their single eye is lost,
>   They their own high attainments boast,
>   Their purity and zeal,
>   In paths of wild delusion stray,
>   Mistaking for the heavenly ray
>   The flashy gleams of hell. (p. 176)

Lk. 11:42, *Ye pass over judgment, and the love of God.*

> What Pharisees can do
> Is but the outward part:
> Religion undefil'd and true
> Is seated in the heart:
> His kingdom from above,
> His nature we partake,
> When God appeas'd in Christ we love,
> And all men for his sake. (pp. 177–8)

Lk. 11:46, *Ye lade men with burthens grievous to be borne, and ye yourselves touch not, &c.*

> The Scribes a sinner load
> With vain performances,
> Nor keep themselves the law of God,
> Nor God desire to please:
> A man of faith and love
> Doth with the sufferer share,
> His misery from the wretch remove,
> And all his burthens bear. (p. 178)

Lk. 11:52, *Woe unto you lawyers: for ye have taken away the key of knowledge; ye entred not in, etc.*

> 1. Woe to the men that cry
> "We are the guides who show
> "Your way to heaven; on us rely,
> "And seek no more to know!"
> Blind leaders of the blind,
> They seize the sacred key,
> Nor suffer souls the Truth to find
> Who fain would Jesus see.

2.   The hateful light they shun,
They contradict the way,
(The way themselves have never known)
    And force the flock to stray;
Their tyrannizing power
    Thro' ignorance maintain,
And lengthen out the dreary hour
    By which alone they reign. (p. 178)

Lk. 11:53–4, *The Pharisees began to urge him vehemently and to provoke him, &c.*

Thy wisdom and thy light,
    Jesus, on us bestow,
And teach us how to speak aright
    To each provoking foe:
From false insidious men
    Thy messengers defend,
And guard whoe'er thy truths maintain,
    And keep us to the end. (p. 179)

Lk. 12:2, *There is nothing covered, that shall not be revealed.*

Sinners to the shades may run,
    Hide them from the sight of men,
But the Judge they cannot shun,
    All their thoughts by him are seen;
Dark and light's to him the same;
    He will all their hearts reveal,
Drag them out to open shame,
    Chase the hypocrites to hell. (p. 179)

Lk. 12:4, *I say unto you my friends, Be not afraid of them that kill the body, &c.*

1. What can harm the friends of God?
    Us who on thy love depend,
   Us the purchase of thy blood
    Wilt thou not thro' life defend?
   Yes; we dwell secure from ill,
    Safe, tho' fire and sword be near:
   Yet the world our bodies kill,
    God, and none beside we fear.

2. Man may soul and body part,
    Still they both are join'd to Thee,
   Thou of both the Saviour art,
    Christ our immortality:
   Who thy nature here receive,
    We the darts of death defy,
   We who in thy death believe
    One with God can never die. (p. 180)

Lk. 12:5, *Fear him, which after he hath killed hath power to cast into hell.*

Nought we love which man can give,
 Nought which man can take away,
When thy sayings we receive,
 When we only Thee obey:
Then thy greatness we revere,
 When the Judge of all we own,
Tremble while we sojourn here,
 Fear, and love our God alone. (p. 180)

Lk. 12:8, *Whosoever shall confess me before men, him shall the Son of man also, etc.*

Pure in heart, in word, and deed
 Gladly, Lord, I would confess,
Walk as by thy Spirit led,
 Following after righteousness;

Sure that Thou in whom I trust
  Wilt acknowledge me for thine,
Praise before thy heavenly host,
  Share with me the throne Divine. (pp. 181–2)

Lk. 12:9, *He that denieth Me before men shall be, &c.*

Whither, when his Saviour leaves,
  Must the desperate sinner go?
Him the murtherer receives
  Fitted for eternal woe:
Whom the Lord of life denies,
  Justly, finally forsakes,
Satan claims as lawful prize,
  To his place of torment takes. (p. 182)[30]

Lk. 12:12, *The Holy Ghost shall teach you in the same hour what ye ought to say.*

Holy Ghost, I trust in Thee
  The needful grace t'impart,
Thou my mouth and wisdom be,
  The Teacher of my heart:
Help me in the trying hour
To speak those given words of thine,
  Fill'd with faith, and love, and power,
    And eloquence divine. (p. 182)

Lk. 12:14, *Who made Me a judge or a divider over, &c.*

1. Jesus declines the umpire's place
      Whose word had made their difference end,
    To teach the stewards of His grace
      Above all earthly views t'ascend;
    No secular concerns to know
    Or charge themselves with things below.

____

30. [The second half of this verse appears in *Poet. Works*, XI, p. 209.]

2. 'Tis not for Jesus' messengers
    Partitions of estates to make,
    The burthen of external cares,
    The needful charge let others take,
    True ministers of Christ the Lord
    Should only live to preach his word. (p. 182)[31]

Lk. 12:15, *A man's life consisteth not in the abundance, &c.*

[I]

1. Sinners, to you the source we show
    From whence all human discord springs,
    That origin of evil know,
    That direful lust of earthly things,
    And ask your Lord, in instant prayer,
    The root out of your hearts to tear.

2. Your life on needful things depends,
    Not on superfluous treasures vain:
    A little serves for nature's ends;
    And if a world of wealth ye gain,
    Ye nothing gain with all your care
    But food to eat and cloathes to wear. (p. 183)[32]

Lk. 12:15.

II

1. Misers, the name belongs to you,
    Who thrive by lawful means alone,
    Nor rob your neighbour of his due,
    But, too tenacious of your own,
    Indulge your appetite for gold,
    Your sateless lust to have and hold.

31. [The first four lines of verse 1 are combined with the last two lines of verse 2 to form one verse in *Poet. Works*, XI, p. 209.]
32. [Verse 2 appears in *Poet. Works*, XI, p. 209, with the alteration of "your" to "our," etc.]

2. What can your hoarded earth avail,
   When justice doth your souls require?
   No riches will ye find in hell,
   Tho' Satan pays his slaves their hire,
   While naked out of life ye go,
   To greet your shouting friends below. (pp. 183–4)

Lk. 12:19, *Soul, thou hast much goods laid up for many years; take thine ease, etc.*

1. "Much goods for many years laid up!"
   Vain sinner, to the future blind,
   Lean not on that deceitful hope,
   Nor trust those many years behind:
   Inslav'd to appetite and sense,
   Voluptuous soul, of life secure,
   When death and judgment call thee hence,
   Who shall another hour insure?

2. How many rich in pleasures live,
   In pride, and sloth, and sensual joy!
   Their consolation they receive,
   They look upon their wealth — and die!
   No real bliss in life they know
   By various gusts of passion driven,
   And hopeless at their death they go
   From earth, to be shut out from heaven. (p. 185)[33]

Lk. 12:22–3, *Therefore I say unto you, Take no thought for your life, etc.*

1. Anxious thought to avarice tends,
   Anxious thought our Lord forbids,
   To the birds and lilies sends:
   He who all his creatures feeds,
   If we dare in Him confide,
   Will he not for man provide?

33. [Verse 1 appears in a different metre in *Short Hymns*, II, p. 210.]

2. He who form'd our curious frame,
   He in whom till now we live,
   Is he not in love the same,
   Ready all we want to give?
   Thoughtless then for clothes and food,
   Cast we all our care on God. (p. 186)

Lk. 12:35, *Let your loyns be girded about, and your lights burning.*

1. Servants of Christ, arise,
   To do your Master's will,
   Soldiers, be bold to win the prize,
   On that celestial hill;
   Ye travellers, hold on,
   Impatient to remove,
   Gird up your loins, and swiftly run
   The race that ends above:

2. Inkindled at the word
   Your faith by works maintain,
   Your burning lamps with oil be stor'd,
   With love to God and man:
   (That oil the Spirit supplies,
   He sheds that love abroad),
   Go forth to meet him in the skies,
   Your dear returning God. (p. 189)

Lk. 12:[36], *And ye yourselves like unto men that wait for their Lord, &c.*

In fixt attention wait
Till Christ the Bridegroom come,
His ready servants to translate
To their eternal home:
With eager joy receive
The soul-dismissing word,
And die into his arms, and live
Triumphant with your Lord. (p. 189)

Lk. 12:37, *Blessed are those servants, whom the Lord, &c.*

1.   Jesus, the power impart
Thy coming to attend,
And mark the motions of my heart,
    Till life and care shall end:
That last important hour
Be ever in my sight,
Till mounting from the watchman's tower,
I greet my friends in light.

2.   Till Thou appear again,
O may I live for Thee,
And watching unto death obtain
    Thy saints' felicity,
Numbred among the blest
Thine open face survey,
And on thy glorious fulness feast
In that eternal day. (p. 190)[34]

Lk. 12:38, *And if he shall come in the second watch, &c.*

    That blessing to secure,
That joy beyond the skies,
May I the vigilant toil endure,
    And never close mine eyes,
Incessant ask the power
My soul on Thee to cast,
And watch and live thro' every hour
As each would prove the last. (p. 190)

Lk. 12:40, *Be ye therefore ready also: for the Son of man cometh at an hour when ye think not.*

    Ready that I may be,
I work the works of God,
And keep my conscience clear and free
    Thro' the atoning blood:

34. [Verse 1 appears in *Poet. Works*, XI, p. 213.]

So shall I without fear
Meet the great day unknown,
And shout to see the Judge appear,
And hail him on his throne. (pp. 190–1)

Lk. 12:45, *If that servant say in his heart, My Lord delayeth his coming, etc.*

Those who think He tarries long
   Their Master's charge forget,
Smite their brethren with the tongue,
   Their fellow-servants beat,
Proud of temp'ral dignities
Their lusts and passions gratify,
   Live in pleasures, sloth, and ease,
      As never born to die. (p. 192)

Lk. 12:46, *The Lord of that servant will come in a day when he looketh not for him, &c.*

Sudden, unexpected death
   The wicked shall surprize,
Dying with the fiends beneath
   A death that never dies:
O that I, till life is o're,
May every hour and moment fear,
   Feel — The Judge is at the door,
      And heaven or hell is here! (p. 193)

Lk. 12:48, *But he that knew not, and did commit things worthy of stripes, shall, etc.*

Whose hope on ignorance is built
   Upon a broken reed he leans,
It never can exempt from guilt,
   Or save him from his damning sins:
It cannot quench or cool his hell,
   Or mitigate his sad despair,
Far hotter flames that others feel,
   And dwell in fiercer torments there. (p. 193)

Lk. 12:48, *Unto whomsoever much is given, of him shall be much required.*

1. Shall one in perfect love renew'd
     No holier than th'imperfect live?
    The second benefit of God
     Doth he not then in vain receive?
    But all that bear his image here,
     His Spirit's promis'd fulness know,
    Most like their Saviour they appear,
     The ripest fruits of grace they show.

2. Who much receive should much restore,
     The Lord that forms our souls again
    Expects not from an infant's power
     The service of a perfect man:
    But who his depths of Godhead prove
     Should his whole mind and life express,
    In meekness of all-patient love,
     In humble, perfect nothingness.

3. Tremble, thou favour'd saint, on whom
     Thy bounteous Lord hath much bestow'd,
    Thy talents use, till Jesus come,
     And lay out all thy soul for God:
    He bids thee all his gifts improve:
     But if thou waste the grace divine,
    But if thou boast thy perfect love,
     The doom of Lucifer is thine. (p. 194)

Lk. 13:5, *Except ye repent, ye shall all likewise perish.*

1.   Meer mercy doth repeat
      The warning to mankind,
    But sinners wilfully forget
      And cast his words behind:
      Yet God appoints it so,
      That all the truth should feel,
    Repentance, or damnation know,
      And mourn in earth, or hell.

2.   Jesus, what shall I do,
      The salutary pain,
The permanent contrition true,
      The blessed grief to gain:
      I only live to mourn
      My sins and follies past:
Display thy wounds, my heart to turn,
      And let me breathe my last. (pp. 197–8)

Lk. 13:6, *A certain man had a figtree planted in his vineyard, and he came and sought, etc.*

      I the barren figtree am,
          Planted here in sacred ground:
      Oft to me my Planter came,
          Fruit he sought, but none he found,
      Void of vital piety,
      No good works were wrought by me. (p. 198)

Lk. 13:7, *Then said he — Cut it down, &c.*

      God at last in anger said
          (Leaving judgment to his Son),
      "Slay the soul already dead,
          Cut the formal Christian down,
      Let his gracious day be o're,
      Let him clog the church no more." (p. 198)

Lk. 13:8–9, *And he answering said unto him, Lord, let it alone this year also, &c.*

1.   Mild my Advocate replied,
          "Grant him still a longer space,
      Till I for his cause have tried
          All the methods of my grace;
      Let this barren soul alone,
      I have made his curse my own."

143

2. Rescued by thy powerful prayer,
   Thee I bless for my reprieve:
Since Thou dost in mercy spare,
   Let me for my Saviour live;
Now th'effectual work begin,
Clear my life and heart from sin.

3. Jesus, dig about my root,
   Shower thy blessings from above;
If at last I bring forth fruit,
   Works of humble faith and love,
Thou shalt all the glory have,
Saving whom Thou diedst to save. (pp. 198–9)

Lk. 13:13, *And immediately she was made straight, and glorified God.*

1. Nor time nor means my Lord can need
   T'accomplish thy own work in me:
Speak, and my soul from sin is freed,
   Is loos'd from its infirmity:
My heart and spirit rectify,
   Remove my nature's bent to ill,
And while thou dost the rule apply,
   Conform me to thy perfect will.

2. O that I now my heart could raise
   Transferr'd from earth to things above,
And only live to spread thy praise,
   To magnify thy healing love!
O that in every word and thought
   And deed I might thy glory show,
Who hast on me such wonders wrought,
   That all may thy salvation know! (p. 200)[35]

35. [The last four lines of verse 1 and verse 2 appear as part of a longer hymn in *Poet. Works*, XI, pp. 218–19.]

Lk. 13:18[–19], *The kingdom of God is like a grain of mustard seed, &c.*

1. O how unlike the thoughts of man
    The kingdom of thy grace below!
    We look, that the minutest grain
    Should swiftly to perfection grow,
    With sudden full maturity
    Shoot up at once into a tree.

2. But small at first thy kingdom, Lord,
    Doth greatly in the end increase,
    The gospel seed, th'ingrafted word
    By imperceptible degrees
    Shall stately as the cedar rise,
    Fair as the trees of paradise. (p. 201)[36]

Lk. 13:21, *It is like leaven, which a woman took and hid in three measures of meal, etc.*

1. By silent, slow, unnotic'd means
    The heavenly principle proceeds,
    And while its secret way it wins,
    Its sanctifying virtue spreads
    Thro' all we think, and speak, and do,
    And makes our life and nature new.

2. Long in the heart of man conceal'd
    And cover'd up the grace remains,
    But more and more diffus'd, reveal'd,
    O're every bosom-lust it reigns,
    Till all our powers its influence prove,
    And all our souls are peace and love. (p. 202)

36. [An alternative last line appears in the margin of the MS: "One with thy kingdom in the skies."]

Lk. 13:22, *He went through the cities and villages teaching and journeying toward Jerusalem.*

> Jesus, Prince of pastors, fill
>> The shepherds sent by Thee
> With thy own intrepid zeal,
>> And fervent charity:
> Then we shall in every place
> Thy people with thy word supply,
>> Live to feed their souls with grace,
>> And in their service die. (p. 202)

Lk. 13:23, *Then said one unto him, Lord, are there few that be saved?*

> My heart's supreme desire,
>> Saviour, to Thee is known,
> Not after other souls t'inquire,
>> But to secure my own:
> What shall I do to gain
> A lot among the blest,
> Or how by labouring here attain
>> To heaven's eternal rest? (pp. 202–3)

Lk. 13:25, *When once the Master of the house is risen up, and hath shut the door, &c.*

> Now is the season to repent,
>> Now is the gracious day,
> I may those endless woes prevent,
>> And cast my sins away:
> Now, Saviour, now I cease from sin,
>> I knock at mercy's gate,
> This moment seek to enter in:
>> The next may be too late. (p. 204)

146

Lk. 13:26, *We have eaten and drunk in thy presence, and thou hast taught in our streets.*

1. The Jews beheld the Lord most high,
       When God on earth appear'd,
   His wonders saw with careless eye,
       His slighted sayings heard:
   They would not own that Christ was He,
       The true, eternal God,
   Held fast their incredulity,
       And perish'd in their blood.

2. Professors still his name abuse,
       His sacraments and word,
   Subjection to his will refuse,
       And falsely call him Lord:
   But O, what profit wilt thou find,
       Thou Christian infidel,
   To sorer punishment consign'd,
       And to an hotter hell! (p. 204)[37]

Lk. 13:27, *But he shall say, I tell you, I know not whence ye are: depart, etc.*

   Who would not for their Master own,
       Or his commands obey,
   They justly are by Christ unknown
       In that decisive day:
   Who far from God in will and heart
       Themselves on earth remov'd,
   To hell eternally depart
       From him they never lov'd. (p. 205)

37. [Verse 1 and the first four lines of verse 2 appear in *Poet. Works*, XI, pp. 220–1. Verse 2 is completed by adding the first four lines of the following poem, "Who would not for their Master own."]

Lk. 13:32, *I cast out devils, and I do cures today and, &c.*

1. Jesus, if Thou thy Spirit give,
   We all the serpent's wiles perceive,
   Faithful and firm perform thy will,
   Our ministry with joy fulfil,
   Give up our all, and win the prize
   When death completes our sacrifice.

2. The office we from Thee receive
   For this a few short days we live;
   We only live the fiends to chase,
   And minister thy healing grace,
   And then our willing souls resign
   By sufferings perfected, like thine. (pp. 206–7)[38]

Lk. 13:35, *Behold, your house is left unto you desolate.*

1. The sinner left by Truth Divine
       Is dark and void of every good:
   When Jesus doth no longer shine
       How frightful is the solitude!
   O may I tremble at thy word,
       The day of my salvation see,
   Nor e'er provoke my gracious Lord
       In justice to abandon me!

2. A thousand offers I confess,
       A thousand calls I have withstood,
   But now I would be sav'd by grace,
       Lover of souls, Thou knowst I wou'd:
   Beneath thy mercy's wings receive
       To which I now for refuge fly,
   And let me in thy favor live
       And let me in thine image die. (p. 208)

38. [Verse 1 appears with slight alterations in *Poet. Works*, XI, p. 222.]

Lk. 14:8, *Sit not down in the highest room.*

> Nature would shine above the rest,
> Appropriate to itself the best;
> But he who knows the truth of grace
> Delights to take the lowest place:
> The humble man remains unknown
> The saint prefers himself to none,
> Least in his own, he waits behind,
> Least in the eyes of all mankind. (p. 210)

Lk. 14:9, *Begin with shame to take the lowest room.*

> 1. O thou who at the gospel-feast
>   Seatest thyself above the rest,
>   Superior honours bold t'assume,
>   And challenging the highest room;
>   Before his justice cast thee down,
>   Instructed by the Master's frown,
>   Vain boaster of thy perfect grace,
>   Go, take with shame the lowest place.

> 2. Less than the least who Jesus know,
>   Or in his steps desire to go,
>   Less than the penitents sincere,
>   The abject slaves of legal fear,
>   Low at their feet, the harlots see
>   And publicans prefer'd to Thee,
>   And loath thyself in thy own eyes,
>   Till Christ exalt thee to the skies. (p. 367)

Lk. 14:15, *Blessed is he that shall eat bread in the kingdom of God.*

> Happy he, whose wickedness
> Is cover'd and forgiven!
> In the kingdom of thy grace
> He eats the bread of heaven:

In thy dazling realms above
He soon shall live supremely blest,
Banquet on thy richest love,
    The saints' eternal feast. (p. 213)

Lk. 14:17, *And sent his servant at supper time to say, &c.*

1.   When the time was now fulfil'd
        Thou didst send forth our Lord;
    In a servant's form reveal'd
        He preach'd the gospel word,
    Show'd the heavenly kingdom nigh,
    Invited sinners to the feast,
        "Weary souls, on Me rely,
        And I will give you rest.

2.   "I will give you drink, and feed
        Your hungry souls with love,
    To the feast eternal lead,
        And be your Life above;
    I have there prepared your place
    Who to My yoke your spirits bow;
        Now receive My word, and grace
        And heaven is ready now."

3.   Daily sent in Jesus' name
        Thy gospel-servants go,
    Tidings of great joy proclaim
        Of heaven begun below:
    Christ is ready to receive
    The souls he did by death redeem,
        Waits his precious Self to give,
        And grace and heaven in Him. (pp. 213–14)[39]

39. [Verses 1 and 2 appear in *Poet. Works*, XI, pp. 227–8.]

Lk. 14:18, *The first said, I have bought a piece of ground, and I must needs, etc.*

Nothing more the wealthy need,
Of outward good possest,
Slight the true, substantial bread,
The evangelic feast:
Lost in ease and idleness,
They live to eat, and drink, and play,
More and more of earth they seize,
And cast their souls away. (pp. 214–15)

Lk. 14:20, *And another said, I have married a wife, and therefore I cannot come.*

1. Men the choicest gift abuse,
    And to a curse pervert,
    Married who their God refuse,
    Nor give to Christ their heart;
    The supreme felicity
    They in his proffer'd grace disclaim;
    Such alas, shall never see
    The marriage of the Lamb.

2. Why should that a hindrance prove
    Which God a help intends?
    Sinner, gain in Jesus' love
    The bliss that never ends;
    Come, thou oft-invited guest
    Whom God Himself vouchsafes to woo,
    Hasten to the gospel-feast,
    And bring thy consort too. (p. 215)[40]

40. [Verse 2 appears in *Poet. Works*, XI, p. 229, as part of a longer poem.]

Lk. 14:21, *Bring hither the poor, and the maimed, and the halt, and the blind.*

> Needy, impotent to good,
>   Disabled, halt, and blind,
> Hungring after heavenly food
>   Our souls may mercy find:
> Sinners poor invited are
> To what the rich and full despise,
>   Feasted here on Christ, they share
>   His banquet in the skies. (p. 216)

Lk. 14:34, *If the salt have lost its savour, wherewith shall it be seasoned?*

1. Who lose the salt of grace,
      The humble, loving zeal,
    Most dreadful is their case,
      Most irretrievable,
    Insipid souls, and only fit
    For Satan and his hellish pit!

2. O may I ever be
      The least in my own eyes,
    Retain my poverty,
      And labour for the prize,
    And always dread th'apostate's doom
    And watch, and pray, till Jesus come! (p. 220)

Lk. 15:1, *Then drew near unto him all the publicans and sinners for to hear him.*

> Why did God on earth appear?
>   That to a Physician kind
> Sinsick sinners might draw near,
>   Might in Him salvation find,
> That the blind his light might see,
>   Ignorant his truth receive,
> Slaves, regain their liberty,
>   Dead, by faith in Jesus live. (p. 220)

Lk. 15:2, *This Man receiveth sinners, and eateth with them.*

1. Yes; for Thou hast receiv'd
    The sinners' chief in me:
    Through mercy I believ'd,
    And favour found with Thee:
    A wandring sheep to Satan sold,
    Thou hast brought back into thy fold.

2. This heav'n-descended Man
    God over all I own,
    Who doth my soul sustain
    With living bread unknown;
    Admitted on thy grace to feast
    O take me to thy endless rest. (pp. 220–1)[41]

Lk. 15:6, *And when he cometh home, he calleth together his friends and neighbours, saying unto them, Rejoice with me; for I have found my sheep which was lost.*

Jesus now gone up on high
    Calls his family above,
Bids his friends and neighbours cry,
    "Glory to the God of love!"
Triumph all the heavenly host,
    Earth repeats the joyful sound,
"Christ hath sav'd a sinner lost,
    "Christ his wandring sheep hath found!" (pp. 221–2)[42]

Lk. 15:7, *Likewise joy shall be in heaven over one sinner that repenteth more than,* etc.

Jesus' bliss the church inspires,
    Who before his Face appear;
Angels strike their sounding lyres
    For a soul repenting here:

41. [Verse 1 appears in *Poet. Works,* XI, p. 232, although there lines five and six are replaced by the last two lines of verse 2.]
42. [In *Poet. Works,* XI, p. 233, the first four lines of this verse appear in a longer poem combined with the first four lines of the following poem on Lk. 15:7.]

Jesus' most stupendous grace
To a prodigal forgiven
Challenges their loftiest *praise*,[43]
Heightens all the joys of heaven. (p. 222)

Lk. 15:8, *What woman having ten pieces of silver, if she lose one, &c.*

1. Pure the soul at first was made,
     Mark'd with God's authentic sign,
   But the image is decay'd,
     Wholly lost the stamp Divine:
   Lost himself the sinner lies,
     Sunk in sin and trampled down,
   Till the Lord of earth and skies
     Finds, and claims him for his own.

2. Then the sinner seeks thy grace,
     By the candle of the word,
   Sweeps the house, th'inlighten'd place,
     Waiting to receive his Lord:
   Still he searches after Thee,
     And, when Thou discover'd art,
   Feels the joyful extasy,
     Finds the image in his heart. (pp. 222–3)

Lk. 15:12, *And he divided unto them his living.*

The Father by his clamours prest
In anger grants the bold request
   Of his presumptuous son:
And hurrying on by swift degrees
To gain the heights of wild excess,
   He flies to be undone. (p. 223)

43. [The MS margin has "lays" as an alternative to "praise."]

Lk. 15:14, *He began to be in want.*

1. The wanderer from his Father's face,
   Who now has wasted all his grace,
   On earth can nothing find
   To satisfy his soul with food,
   Or give the smallest taste of good
   To his immortal mind.

2. Who happy without God would be
   Finds only want and misery
   When God is quite remov'd:
   How void the spirit if God depart,
   And O, what famine in the heart
   Where Jesus is not lov'd. (p. 224)[44]

Lk. 15:17, *How many hired servants of my father's, &c.*

1. The steps of man's conversion see!
   Perceiving his own misery
   He to himself returns,
   Made conscious of his spirit's wants,
   As perishing for hunger faints,
   And after God he mourns.

2. When to his sober mind restor'd,
   He envies those that serve the Lord
   With every good supplied,
   Who in his family possess
   The true substantial happiness,
   And nothing want beside. (p. 226)[45]

Lk. 16:3, *What shall I do? I cannot dig, to beg I am ashamed.*

Who Jesus and his grace has lost,
What hast thou, soul, whereof to boast?
Sin, only sin remains to thee,
Proud want, and slothful poverty:

44. [Verse 2 appears with variants in *Poet. Works*, XI, p. 234.]
45. [Verse 2 appears in *Poet. Works*, XI, p. 235.]

How justly impotent to good,
Who wou'dst not use the power bestow'd,
Thou canst not help thy desperate case,
Or strive, or ask, or hope for grace. (p. 231)

Lk. 16:4, *I am resolved what to do, that when I am put out of the stewardship, etc.*

But when on earth I cease to live,
Who shall my naked soul receive,
Nourish my soul which cannot die,
And all its endless wants supply?
Jesus, my sole resource Thou art,
Relieve my poverty of heart,
And let me my true riches see;
And find them all contain'd in Thee. (p. 231)

Lk. 16:8, *The children of this world are in their, &c.*

1. The men who seek their portion here,
        To their own worldly interest true,
    Consistent with themselves appear,
        With steady aim their end pursue,
    Contrivance, care, and foresight show
    T'insure the good they prize below.

2. Not half so wise the sons of light
        The one thing needful to secure!
    Toiling henceforth both day and night
        To make our heavenly treasure sure,
    O might we every means improve,
    And Jesus every moment love!

3. Saviour, our want of even zeal,
        Our past improvidence forgive,
    That proving all thy perfect will
        To Thee we may intirely live,
    Accomplishing thy whole design,
    Receiv'd into that house Divine. (p. 232)[46]

46. [Verses 1 and 2 appear in *Poet. Works*, XI, pp. 240–1.]

Lk. 16:9, *Make to yourselves friends of the mammon,* &c.

1. Whate'er Thou dost to us intrust,
      With thy peculiar blessing blest
    O make us diligent and just,
      As stewards faithful in the least,
    Indow'd with wisdom to possess
    The mammon of unrighteousness.

2. Help us to make the poor our friends,
      By that which paves the way to hell,
    That when our loving labour ends,
      And dying from this earth we fail,
    Our friends may greet us in the skies
    Born to a life that never dies. (pp. 232–3)[47]

Lk. 16:10, *He that is faithful in that which is least, is faithful also in much.*

1. The meanest gifts, my substance here,
      Lord, if I faithfully improve,
    And to thy members minister,
      Wilt thou not to the things above
    My heart and purg'd affections raise,
    And teach me to improve thy grace?

2. Wilt thou not bless me with the skill
      To use my precious time aright,
    To labour up the heavenly hill,
      To mingle with the saints in light,
    And happy at thy side sit down,
    Deck'd with an everlasting crown? (p. 233)

47. [Verse 2 appears in *Poet. Works*, XI, p. 241.]

Lk. 16:11, *If therefore ye have not been faithful in the unrighteous mammon, who, etc.*

1. Riches by fraudful crimes acquir'd,
     Possest by powerful villainy,
   By worldlings valued and admir'd,
     They cannot the true riches be,
   Cause of unnumbred ills below
   They cannot happiness bestow.

2. Saviour, from these defend thine own
     And with the real riches bless,
   Riches unsearchable, unknown,
     Riches of unexhausted grace,
   And bless us with the wealth above,
   Thy rich, inestimable love. (pp. 233–4)

Lk. 16:14, *The Pharisees who were covetous, heard all these things, and they derided him.*

   The eager for esteem and gold,
   To avarice and ambition sold,
   In every age deride the word
   Of a poor self-denying Lord:
   And should he now to earth return,
   The rich would still their Saviour spurn,
   His counsels slight, his yoke disdain,
   And nail him to his cross again. (p. 235)

Lk. 16:15, *Ye are they which justify yourselves before men, but God knoweth your hearts, etc.*

1. Thou Pharisee who, blind and proud,
     Dost righteous before men appear
   What art thou in the sight of God?
     A rotten, painted sepulchre!
   Thine inward wickedness he sees,
     And will to all mankind reveal,
   Thy filthy rags of righteousness,
     Thy title not to heaven, but hell.

2. Ye pillars in your own esteem,
   Vain is the praise which man bestows:
   Just, to yourselves and men ye seem,
   But all your hearts th'Omniscient knows:
   Men, foolish men, the state approve
   Of saints intirely sanctified,
   Admiring that as perfect love
   Which God abhors as perfect pride. (pp. 235–6)

Lk. 16:16, *The law and the prophets were until John; since that time the kingdom, etc.*

The kingdom promis'd and foreshow'd
   By legal types and ancient seers,
The church, the hierarchy of God
   Establish'd now on earth appears;
And sinners, sav'd for Jesus' sake,
   May all into the kingdom press,
Its glory, power, and joy partake,
   And seize the crown of righteousness. (p. 236)

Lk. 16:17, *And it is easier for heaven and earth to pass, than one tittle of the law to fail.*

When Jesus' kingdom is reveal'd,
The law's in every point fulfil'd,
Its shadows to the light give place,
Its figures to the truth of grace.
Th'event, when we on Christ rely,
Accomplishes the prophecy,
The promise in th'effect we prove,
And fear forever lost in love. (pp. 236–7)

Lk. 16:25, *But now he is comforted.*

1. Happy the child of misery,
   Who doth on earth affliction see,
      And Jesus' cross embrace,
   Who evil patiently receives,
   In indigence and sorrow lives
      The life of righteousness.

2. For momentary sufferings here
The Saviour shall his follower chear,
    Before he hence remove,
With tastes of bliss unspeakable;
And when he leaves the weeping vale,
    With all the joys above. (pp. 240–1)

Lk. 16:25, *And thou art tormented.*

1. How wretched is the man possest
Of all his wish, by blindness blest,
    Who no affliction knows,
Nor sorrow feels, or cross sustains;
His pleasure promises his pains,
    And everlasting woes.

2. He hath his consolation here:
And mem'ry terribly severe
    Shall tell him so beneath,
While he who once would nothing bear,
Gnaws his own tongue in fierce despair,
    And dies the second death. (p. 241)

Lk. 16:29, *They have Moses and the prophets.*

1. We have them too; and Christ beside:
His word and Spirit is our guide
    In the celestial way;
His gospel and apostles show
The means t'escape that hellish woe,
    "Repent, believe, obey!"

2. The word Divine we rightly hear,
Who read with faith and humble fear,
    To it for counsel fly,
Who pray and live it o're and o're,
And Him that speaks in truth adore,
    In spirit glorify. (pp. 242–3)[48]

48. [Verse 1 appears in *Poet. Works*, XI, p. 247.]

Lk. 17:4, *If he trespass against thee seven times in a day, &c.*

1. Let mine injurious brother own
      His oft-reiterated sin,
    Receiv'd for Jesus' sake alone,
        As the offence had never been,
    I to my confidence restore,
    And love, and prize him as before.

2. Yes, if sufficient proof he give
      That he doth really repent,
    Again I to my arms receive,
        Again I count him innocent,
    With cordial amity embrace,
    And set him in his former place.

3. But if his stubborn pride disdain
      The frequent evil to confess,
    Lord, shall I trust my foe again
        Or as my bosom-friend caress?
    I must, I will with love receive
    And twice ten thousand times forgive.

4. Hardned in his impenitence
      For him I now in secret mourn,
    Remit unask'd the hundred pence,
        And pray my God his heart to turn,
    And treat him, when the change I see,
    As kindly as Thou treatest me. (p. 245)[49]

Lk. 17:6, *If ye had faith as a grain of mustard-seed, ye might say unto this sycamine, etc.*

1.   Lord, the virtue of thy love
        Omnipotent exert,
      Sin t'extirpate, and remove
        Its nature from my heart;

---

49. [Verses 1, 3, and 4 appear in *Short Hymns*, II, p. 227 and in *Poet. Works*, XI, p. 248.]

Cast it out, th'accursed tree,
The carnal mind abhorring God,
Sink it, Jesus, in the sea
Of thy all-cleansing blood.

2.   Surely faith's minutest grain
Shall do the mighty deed,
Form my sinless soul again
From every evil freed:
Nature shall obey thy word,
From all concupiscence and pride
Sav'd, and perfectly restor'd,
And wholly sanctified. (pp. 246–7)

Lk. 17:12–13, *There met Him ten men that were lepers.*

1.   Repentance doth with fear begin,
We feel the baseness of our sin,
Not bold salvation to demand,
Or snatch the grace out of His hand,
Not worthy before God t'appear,
We come, yet tremble to draw near.

2.   Foul lepers, by ourselves abhorr'd,
Asham'd to meet an holy Lord,
Our nature's loathsomeness we feel,
Our heart and life deserving hell,
And cry with lifted voice aloud,
Immeasurably far from God.

3.   Saviour of men, to thee we cry,
Whose blood was shed to bring us nigh,
Apply it, Lord, to purge our sin,
To make our filthy conscience clean;
Thy love infuse, thy mercy show,
And wash the lepers white as snow.

4. When Thou from sin hast set us free,
Our Master and Instructor be,
Teach by thy salutiferous[50] grace
And guide us thro' our happy days,
Let mercy all our steps attend,
Till time in life eternal end. (p. 248)[51]

Lk. 17:14, *And when he saw them, he said unto them, Go, show yourselves unto the priests, &c.*

Jesus, Thou hast with pity seen,
And heal'd a croud of leprous men;
While to the priests ourselves we show'd,
Attending in the courts of God,
Thy pity bad our sins depart,
And pardon purified our heart. (p. 249)

Lk. 17:20, *The kingdom of God cometh not with observation.*

Not with outward pomp and state
Comes thy kingdom here below,
Those that would be rich or great
Cannot its true nature know,
The dim eyes of flesh and blood
Never can its glory see:
But when I embrace my God,
Then I find thy throne in me. (pp. 251–2)

Lk. 17:21, *The kingdom of God is within you.*

Love, the power of humble love,
Constitutes thy kingdom here:
Never, never to remove
Let it, Lord, in me appear,

50. [The *Oxford English Dictionary* defines this word as "conducive to safety, well-being, or salvation," and notes that the word is very common in the seventeenth century, but quotes only two examples in the eighteenth century (1756, 1760), and none later.]
51. [Verses 1–3 appear in *Poet. Works*, XI, p. 251.]

> Let the pure, internal grace
> Fill my new-created soul,
> Peace, and joy, and righteousness,
> While eternal ages roll. (p. 252)

Lk. 17:22, *The days will come when ye shall desire to see one of the days of the Son of man, etc.*

1.　　The times of Jesus' grace
　　　We should with care improve,
　　The joyous, evangelic days
　　　Of our first rapt'rous love;
　　　That when the light withdraws,
　　　And troublous times succeed,
　　We boldly may take up our cross,
　　　And suffer with our Head.

2.　　To Thee for help I cry,
　　　While yet thy days I see;
　　When darkness & temptation's nigh,
　　　My Lord, remember me:
　　　Thro' death's tremendous night
　　　By angel-hosts convey
　　My fearless soul, to see the light
　　　Of thine eternal day. (p. 252)

Lk. 17:23–4, *They shall say to you, See here, or see there: go not after them, etc.*

1.　All parties furiously contend
　　　With the great Babylon of Rome,
　　Dispute, and wrangle without end,
　　　"To us for true religion come,"
　　Christ among them they bid us seek,
　　As every sect were Catholic.

2.　But shall we their disciples be
　　　Who would Immensity confine?
　　We need not wander far to see
　　　The universal Lightning shine:
　　Look, sinner, look, where'er thou art,
　　For Christ's appearing — in thy heart. (p. 253)

164

Lk. 17:25, *But first must he suffer many things, and be rejected of this generation.*

> The same necessity
> Is on the members laid;
> And hated by the world like Thee
> We imitate our Head,
> Pursue the narrow way,
> Beneath thy burthens groan;
> And thus prepar'd we see thy day
> While sharers of thy throne. (p. 253)

Lk. 17:26, *As it was in the days of Noah, so shall it be also in the days of the Son of man.*

1. Thy judgments, Lord, in ages past
    Are types and figures of the last,
        And warn us to repent,
    Yet millions make thy warnings vain,
    Secure in sin they still remain,
        And die impenitent.

2. The world we now, like Noah's, see,
    Drunk with the same stupidity,
        In present things employ'd,
    For sensual joy and vain delight
    The everlasting goods[52] they slight
        And dare the wrath of God. (pp. 253–4)

Lk. 17:27, *They did eat, they drank — till the day that Noah entred into the ark, etc.*

1. The world thine oracles despise,
    The Christian world, with careless eyes
        Thine ancient judgments see,
    Nor will they shun their doom foretold,
    Or know they read in those of old
        Their own sad history.

---

52. [Wesley clearly intended "good" here.]

2. As born their appetites to please,
   Their own conveniency and ease
      They only live t'insure,
   Add house to house, and field to field,
   Marry, and feast, and plant, and build,
      To make their names endure. (p. 254)

Lk. 17:29, *The same day that Lot went out of Sodom, it rained fire and brimstone, etc.*

1. A moment more had Lot delay'd,
   A moment more in Sodom stay'd,
      The fire had stopt his flight,
   Had swept away his tardy soul,
   And sunk him in the sulphe'rous pool
      With all the sons of night.

2. But warn'd out of the flames he fled,
   That we with instantaneous speed
      May from destruction run,
   Like Lot, our all forego, despise,
   Before the venge[a]nce of the skies
      In fiery storms come down. (pp. 254–5)

Lk. 17:30, *Even thus shall it be on the day when the Son of man is revealed.*

1. The threatning will be soon fulfil'd,
   In flaming fire from heaven reveal'd
      The Son of man shall come
   Full vengeance on his foes to take,
   Who light of all his judgments make,
      And mock at Sodom's doom.

2. Sinners shall be surpriz'd again;
   The wrath of God pour down like rain,
      And to a deluge swell,
   Justice as in a moment's space
   Shall swallow up all the faithless race,
      Shall sweep the world to hell. (p. 255)

Lk. 17:31, *He which shall be upon the housetop, and his stuff in the house, let him not, etc.*

> Who Jesus' warning words receive,
> The perishable goods we leave
>   Ev'n now in heart and mind,
> Our souls to save without delay
> We fly, and cast the world away,
>   And never look behind. (p. 255)

Lk. 17:33, *Whosoever shall lose his life, shall preserve it.*

> That happy loss I long to know,
> To lose myself, a man of woe,
> A man of lips and heart unclean,
> A wretched man of inbred sin:
> O could I gasp my parting breath,
> And find myself redeem'd from death,
> Impassive, innocent above,
> Fill'd with the glorious God of love! (p. 256)

Lk. 17:34, *In that night there shall be two men in one bed; the one shall be taken, etc.*

> 1. The Saviour knows and eyes his own
>   Who live and die for Him alone,
>   A difference in their favor makes,
>   Preserves, and from the evil takes;
>   In tribulation's darkest night
>   He keeps the children of the light,
>   Kindly forbids their faith to fail,
>   And guides them thro' the mortal vale.

> 2. O may we watch, and pray, and strive,
>   Before our dreary hour arrive,
>   Before our gracious day be o're,
>   And man can work for God no more:
>   We yet may 'scape the coming snare,
>   We yet may for our Lord prepare,
>   Make our election sure, and prove
>   Pure vessels of his saving love. (pp. 256–7)

Lk. 17:36, *Two women shall be grinding, &c.*

Hard-labouring for the body here,
How few th'approaching judgment fear,
Expect the Judge, for mercy cry,
And to the arms of Jesus fly!
Yet some midst life's tumultuous cares
The Saviour in his bosom bears,
Till far above the storm they soar,
And reach with Him the heavenly shore. (p. 257)

Lk. 17:37, *Wheresoever the body is, there will the eagles be gathered together.*

Th'elect on wings of eagles borne
Shall soon with rapid joy return,
To Jesus gather'd in the skies
Behold their God with eagles' eyes:
The sight shall make their heavenly feast;
The saints with his full presence blest
Shall live to sing, and love and gaze
An age of everlasting days. (pp. 257–8)

Lk. 18:9, *He spake this parable unto certain, which trusted in themselves that they, etc.*

1. Professors good in their own eyes,
       In their own vain opinion just,
   Who dare the worst of men despise,
       And in their own perfections trust,
   They, dead in sin, themselves deceive,
   And only have a name to live.

2. Themselves they never yet have known
       Themselves who proudly justify,
   On publicans with scorn look down,
       "Stand by thyself" to sinners cry,
   And glory in their sordid dress,
   The clouts of their own righteousness. (p. 261)

Lk. 18:11–12, *God, I thank thee, that I am not as other men are,*
&c.

> The modern Pharisee is bold
> In boasting to surpass the old:
> Triumphant in himself, he stands
> Conspicuous with extended hands,
> With hideous screams and outcries loud
> Proclaims his goodness to the croud,
> Glories in his own perfect grace,
> And blasphemies presents for praise!
> "Again I thank thee, and again,
> "That I am not as other men,
> "But holy as thyself, and pure,
> "And must, O God, like thee indure:
> "Thyself I now to witness call,
> "That I am good, and cannot fall,
> "Thee to exalt, repeat the word,
> "And thus I glory — in the Lord!" (pp. 262–3)

Lk. 18:13, *The publican standing afar off, would not lift up so much*
as his eyes to heaven, etc.

1.   A penitent indeed
         Has nothing good to plead,
     Guilt confesses with his eyes,
         Dares not lift them up to heaven,
     Not so much in words, as sighs
         Prays, and begs to be forgiven.

2.   O'rewhelm'd with conscious fear
         He trembles to draw near;
     Far from the most holy place,
         Far from God his distance keeps,
     Feels his whole unworthiness,
         Feels — but shame has seal'd his lips.

3.   Labours his strugling soul
    With indignation full;
  With unutter'd grief opprest,
   Grief too big for life to bear,
  Self-condemn'd he smites his breast,
   Smites his breast — and God is there!

4.   Loos'd by the power of grace,
    Behold, at last he prays!
  Pleads th'atoning sacrifice
   For meer sin and misery,
  Humbly in the Spirit cries,
   "God be merciful to me!" (pp. 263–4)

Lk. 18:14, *I tell you, This man went down to his house justified,*
and not the other, etc.

1.   Jesus doth the truth declare;
    The boaster bears his load,
  Hastning from the house of prayer
   Beneath the curse of God:
  God the publican receives;
  And conscious of the blood applied,
  He with joy the temple leaves,
   A sinner justified.

2.   God resists the proud and vain
    Of their own righteousness,
  Every self-exalting man
   Almighty to abase:
  All themselves who justify
  He dooms his endless wrath to feel,
  Bold invaders of the sky
   He *brings* them down to hell.[53]

3.   Sinners self-condemn'd he chears
    With blessings from above,
  Grace, abundant grace confers,
   And sweet forgiving love;

53. [The MS margin has "thrusts" as an alternative to "brings."]

Strangely condescends to stoop,
And dwell with every contrite one,
Lifts the humbled mourner up,
And seats him on his throne. (pp. 264–5)

Lk. 18:21, *All these things have I kept from my youth.*

How blind the heart of man
Who thinks he all has done,
Yet never yet his work began,
Or lov'd the God unknown!
Commanded to sell all,
He will with nothing part,
But stops his ears against the call,
"My son, give me thy heart." (p. 266)

Lk. 18:22, *Yet lackest thou one thing.*

One thing is lacking still
But one which all implies,
To offer up thy heart and will,
And life in sacrifice;
With gladness to restore
Whate'er thy God hath given,
And thro' his deputies the poor
Lay up thy wealth in heaven. (p. 266)

Lk. 18:23, *When he heard this, he was very sorrowful, for he was very rich.*

When God severely kind
A blessing hath remov'd,
We then our close attachment find
To what too well we lov'd:
Our sad reluctant pain,
Our lingring grief to part,
Too sensibly alas, explain
The fondness of our heart. (p. 266)

171

Lk. 18:24, *Jesus said, How hardly shall they that have riches enter into the kingdom of God!*

> Who cleave to earth and sin,
> Believe what Christ doth say,
> (He makes the terms of entring in,
> He is the Door, the Way):
> For you with wealth to part,
> For you your all to sell,
> The Searcher of the worldly heart
> Declares Impossible. (pp. 266–7)

Lk. 18:25, *It is easier for a camel to go through the eye of a needle, than for a rich man, etc.*

> Who wealth possesses here,
> And is by wealth possest,
> Can never in his sight appear
> By whom the poor are blest:
> His riches he injoys,
> On them for help relies,
> And loses for terrestrial toys
> A kingdom in the skies. (p. 267)

Lk. 18:26, *And they that heard it said, Who then can be saved?*

> Few of the wealthy fear
> The formidable word,
> For few will condescend to hear
> A mean, rejected Lord:
> The poor his truth believe,
> And with their idols part,
> Convinc'd, till Jesus they receive,
> They still are rich in heart. (p. 267)

Lk. 18:27, *The things which are impossible with men, are possible with God.*

> To save the rich from hell,
> Above the world to raise,
> There needs a double miracle
> Of thine almighty grace:
> But if to Thee he run,
> Thy riches he receives,
> And then he trusts thy love alone,
> And poor in spirit lives. (pp. 267–8)

Lk. 18:28, *Lo, we have left all and followed thee.*

> It matters not how small
> The sacrifice we make,
> For Christ we then forsake our all,
> When we our hopes forsake,
> Our every vain desire,
> Our every creature-love,
> And nought on earth but Christ require,
> And nought but Christ above. (p. 268)

Lk. 19:10, *For the Son of man is come to seek, and to save the lost thing.*[54]

> 1. To save the lost thing,
>   From heaven He came,
>   And pardon to bring
>   Thro' faith in his name,
>   The great Mediator
>   Has sav'd us by grace,
>   Assuming the nature
>   Of all the lost race.

54. [It is not clear why Charles Wesley substituted the words, "the lost thing," for the AV, "that which was lost."]

173

2. One body we were
    Corrupt thro' the fall:
But Jesus did bear
    The burthen of all,
Our sorrows he suffer'd,
    For sin to atone,
Our life He recover'd,
    By losing his own. (pp. 274–5)

Lk. 19:11, *They thought that the kingdom of God should immediately appear.*

1. Now, ev'n now, the kingdom's near,
    Peace, and joy, and righteousness,
Soon it shall in us appear;
    Reverent joy, victorious peace,
Real righteousness brought in
    Roots out selfishness and pride,
Finishes the inbred sin,
    Makes us like the Crucified.

2. Nature cannot comprehend
    Jesus reigning on the cross,
That we may on Him depend,
    Suffering, dying in his cause:
Nature would in pomp and state
    High at his right-hand sit down,
Suddenly be rich and great,
    Shun the cross, but snatch the crown. (pp. 275–6)

Lk. 19:14, *We will not have this man to reign over us.*

1. The world that bear the Christian name,
    Thy authority disclaim,
        Against thy laws rebel:
And who thy government refuse
The yoke of sin they madly chuse,
        And serve the prince of hell.

174

2. Jesus, preserve thy grace in me
   Willing to be rul'd by Thee,
   By Thee my Lord alone:
   My only rightful King Thou art;
   Restore, and stablish in my heart
   Thine everlasting throne. (p. 276)

Lk. 19:15, *He commanded those servants to be called, to whom he had given the money, etc.*

1. When we before our Judge appear
   The day shall all our lives reveal,
   How we employ'd our substance here,
   Our time, and intellect, and will;
   What gain'd we by the heavenly trade,
   How many souls we won for God,
   What use of all his graces made,
   What use of Jesus, and his blood.

2. But O, what answer at the throne
   Will that unfaithful pastor give,
   Who call'd his Master's goods his own,
   And for his God refus'd to live,
   Who dar'd his talents misemploy,
   In sloth, and luxury, and pride,
   Nor fear'd to stumble and destroy
   The souls for whom his Saviour died. (p. 277)

Lk. 19:20, *Lord, . . . here is thy pound, which I have kept, &c.*

1. Tremble, thou careless minister,
   Who standest all day long
   Idle in Jesus' vineyard here,
   Yet think'st thou dost no wrong;
   Content in indolence to live,
   As for thy pastime born,
   Thou dost from Christ the pound receive,
   And make Him no return.

2. Not to improve them, is to lose
   The talents of thy God,
   The gifts which for his church's use
   He hath on thee bestow'd;
   Not to do good is to do ill;
   Thy sacred ministry
   Not to discharge, not to fulfil,
   Is wickedness in thee.

3. Rest is in labourers a crime,
   Before their work is done:
   Thy power, authority, and time,
   And life are not thy own:
   Prepare a strict account to give,
   When Jesus bows the sky;
   And now his zealous servant live,
   Or then — forever die. (pp. 277–8)[55]

Lk. 19:24, *Take from him the pound, and give it to him that hath ten pounds.*

1. The evangelic minister
   Should above others have
   A zeal for God, an active care
   Immortal souls to save:
   But if his duty he neglect,
   His long-offended Lord
   The slothful servant will reject,
   And quite revoke the word.

2. The word, and care, the labouring zeal
   He *doth* to others give:
   And laymen now of Jesus tell,
   And urge us to believe;
   Unlearn'd they rise and scale the sky,
   While scribes who all things know
   Live ignorant of Christ and die,
   And find their place below. (pp. 278–9)

55. [Verses 1 and 2 appear in *Poet. Works*, XI, p. 266.]

Lk. 19:26, *Unto every one which hath shall be given.*

1. The more his faith by works he shows,
   The more a true believer grows,
   His toil and strength at once increase,
   His fruits and life of righteousness,
   And daily doth the saint improve
   In zeal, humility, and love.

2. Using the grace his Saviour gives,
   He more abundant grace receives,
   Less, and still less in his own eyes,
   Who every talent occupies,
   The plenitude of grace shall gain,
   And crown'd at last with Jesus reign. (p. 279)

Lk. 19:27, *Those mine enemies . . . slay them before me.*

1. Who will not to their Saviour go
      For mercy, life and heavenly peace.
   Drag'd to the judgment-seat shall know
      His power, and truth, and righteousness,
   And bear their punishment beneath,
   And die an ever-living death.

2. Depriv'd of every gracious gift,
      Who would not yield that Christ should reign,
   Their eyes they shall in torments lift,
      And gnaw their tongues in hopeless pain,
   Cast out, and banish'd from his sight
   To horrors of eternal night.

3. But lo, the sentence to prevent,
      While yet Thou may'st be found I come,
   Thy foes and mine to Thee present;
      Jesus, to swift destruction doom
   My sins, and rebel lusts, not me,
   Who groan beneath their tyranny.

4. These lords thy subject have oppress'd,
   And never will thy laws obey:
Expel the tyrants from my breast,
   Th'usurpers by thy Spirit slay,
Slay by the brightness of thy face,
And let thy glory fill the place. (pp. 279–80)[56]

Lk. 19:28, *He went before them, ascending up to Jerusalem.*

1. Our great Example and our Head
   Before us goes to mortal pain:
Shall we not in his footsteps tread,
   His sufferings and his cross sustain,
Offer our souls in sacrifice,
And die where our Redeemer dies?

2. Expos'd to all temptations here,
   From conquering we to conquer go,
By Jesus led disdain to fear,
   When grapling with our latest foe,
We trample death beneath our feet;
And then our victory is compleat. (pp. 280–1)

Lk. 19:36, *As he went, they spread their clothes in the way.*

1.   The power of Christ is seen
         Over the hearts of men!
Suddenly they all agreed,
   Worship Him with one accord,
In the way their garments spread,
   Aid the triumph of their Lord.

2.   But soon a countless race
         Shall magnify his grace,
Pleasure spurn beneath their feet,
   Riches, and the world's esteem,
Glad to Jesus' cross submit,
   All renounce, and follow Him.

56. [Verses 3 and 4 appear in *Poet. Works*, XI, p. 267.]

3.   Myriads hosanna cry
     And praise the Lord Most-high;
  Myriads shall pour out their blood,
   Joyfully their lives lay down,
  Die, to glorify their God,
  Die, to win the martyr's crown. (p. 281)

Lk. 19:37–8, *The whole multitude of the disciples began, &c.*

1. Descending from the mountain
    Still thy disciples meet Thee,
      With songs of praise
      Extol thy grace,
    With loud hosannas greet Thee:
This, this we all acknowledge
    Our time of visitation,
      And see and own
      What Thou hast done
For us and our salvation.

2. Sent from thy Father's bosom,
    Honour, and might, and blessing,
      And glory we
      Ascribe to Thee,
    And praises without ceasing:
Jehovah from Jehovah
    Thou art to sinners given;
      Thy Spirit seals,
      Thy peace reveals
Our peace with God in heaven.

3. Come in thy gracious kingdom,
   We now by faith adore thee;
     But wait to see
     Thy Majesty,
   And all thy heavenly glory;
   Thy last triumphant coming
   Shall from the grave deliver;
     And then we rise
     Above the skies
   And praise our King forever. (pp. 281–2)[57]

Lk. 19:39, *The Pharisees said, Master, rebuke thy disciples.*

The praise of Christ offends the ear
  Of envious Pharisees,
Who hate to see his power appear,
  And fight against his peace;
The kingdom of his grace within
  They impiously deny,
And scorning Him that saves from sin
  In unbelief they die. (p. 282)

Lk. 19:43–4, *Thine enemies . . . shall lay thee even with the ground . . . and not, etc.*

1. Who can the dreadful state explain,
     The misery of a soul conceive,
   Whom God abandons to his pain,
     Whom Justice doth to Satan leave?
   A sinner damn'd, of hope bereft,
     To all his foes implacable,
   Like a rebellious city left,
     And plunder'd by the hosts of hell!

2. For God originally made
     The city is by fiends possest,
   As Babylon in ruins laid,
     The serpent's home, the dragon's nest:

57. [The last five lines of verse 1 and the first five lines of verse 2 are combined to form one verse which appears along with verse 3 in *Poet. Works*, XI, pp. 267–8, as a poem of two verses.]

No token or remains of good,
Of hope, or penitent desire,
To show where once the city stood
Burnt up with everlasting fire. (p. 284)

Lk. 19:46, *Ye have made it a den of thieves.*

Jesus' zeal can never bear
Simon's followers profane,
Miscreants who the house of prayer
Turn into a robber's den:
God abhors the priestly thieves,
Holy things who buy and sell:
And when He the hirelings leaves,
Satan pays his slaves in hell. (p. 285)

Lk. 19:47, *He taught daily in the temple.*

1. While to the temple we repair,
The house of truth as well as prayer,
God in the means injoin'd,
Instructor of the faithful race,
God in the ministers of grace,
And at his feast we find.

2. Daily he doth his people teach,
The gospel of salvation preach,
The news of sin forgiven,
While Jesus his own word applies,
Comes in his Spirit from the skies,
And bears our souls to heaven. (p. 285)

Lk. 20:1–2, *As he taught the people in the temple, and preached the gospel, etc.*

1. Rulers, high-priests, and scribes employ
Their power and art in every age,
Jesus, thy gospel to destroy;
Against thy ministers they rage,
And question our authority,
To teach the truth receiv'd from Thee.

2. But arm us with thy wisdom, Lord,
    Their craft and malice to defeat,
And vanquish'd by thy Spirit's sword,
    The world and tempter shall retreat,
Their Conqueror own with silent shame,
And bow to thine Almighty name. (p. 286)

Lk. 20:9, *He went into a far country for a length of time.*[58]

1.   Jesus to heaven is gone,
            That distant land unknown;
    Long He from his vineyard stays,
            Doth not in his flesh appear;
    Yet in his protecting grace
            Every day we find Him here.

2.   Still the Invisible
            With men vouchsafes to dwell;
    Present in his house we prove,
            Present at his mystic feast,
    Present by the Spirit of love,
            Present in the faithful breast.

3.   Who on his word rely,
            We live beneath his eye,
    Think him always at the door,
            Witness of our industry,
    Labour on with all our power,
            Thus expect his face to see.

4.   The slothful worldly throng
            Suppose He tarries long;
    Life appears an age to them,
            Till th'important moment's o'er,
    Then they wake out of their dream,
            See the Judge, and sleep no more. (p. 287)[59]

58. [The AV reads: "a long time." Once again Charles Wesley made his own translation.]
59. [Verses 1 and 4 appear in *Poet. Works,* XI, p. 270.]

Lk. 20:14, *Come, let us kill him, that the inheritance may be ours.*

> Ambitious, covetous, and vain,
> Priests who in ease and pleasure live,
> They persecute their Lord again,
> His members vex, his Spirit grieve;
> Souls by their negligence they kill,
> Jesus afresh they crucify,
> And eat, and drink, and sport their fill,
> And let the poor thro' hunger die. (p. 288)

Lk. 20:15, *So they cast him out of the vineyard, and killed him.*

> Who love his name, and keep his word,
> And Jesus for our Pattern take,
> The church, the vineyard of our Lord,
> We never, never will forsake:
> Let wicked priests, if God permit,
> Out of the pale with fury cast,
> The servants as the Master treat,
> And nail us to his cross at last. (p. 288)

Lk. 20:16, *He shall come and destroy these husbandmen, and shall give the vineyard to others.*

1. Who his coming shall abide,
    Stand his day, when Christ appears?
   Not the violent sons of pride,
    Not th'unfaithful ministers:
   Those who made his precepts void
    Cannot from his judgments flee,
   Cast out of his sight, destroy'd,
    Damn'd to all eternity.

2. Idle, mercenary, proud,
    Robbers of the church and poor,
   Would ye 'scape the wrath of God,
    Wrath that always shall endure?

While ye hear your punishment,
    To the righteous sentence bow,
Let yourselves the doom prevent,
    Let your lives forbid it now. (pp. 288–9)

Lk. 20:17, *The Stone which the builders rejected, the same is become
the head of the corner.*

1. Who builders should by office be,
    Or pillars to support the dome,
They will not own that Christ is he,
    Or hear him, now the Prophet's come,
Or for their rightful King receive,
Or by his death *consent*[60] to live.

2. The Basis of his church below,
    The Cement, Corner-stone, and Head,
They wilfully refuse to know,
    On Jesus and his members tread,
Till all compleat the Temple rise,
And shine eternal in the skies. (p. 289)

Lk. 20:24, *Whose image and superscription hath it?*

1.   Thy name, O Christ, I bear,
      Thy ruin'd character:
Hardly legible thy name,
    Yet I still belong to Thee;
Marr'd by sin thine image claim,
    Challenge thy own property.

2.   The value I receive
      Which Thou art pleas'd to give:
Stamp me with thy mind restor'd,
    Real righteousness divine,
Render'd to my rightful Lord,
    Keep me then forever thine. (p. 291)

---

60. [The Word "submit" is written in the margin as an alternative to "consent."]

Lk. 20:44, *David therefore calleth him Lord, how is he then his Son?*

1.   In Jesus Christ we see
       The depths of deity,
Compound strange of God and man,
       Creature and Creator join'd!
Who the myst'ry can explain,
       Fathom the eternal Mind?

2.   Lowliness meets in Him
       With majesty supreme,
Poor, dependant, and unknown,
       Scorn'd on earth, by heaven ador'd,
David's uncreated Son,
       David's Son, and Sovereign Lord.

3.   Wisdom and Power Divine
       Unfold his love's design,
Bid us stedfastly believe
       God became the Son of man,
That we may his life retrieve,
       Sons of God with Jesus reign.

4.   Lord, we with joy confess
       The myst'ry of thy grace:
God and man because Thou art,
       God and man shall still agree;
God and man no more shall part,
       One in all thy saints, and me. (p. 293)[61]

61. [*Rep Verse*, No. 173, p. 217.]

Lk. 20:46–7, *Beware of the scribes, which desire to walk, &c.*

1. Alas for us, who need beware
   Of men that sit in *Moses'* chair,
       And should to heaven the people guide!
   Men with the pomp of office clad,
   In robes pontifical array'd,
       But stain'd with avarice and pride:
   They love to be prefer'd, ador'd,
   Affect the state and stile of *lord*,
       And shine magnificently great;
   They for precedency contend,
   And on ambition's scale ascend
       Hard-labouring for the highest seat.

2. The church they call their proper care,
   The temple of the Lord they are,
       Abusers of their legal power;
   Greedy the church's goods to seize,
   Their wealth they without end increase,
       And the poor widow's house devour.
   O what a change they soon shall know,
   When torn away by death, they go
       Reluctant from their splendid feasts,
   Condemn'd in hottest flames to dwell,
   And find the spacious courts of hell
       Pav'd with the skulls of Christian Priests![62] (pp. 294–5)[63]

---

62. A saying of Chrysostom.
63. [The first six lines of each verse appear in *Poet. Works*, XI, p. 273, as two six-lined verses. The whole is in *Rep. Verse*, No. 269, p. 306.]

Lk. 21:2, *He saw also a certain poor widow, casting in thither two mites.*

1. Thousands when the wealthy give
    From their superfluity,
    Christ their offering doth receive;
    Doth with more complacence see
    One contented to be poor,
    Fed with manna from above,
    One who offers all his store
    Only lives by faith, and love.

2. To the actions of the great
    God a mourner's heart prefers,
    One who in a des'late state
    Feeds as on the widow's tears,
    For the heavenly Bridegroom sighs,
    Life and all by Christ bestow'd
    Rendring back in sacrifice,
    Thinks he nothing gives to God. (pp. 295–6)

Lk. 21:4, *But she of her poverty hath cast in all the living that she had.*

God his mighty power displays,
    God his love to sinners shows;
Free, and disengag'd by grace
    Then the poor his all bestows;
Let his whole provision fail,
    He his confidence approves,
Feasts a Friend invisible,
    One whom more than life he loves. (p. 296)

Lk. 21:14, *Settle it therefore in your hearts, not to meditate before what ye shall answer.*

Jesus, fix it in my heart
    That human help is vain;
If my Advocate Thou art,
    Thou wilt my cause maintain:

Casting then my care away,
I on thine only grace rely;
Thou shalt teach me in that day,
And by my mouth reply. (pp. 298–9)

Lk. 21:15, *I will give you a mouth and wisdom which all your adversaries shall not be able, etc.*

Other wisdom I disclaim
Than that Thou dost bestow;
Eloquent enough I am,
If I my Saviour know:
None can stand against my word,
To Thee when I my all resign,
Join'd to an Almighty Lord,
And arm'd with Love Divine. (p. 299)

Lk. 21:17, *Ye shall be hated of all men for my name's sake.*

The dear portion of my Lord
With humble joy I take,
Let me live despis'd, abhor'd
Of all men for thy sake:
Only Thou my heart renew,
And me begotten from above
Let the world to death pursue,
Because my God I love. (p. 299)

Lk. 21:21, *Let them which are in Judea flee to the mountains.*

We who our Saviour's word receive,
The city of destruction leave,
Anticipate the coming woe,
Withdraw our hearts from all below;
From sin we take our hasty flight,
Contending for the mountain's height,
The world forsake for Jesus' love,
And find our life conceal'd above. (p. 301)

Lk. 21:27, *Then shall they see the Son of man coming,* &c.

1. Meet and right it is that Thou,
    Jesus, shouldst the heavens bow,
    Once an humble Son of man,
    Our salvation to obtain,
    Shouldst display Thy greatness here,
    Glorious like Thyself appear!

2. Sovereign Lord, for this we wait:
    Come in thy sublime estate,
    Hasten the expected hour,
    Come with all thy pomp and power,
    Come, the Father's only son,
    Shining on thine azure throne.

3. Come, thine exiles to remove,
    Us who thy appearing love;
    Prays the Spirit in the bride,
    Come and take us to thy side,
    Take to our celestial home,
    King of saints, triumphant come.

4. Let thy well-known sign appear,
    Let us soon behold thee here,
    Wonder at thy crimson scars,
    Shout with all the morning stars,
    Fall before thy majesty,
    Face to face forever see! (pp. 301–2)[64]

Lk. 21:28, *Look up, and lift up your heads, for your redemption draweth nigh.*

1.   May we not now look up,
       And lift our hearts to Thee
    In sure and comfortable hope
       Thy kingdom soon to see?

---

64. [Verses 1–3 appear in *Poet. Works*, XI, p. 278.]

Wilt thou not quickly, Lord,
In our behalf appear,
Accomplish thy redeeming word,
And save thy people *here*?

2.   Our utmost Saviour Thou,
Our all-victorious Prince,
Redeem us from our troubles now,
Redeem us from our sins:
Thou hearst in our complaints
Thy Spirit's earnest groan:
O come and make us sinless saints,
And perfect us in one.

3.   That perfect liberty
We humbly wait to know,
With God's establish'd sons to see
Thy throne set up below;
To see thy spotless bride
Fair as the church above,
And share with all the sanctified
Thy most consummate love.

4.   Then, then these eyes shall view,
Our full Redemption come,
To change our mortal bodies too,
And ransom from the tomb,
Gaze on the Man Divine,
Partake thy majesty,
Bright as thy glorious body shine,
Forever one with Thee. (pp. 302–3)

Lk. 21:32–3, *This generation shall not pass away, till all be fulfilled. Heaven and earth, etc.*

> Every word of God is sure,
>   All his threatned woes are near,
> All his promises endure,
>   When the worlds no more appear;
>   When both heaven and earth are fled,
>   Stand whoe'er his will have done,
>   Rise with *joy*[65] upon their head,
>   Share his everlasting throne. (p. 304)

Lk. 21:36, *Watch ye therefore and pray always, that ye may be accounted worthy, etc.*

1. Saviour, we would thy counsel take;
   Awake, and keep our souls awake
       By thy own Spirit's power,
   So shall we always watch and pray,
   And think of that vindictive day,
       And death's tremendous hour.

2. On us a sober mind bestow,
   To watch throughout our course below
       Against the enemy,
   An heart that every moment prays,
   Still hungring after righteousness,
       And still desiring Thee.

3. To us impute thy own desert,
   To us the deepest sense impart
       Of our own worthlessness,
   And hide, for mercy's sake alone,
   Till all the vengeful storms are gone,
       The vessels of thy grace.

---

65. [The word "crowns" is added in the MS margin as an alternative.]

4. So shall we in the judgment stand,
    Boldly appear at thy right hand,
        The glory of our Lord,
    The never-fading crown receive,
    Forever in thy presence live,
        And share thy own reward. (p. 306)

Lk. 22:1, *Now the feast of unleavened bread was nigh, which is called the passover.*

1. My Passover, O Christ, Thou art:
        On Thee that I may duely feed,
    Prepare, and purify my heart,
        My every thought, and word, and deed,
    Expel the old, infectious sin,
    And make mine inmost nature clean.

2. Thou art with all thy fulness nigh
        To souls that hunger after Thee:
    My soul persist to sanctify,
        Dispose for full felicity,
    And purge out all th'accursed leaven,
    And be my endless feast in heaven. (p. 308)

Lk. 22:2, *The chief priests and scribes sought how they might kill him.*

While full of the malicious fiend,
Counsel they take against their Friend;
His thoughts to them are thoughts of peace,
Their hatred he with pity sees,
And bows his head, that they may find
His death the life of all mankind. (p. 308)

Lk. 22:5, *They were glad, and covenanted to give him money.*

1. Tremendous doom, when God the just
        Leaves to themselves the slaves of sin!
    When nothing now obstructs their lust,
        With joy they let the tempter in,
    And lo, the long-sought means they find
    To perpetrate the ill design'd.

192

2. The blackest crimes I should have done,
    Hadst Thou not hedg'd about my way,
    With-held my soul by ways unknown,
    Stood by me in the evil day,
    Oppos'd the violence of my will,
    And mortified my lust to kill.

3. Forever be thy grace ador'd,
    Which would not give me up to die
    Like the old murtherer of my Lord;
      Thy saving name I magnify,
    And humbled into nothing own
    The difference made by grace alone. (p. 309)

Lk. 22:21, *Behold, the hand of him that betrayeth me is with me on the table.*

1. Commemorating our dying Lord
      When to his table we draw near,
    We lift the traitor's hands abhor'd,
      If stain'd with sin our hands appear:
    Refusing from our sin to part,
    We come with Judas in our heart.

2. Who will not let their idols go,
      Who commerce with the world maintain,
    (The world, his sworn inveterate foe)
      Delivering up their Lord again,
    At his own feast they Christ abjure,
    And make their own damnation sure. (p. 313)

Lk. 22:28, *Ye are they which have continued with me in my temptations.*

Jesus vouchsafes his own to praise,
  Their steady faithfulness t'approve,
He glories in his work of grace,
  He triumphs in his guardian love:

With Him our Keeper we abide:
Rewarding what Himself hath given,
Our souls with his temptations tried
He crowns with his own joy in heaven. (pp. 315–16)

Lk. 22:31, *Simon, Simon, behold, Satan hath desired, &c.*

1.   Still our adversary's nigh
        In every place and hour,
      Eager still to tempt, and try
        And sift us, and devour:
      But before he can o'erthrow,
    Or once endeavour to deceive,
      The malicious fiend, we know,
        Must ask our Saviour's leave.

2.   Left by Thee in danger's day
        We no support should find,
      By the tempter borne away,
        As chaff before the wind:
      But if Thou attend our call,
    And give the wheat's solidity,
      Not one sacred grain shall fall,
        Not one be lost from Thee. (p. 317)[66]

Lk. 22:38, *They said, Lord, behold, here are two swords, &c.*

1. Enough for Him who only means
      Himself by yielding to defend,
    To purge, by suffering for, our sins,
      By perfect patience to contend,
    And conquer a rebellious race
    By meekly dying in our place.

66. [Verse 1 appears in *Poet. Works*, XI, p. 287.]

2. Enough, the pattern mild to show,
   And good for evil to repay,
   Enough to make his murtherers know
   They could not force his life away,
   Which freely he for all lays down,
   To buy for all th'immortal crown. (p. 320)[67]

Lk. 22:39, *He went to the mount of Olives, & his disciples also followed him.*

Let us with our Lord retreat,
   To the holy mount repair,
Hallow'd by his bloody sweat,
   By his agony and prayer,
View what there for us was done,
   To the Lamb our spirit join,
Echoing back his deepest groan,
   Sharing in the pangs Divine! (p. 320)

Lk. 22:44, *And being in an agony, he prayed more earnestly.*

Thankful I accept the grace
   Sent in mercy from the sky,
With redoubled earnestness
   To my Comforter apply:
Tempted, above measure prest,
   With redoubled grief and pain,
Never will I let him rest,
   Till my Lord appears again. (pp. 322–3)

Lk. 22:44, *And his sweat was as it were great drops of blood falling down to the ground.*

1. Sentenc'd the first Adam was
   To a common sweat below:
Jesus, to retrieve our loss,
   Sorer toil must undergo:

---

67. [Verse 1 appears in *Poet. Works*, XI, p. 290.]

While he all our sins sustains,
　　See a sweat unseen before!
Forc'd by torture from his veins,
　　Blood transpires at every pore!

2. See the salutary stream
　　Flowing from the sinners' Friend!
Big with virtue to redeem,
　　Large the drops on man descend;
Drops which falling to the ground
　　Purge the universal stain:
There the precious ransom's found,
　　There my peace is seal'd again! (p. 323)[68]

Lk. 22:46, *Why sleep ye? rise and pray, lest ye enter into temptation.*

We to the temptation yield,
　　Sleeping, when we ought to pray,
Then we basely quit our shield,
　　Then by sloth we fall away:
Saviour, lest my foes surprize,
　　Supplicating grace impart,
Bid me, Lord, awake, arise,
　　Speak thy power into my heart. (p. 323)

Lk. 22:49, *They said unto him, Lord, shall we smite with the sword?*

Not govern'd by his word,
　　But furious, headlong zeal,
We seemingly consult the Lord,
　　And ask to know his will;
By passion borne away,
　　Before his will is known,
We rush, impatient of delay,
　　And madly act our own. (p. 324)

68. [Verse 2 appears in *Poet. Works*, XI, p. 292, as verse 2 of a poem based on Luke 22:43.]

Lk. 22:50, *One of them smote the servant of the high priest, and cut off his right ear.*

> A sinner's blindfold will
> Without the light of grace
> Cannot the mind of Christ fulfil,
> Or work his righteousness:
> Whom fiery zeal inflames,
> Push'd on by nature's power,
> To serve his God the more he aims,
> He vexes him the more. (p. 324)

Lk. 22:60, *Peter said, Man, I know not what thou sayest.*

1. In Peter's threefold fall we see,
   A threefold proof of Adam's fall,
   That spirit of infirmity
   By which his sin hath bound us all,
   That frailty of the heart, unknown,
   Or manifest to God alone.

2. He lets the pastor fall, t'explain
   Our depths of infidelity,
   To show the sheep what is in man,
   Left to myself what is in me;
   And while my weakness I confess,
   To arm my soul with all his grace. (p. 326)

Lk. 22:61, *And the Lord turned, and looked upon Peter, &c.*

1. The cock had crow'd and Peter hears,
   Nor calls his Master's word to mind,
   Till Jesus mournfully appears,
   T'upbraid his treachery unkind,
   Repentance by a look t'impart,
   And break his hard, ungrateful heart.

2. A look like that what heart can bear!
    O that it now were cast on mine!
    To snatch from Judas's despair,
    To pierce me with remorse divine,
    To make mine eyes with tears o'reflow,
    And fill my heart with Peter's woe!

3. On me those eyes of mercy turn,
    And suffer me a while to live
    My base unfaithfulness to mourn,
    The sins I never can forgive,
    The sins I must till death bemoan,
    Tho' Thou hast made them all thy own. (pp. 326–7)

Lk. 22:64, *When they had blindfolded [him], they struck him on the face, saying, Prophesy, etc.*

[I]

For our abuse of sight t'atone,
Jesus submits to lose his own,
His bandag'd eyes have open'd ours,
And blest our soul with visual powers;
And lo, I now my Saviour see,
Whose blindness bought the grace for me,
Points out the bright celestial prize,
And shows my way to paradise. (p. 328)

Lk. 22:64.

II

The soldiers struck their God unknown,
    But Christians bold in wickedness
Insult him whom in creeds they own,
    And outrage, while their lips confess;
They buffet all that Christ adore,
    They smite his members with their tongue,
As Jesus still the bandage wore,
    And only guess'd who did the wrong. (p. 328)

Lk. 22:66, *The elders of the people, and the chief priests and scribes come together, &c.*

Learning and authority
By grace unsanctified,
Fight against thy church and Thee
With sacerdotal pride:
Mighty men, and wise, and great
In every age their powers employ
Thee with rancour to intreat,
And in thy saints destroy. (p. 329)

Lk. 22:70, *Then said they all, Art thou then the Son of God? And he said unto them, etc.*

The truth which all his martyrs made,
And join'd them to his host on high,
Their Captain and almighty Head
He first in death should testify:
He dies, in proof that God was born,
Jehovah's Son, Jehovah's heir,
That Christ shall in the clouds return,
And all mankind adore him there. (p. 330)

Lk. 23:10, *The chief priests and scribes stood, and vehemently accused him.*

Teachers and priests corrupt assail
The truth, with rage implacable
Against the saints combine:
Their vehemence, which all bounds exceeds,
Their malice, which no answer needs,
Defeats its own design. (p. 333)

Lk. 23:11, *Herod with his men of war set him at nought, &c.*

Herod and his men of war
The Saviour still despise,
Mock whoe'er his followers are,
Whoe'er his service prize:

What have camps and courts to do
With Christ, the humble Prince of Peace?
Only to deride anew
In all his witnesses. (p. 333)

Lk. 23:12, *The same day Pilate and Herod were made friends.*

Jesus, thro' thy death alone
Both Jews and Gentiles join'd
Cordially consent to own
The Saviour of mankind:
Who thy loving Spirit receive,
One body reconcil'd to God,
Each to each they closely cleave,
Cemented by thy blood. (p. 334)

Lk. 23:19, *Who for a certain sedition made in the city, and for murder, was cast, etc.*

1. How blind the judgment of the croud!
   A thief, a stirrer up of strife,
They chuse before the Son of God,
   The Author of eternal life,
They to the Prince of peace prefer
A vile, seditious murtherer.

2. The sovereign God would stoop so low,
   To raise the abject sons of men,
That we his power divine might know,
   Might all his great salvation gain;
He bore the foul indignity,
To purchase grace and heaven for me. (pp. 334–5)

Lk. 23:20, *Pilate, willing to release Jesus, spake again to them.*

His life to save with vain desire
   The judge doth impotently strive;
Our louder sins his death require,
   They will not suffer him to live
Who came for all mankind t'atone,
And makes our punishment his own. (p. 335)

Lk. 23:23, *They were instant with loud voices, requiring that he might be crucified, etc.*

Reason, and truth, and justice fail,
    While earth and hell their powers employ;
Satan and the chief priests prevail,
    And Innocence himself destroy;
So loud our sins for vengeance cry,
To save the world, its God must die. (pp.335–6)

Lk. 23:25, *He delivered Jesus to their will.*

Abandon'd to the will of man,
Jesus, thou dost for me obtain
A power my spirit to resign
Intirely to the will Divine. (p. 336)

Lk. 23:31, *If they do these things in a green tree, what shall be done in the dry?*

If Jesus, the Immortal Tree,
    Full of all truth and grace,
So rig'rously entreated be
    For man's accursed race;
What have the wicked world to dread?
    Barren alas, and dry,
Cut from the stock, and doubly dead
    They must forever die. (p. 339)

Lk. 23:32, *There were also two other, malefactors, led with him to be put to death.*

1.   O my God, what hast Thou done?
        Into what company
    Brought thy well-beloved Son
        Who always lives with Thee!
    Heir of all in earth and sky,
    With thine eternal Spirit one,
        Is he not the Lord Most-high,
        And Partner of thy throne?

2.   Comfort hence, ye saints, receive
        Opprest with shame and pain,
    Link'd to human fiends who grieve
        Beneath the tyrant's chain;
    Hammer'd to the galling oar,
  Or buried in the mines beneath,
      Christ between the thieves adore,
        And die your Saviour's death. (pp. 339–40)

Lk. 23:33, *They crucified Him, and the malefactors, &c.*

1. He dies — a death of pain and shame,
      To the vile death of slaves submits,
  And thus the humble patient Lamb
      His own great sacrifice compleats!
  The universal sin He bears,
      Conquers the world, and death, and hell,
  And balm in His own blood prepares
      The wounds of all mankind to heal.

2. Saviour of men, Physician good,
      The medicine to my soul apply,
  Apply thine efficacious blood
      To purge, and save, and sanctify:
  The true, substantial holiness
      O might I in thy nature prove!
  Thy Spirit breathe, thy name impress,
      And fill my heart with humble love. (pp. 340–1)[69]

Lk. 23:34, *They parted his garments.*

Thy garments made by hands of men
    Thou dost to thy destroyers leave,
But richest ornaments unseen
    We in thy Spirit's gifts receive,
Cloth'd with divine humility,
    Meekness, and love, and every grace;
And when by faith we put on Thee,
    Our souls are fill'd with righteousness. (p. 341)

69. [Verse 1 appears in *Poet. Works*, XI, pp. 301–2.]

Lk. 23:35, *He saved others: let him save himself, if he be the Christ, the chosen of God.*

Life of the world, I worship Thee,
My Saviour dying on the tree,
Thee the Messiah true adore,
Who dost on all thy Unction pour;
The Chosen One of God confest,
The Head including all the rest,
Who know the virtue of thy blood,
And thro' thy wounds return to God. (pp. 341–2)

Lk. 23:38, *This is the King of the Jews!*

Glory doth to Thee belong,
    Tho' on that shameful tree,
Just it is that every tongue
    Should give the power to Thee:
Lord, we own the kingdom thine,
The kingdom of a dying God,
    Won by agonies divine,
    And bought with all thy blood! (p. 342)

Lk. 23:39, *One of the malefactors, which were hanged, railed on him.*

1. Can sufferings without grace avail
        The adamantine heart to move?
    A sinner on the verge of hell,
        A wretched stranger to thy love,
    Will louder for his torments cry,
    And curse th'avenging God, and die.

2. The sufferer without faith or hope
        Anticipates his doom below,
    Drinks upon earth the dreadful cup
        Of dire, unmixt, infernal woe,
    And pain unhallow'd, Lord, by Thee,
    Expires in endless blasphemy. (p. 343)

[Lk. 23:46], *Into thy hands I commend my spirit.*

1. The holy Jesus rests in Hope,
   And calm in Death on God relies,
   His parting Spirit he gives up,
   Into his Father's Hands & dies.

2. Meek, patient Lamb for us he gives
   The Life which none could take away,
   He lays it down, & GOD receives
   His Soul into Eternal Day.

3. O might I thus my Warfare end,
   Meekly to GOD my Soul resign,
   Into my Father's Hands commend;
   O Jesu, let thy Death be mine.

4. I long with Thee to bow my Head,
   Offered upon thy Sacrifice;
   With Thee to sink among the Dead,
   And in thy Life triumphant rise!

5. Father of Jesus Christ my Lord,
   Conform me to thy Suffering Son,
   And let my Spirit be restor'd
   And let me breathe my latest Groan.

6. Now, let me Now give up the Ghost,
   Now let my Nature's Life be o're,
   Now let me All in Christ be lost,
   And die with Christ to die no more.[70]

70. [MS Thirty, pp. 195–6; MS Richmond, p. 45. Verses 1–4 appear in *Poet. Works*, XII, p. 99. This poem is not included in MS Luke.]

Lk. 23:49, *And all his acquaintance and the women that followed him, stood afar off, beholding, etc.*

Jesus, whom thy grace constrains
To own and follow Thee,
Them thy mercy still detains
Their bleeding God to see:
Fixt I would like them abide,
Nor ever from thy cross remove,
With my Saviour crucified,
A sacrifice to love. (pp. 346–7)

Lk. 23:50,[71] *There was a man named Joseph, a counseller, and he was a good man, & a just, etc.*

1. The righteous man awhile conceal'd
    May for his full commission stay,
    But soon, or late, with courage fill'd
    Appears for Christ in open day,
    His body mystical receives,
    And honour to his members gives.

2. His secret ones to God are known,
    Whom God doth for a season hide,
    But surely they their Lord shall own,
    And suffer with the Crucified,
    Renounce their honourable name,
    And Christ in life and death proclaim.

3. They do not with the world conspire,
    Or to his daily death agree,
    But wait with faith's intense desire
    His reigning power of grace to see,
    And till his heavenly kingdom come,
    They rest themselves in Jesus' tomb. (p. 347)

71. [Charles Wesley incorrectly cited this verse as Lk. 23:52.]

Lk. 23:53, *He laid it in a sepulchre.*

1. With Jesus crucified and dead
    Who the baptismal mystery know,
  A life hid from the world we lead,
    Nothing of the old Adam show,
  Conceal'd, and buried in his grave,
  Till Jesus to the utmost save.

2. As long forgot and out of mind,
    In hope to live with Christ restor'd,
  We wait the quickning power to find,
    The glorious Spirit of our Lord,
  Who perfects all the saints in one,
  And draws the members to his throne. (p. 348)

Lk. 24:2, *They found the stone rolled away from the sepulchre.*

God when we desire to please
    With active faith sincere,
Vanish all the hindrances,
    And mountains disappear:
When we seek our Best-belov'd,
Impossibilities are done,
    Then we find the bar removed,
    And roll'd away the stone. (p. 349)

Lk. 24:4, *As they were much perplexed, behold, two men stood by them in shining garments.*

1. Absent from the sepulchre
    When we seek our Lord in vain,
  In perplexity and fear
    Will he let us long remain,
  Leave us comfortless to mourn,
  Never to our souls return?

2. If he for a time withdraws,
   Our fidelity to prove,
   While we sorrow for his loss,
   While we languish for his love,
   Jesus will himself appear
   Our eternal Comforter. (p. 349)

Lk. 24:10, *It was Mary Magdalen — and other women which told these things unto the Apostles.*

More courageous than the men,
   When Christ his breath resign'd,
Women first the grace obtain
   Their living Lord to find;
Women first the news proclaim,
   Know his resurrection's power,
Teach th'Apostles of the Lamb
   Who lives to die no more. (p. 350)

Lk. 24:12, *Then arose Peter, and ran unto the sepulchre, &c.*

Joyful tidings of their Lord
   His messengers proclaim,
Jesus Christ to life restor'd,
   And pardon thro' his name!
O might I like Peter hear,
   The witnesses' report receive,
Empty find thy sepulchre,
   And wonder and believe. (pp. 350-1)

Lk. 24:16, *But their eyes were holden, that they should not know him.*

1. Who can Jesus' mind explain,
   His mysterious counsels tell,
When he doth with us remain
   Hidden, imperceptible!
Oft by Him upheld we go,
   Walk with him in all his ways,
Yet our Lord we do not know,
   Do not clearly see his face.

2. Lord, mine eyes are holden too,
   Holden, till unseal'd by Thee:
   Thee, whom once in part I knew,
   Now I neither know nor see:
   Or if manifest Thou art,
   Soon Thou vanishest away:
   Come, and purify my heart;
   Then Thou wilt forever stay. (pp. 351–2)[72]

Lk. 24:17, *What manner of communications are these that ye have — as ye walk and are sad?*

Griev'd for having lost our Lord,
   Him we by our sorrow please:
Till he doth his light afford,
   Jesus pities our distress;
Drawn by our infirmity
   He will soon himself reveal,
Give us eyes his love to see,
   With his church forever dwell. (p. 351)

Lk. 24:19, *He said unto them, What things?*

Tho' his glorified estate
   Swallows up the Man of woe,
Can our Lord so soon forget
   All his suffering days below?
No; his changeless love withstands,
   Love retains the bleeding scars,
Still he bears us on his hands;
   Graven on his heart he bears! (pp. 352–3)

72. [Verse 2 appears in *Short Hymns*, II, p. 234, and in *Poet. Works*, XI, p. 307, in a different metre.]

Lk. 24:19, *Jesus was a Prophet mighty in deed and word, before God and all the people.*

> Deeds and words a bishop praise,
> Words of truth and deeds of love;
> Every messenger of grace
> Shows his mission from above;
> Still by Christ he preaches peace,
> Proves his ministerial call,
> By a life of holiness
> Teaching, doing good to all. (p. 353)

Lk. 24:30–1, *He took bread, and blessed it, and brake, and gave it to them. And their eyes, etc.*

1. If Jesus bless, and break the bread,
   And give it hungry souls to feed,
   To sudden sight restor'd
   With faith's inlighten'd eyes they see
   The fulness of the Deity,
   And recognize their Lord.

2. Millions of mournful souls have seen
   Him fairer than the sons of men
   Present at his own feast,
   Injoy'd on earth the blisful sight,
   And lean'd with rapturous delight
   On his beloved breast.

3. Yet who their Saviour truly knew,
   They could not always keep in view
   The beauties of his face:
   From saints he sensibly withdraws,
   And makes them gainers by the loss
   Of that extatic grace.

4. With stronger love for Him they sigh,
   Till Christ returning in the sky
       Their glorious Head they see,
   And then he hides his face no more,
   And then they gaze, admire, adore
       Thro' all eternity. (pp. 355–6)

Lk. 24:37, *They were terrified and affrighted.*

1. Left to itself, the soul of man
       Cannot discern the things of God,
   Mistakes for meer illusions vain
       Uncommon benefits bestow'd:
   The tempter's visits blind and lull,
       With bold security inspire,
   Flatter the visionary soul,
       But never suffer him t'inquire.

2. When God vouchsafes the soul to bless,
       Or sends some heavenly messenger,
   Himself doth on the mind impress
       A jealous awe, an humble fear
   Lest rashly we should all receive
       As surely coming from above,
   And every specious spirit believe,
       Before we try, compare, and prove. (p. 359)

Lk. 24:38, *He said unto them, Why are ye troubled?*

   The visits of unusual grace
       We should with diffidence receive,
   But not with infidel distress
       Which will not on full proof believe:
   Yet, till the Lord fresh grace bestow,
       To guard the former and explain,
   His gifts we neither use nor know,
       But turn his blessings into bane. (p. 359)

Lk. 24:40, *He shewed them his hands and his feet.*

1. The marks of thy expiring love
   In glory, Lord, Thou dost retain,
   The wounds which bought thy crown above,
   That thro' the path of sacred pain
   The members on thy cross may rise,
   And bear thy burthen to the skies.

2. Thy wounds Thou dost to sinners show,
   That we may love those pangs behind,
   After our patient Pattern go,
   Sure refuge in temptation find,
   Succour in perilous distress,
   And fountains of eternal grace.

3. Close not thy wounds against my soul,
   But let them always open be;
   They bleed the balm that makes me whole,
   (Balm of all sin and misery)
   Declare that God and I are one,
   And make my passage to his throne. (p. 360)

Lk. 24:49, *Behold, I send the promise of my Father upon you: But tarry ye in the city, etc.*

1. Before the Comforter's descent,
   We cannot savingly repent,
   Or truly, Lord, in Thee believe;
   But till thy word is ratified,
   We in the outward church abide,
   And look The Promise to receive:
   The Promise of thy Father's Grace,
   Saviour, it must on us take place,
   On us who seek, secure to find,
   Who gasp to meet Him from above,
   The Spirit of power, and faith, and love,
   The Promise made to all mankind.

2. Thou didst to thine Apostles give,
   And still their successors receive
      That ministerial Comforter;
   He all thy messengers ordains,
   And when in them his kingdom reigns,
      Thy genuine gospel they declare:
   He every faithful heart inspires,
   Thy members fills with pure desires,
      With life and real holiness,
   With love omnipotent, divine,
   With all that spotless mind of thine,
      That plenitude of heavenly grace. (pp. 363–4)

THE GOSPEL OF JOHN

THE GOSPEL OF JOHN
(MS John)[1]

Jn. 1:7, *John came to bear witness of the Light, that all men through It[2] might believe.*

1. The first Apostle of the Lamb,
   First witness to the Light he came,
   First confessor of thine;
   Jesus, thy honour'd minister
   He came, thy coming to declare,
   Eternal Word Divine.

2. But shining in the faithless heart,
   Thou only dost the power impart
   His record to receive,
   "That every fallen child of man
   Thro' Thee the saving grace may gain,
   And in Thyself believe." (p. 2)

Jn. 1:10, *He was in the world, and the world was made by him, and the world knew him not.*

1. Jesus, the world was made by Thee,
   That men in all thy works might see
   Thy wisdom, love, & power,
   But thro' their own false wisdom blind,
   Their present God they cannot find,
   Or worthily adore.

1. [Inside the cover Charles Wesley has written a sentence, first in Greek: *Sus eimi Christē, sōson hōs autos theleis;* and then in Latin, *Tuus sum Christe, serva quo velis modo*; (i.e., I am Thine, O Christ, save [or preserve] in what manner Thou wilt). On p. 1 of the flyleaf he continues: "Mem. Nov. 30, 1765: Lent Matthew to Mr Hampson D. 1." (i.e. Dec. 1, 1763). Throughout the MSS John and Acts dates often are entered in Wesley's shorthand and indicate when the poems for each chapter of the biblical book were begun.]
2. [The AV reads: "Him."]

2. In pity for our helpless race,
   Thou cam'st the shades of sin to chase,
      The manifested Word,
   Yet still the world lie wrapt in night,
   And shut their eyes against the Light,
      And will not know their Lord. (pp. 3–4)

Jn. 1:22, *Then said they unto him, Who art thou? what sayest thou
of thyself?*

The humble man by Jesus sent,
   If just authority constrain,
As mercy's meanest instrument
   Speaks of himself with irksome pain,
And chusing to remain unknown,
Fixes our thoughts on Christ alone. (pp. 14–15)

Jn. 1:38, *Jesus turned and saw them following . . . They said unto
him, Master, where dwellest Thou?*

1. We seek the Saviour of mankind,
      If he infuse the good desire,
   But Jesus we can never find,
      Unless we of himself inquire
   Leave every ministerial John,
   And ask for Christ of Christ alone.

2. The law points out the Victim slain,
      And toward Him a few steps we go,
   But never can to Christ attain
      Till He the power of faith bestow,
   Turning to us, Himself impart,
   And speak in mercy to the heart.

3. Master, (as such Thyself I own,)
      My Master and Director be,
   Instruct me in the way unknown,
      Which leads to happiness and Thee,
   And by the lessons of Thy love
   Conduct me to Thy house above. (pp. 11–12)[3]

3. [Verses 2 and 3 appear in *Poet. Works*, XI, p. 328.]

Jn. 1:42, *When Jesus beheld him, he said, Thou art Simon, &c.*

Happy whome'er the God of grace
Beholds with looks of tender love!
His look is[4] saving to our race,
  Our miseries & sins remove,
His looks immortal strength impart,
And reach the poor, expecting heart. (p. 13)

Jn. 1:46, *Philip saith unto him, Come & see.*

By tasting Him we know,
By faith we come & see
Th'Invisible reveal'd below,
  Th'incarnate Deity:
We search the written word,
We weigh & all things prove,
And wait the leizure of our Lord
  To manifest his love. (p. 17)

Jn. 1:47, *Behold an Israelite indeed, in whom is no guile.*

O were I like him sincere,
Blest with Jacob's character,
Artless, innocent, & plain,
Upright both to God & man!
True to all which I profess,
In simplicity of grace,
Lord, I would thy follower be,
Seek the praise that comes from Thee. (p. 17)

Jn. 1:49, *Rabbi, thou art the Son of God, thou art the King of Israel.*

Jesus, thou our Rabbi art,
  Thy sayings we receive
With docility of heart,
  And joyfully believe:

---

4. [In the MS Charles Wesley originally wrote "His looks are," but altered this wording to "His look is;" however, he retained the plural in lines four and five.]

Thee the Son of God confess,
Co-equal with thy Father own,
Israel's King, thy sway we bless,
And hail thee on thy throne. (p. 18)

Jn. 2:4, *When they wanted wine, the mother of Jesus saith unto him,
They have no wine, etc.*[5]

1. Loos'd from the ties of flesh and blood,
Jesus, in all the things of God
Thy messenger should be,
Deaf to the voice of nature's *now*,
To Thee for his instructions bow
And singly look to Thee.

2. Harshly Thou dost thy mother treat,
Least pious parents should forget
Their sons are not their own,
Or plead a right to interfere
In matters where thy minister
Is taught of God alone. (p. 23)

Jn. 2:9, *When the ruler of the feast had tasted the water that was
made wine, &c.*

1. Jesus, to Thee our wants we tell
(But need no Advocate with Thee)
Fountain of life, Salvation's Well,
Divine, imparadizing[6] Tree,
Thou art the true immortal Vine,
Which chears thy saints with heavenly wine.

---

5. [Preceding the entries for chapter 2 in Wesley's shorthand is written: "D. 7" (December 7).]

6. [The *Oxford English Dictionary* lists "to imparadize:" "to place in, or as in, Paradise; to bring into a state of rapture," with occasional examples as late as the nineteenth century; however, it quotes no example of a present participle adjective.]

2. Our thirsty souls the wine require
    Which from thy wounded body flow'd,
    The ben'fits of thy death desire,
    The virtues of thy precious blood;
    The Spirit from thy throne above,
    The full effusion of thy love.

3. Convert our nature into grace,
    Our heart to things of earth inclin'd
    To objects spiritual upraise,
    To heavenly good our groveling mind,
    And give our new-born souls a taste
    Of joys which shall forever last.

4. The vessels of thy mercy fill
    (Till our glad hearts with thanks o'reflow)
    With power to do thy utmost will
    And perfect holiness below,
    Fill up our soul's capacity
    With all the love which is in Thee. (pp. 24–5)

Jn. 2:13, *The Jews' passover was at hand, and Jesus went up to Jerusalem.*

Thou dost the forms commend
Of outward righteousness,
And teach us constantly t'attend
The channels of thy grace:
Thy practise as our law
We gladly, Lord, receive,
And keep thy feasts with sacred awe,
And to thy statutes cleave. (pp. 27–8)

Jn. 2:16, *Take these things hence.*

More odious than the birds and beasts,
Creatures required for sacrifice,
Are careless crouds and worldly priests
Who now provoke Thy glorious eyes,

219

Profane the temple of the Lord,
    Their venial ministry disgrace,
And sell the prayer, the psalm, the word,
    And buy in hell the hottest place. (p. 28)[7]

Jn. 2:18, *What sign shewest thou unto us, seeing thou dost these things?*

No right the house of God to cleanse
    Has he, whose heart remains impure;
But if he chase the creature thence,
    His ministerial call is sure:
A life of apostolic love,
    This is the standing miracle,
This only can his mission prove
    And justify the pastor's zeal. (p. 29)

Jn. 3:4,[*Nicodemus saith unto Him, How can a man be born when he is old?*][8]

Saviour of men, I ask no more,
    How can the wonder be,
But trusting in thy gracious power,
    I leave it all to Thee;
That heavenly birth I wait to prove,
    I look to be restor'd,
In age, to the new life of love,
    The image of my Lord. (p. 32)

Jn. 3:5, *Except a man be born of water & of the Spirit, he cannot enter into the kingdom of God.*

1. The water & the Spirit join,
    The inward grace & outward sign
        In that great mystery
    Thro' which our souls are born again,
    Thy kingdom first on earth obtain,
        And then thy glory see.

7. [This verse appears in *Poet. Works*, XI, p. 337 but with the omission of lines six and eight.]

8. [At the beginning of the entries for chapter 3 in Wesley's shorthand is written: "D. 10" (December 10).]

2. Who the baptismal rite receive,
   And by & in thy Spirit live
      The sinless life unknown,
   Children of God they reign in love,
   Joint-heirs with Thee, O Christ, remove
      To share thy heavenly throne. (pp. 32–3)

Jn. 3:10, *Art thou a master of Israel, and knowest not these things?*

1. The masters of our Israel may
      The fact by sure experience prove,
   May know the Truth, the Life, the Way,
      Born of his Spirit from above,
   In real holiness renew'd,
   By faith the genuine sons of God.

2. But few th'incarnate Word receive,
      Author of that mysterious birth;
   They will not in his name believe,
      Or quit for heaven the things of earth,
   But on the outward sign rely
   Till Christ-less in their sins they die. (p. 36)

Jn. 3:12, *If I have told you earthly things, and ye, &c.*

   Who will not now the word believe,
      And feel that wondrous birth below,
   How shall their carnal hearts conceive
      The joys which in thy presence flow,
   The rivers of unmixt delight,
      The pleasures of thy house above,
   The soul-beatifying sight,
      The extasies of glorious love! (p. 38)[9]

9. [The first half of the verse appears in *Poet. Works*, XI, p. 344.]

Jn. 3:15, *That whosoever believeth in him, should not perish, but have eternal life.*

1. O Thou who hast our sorrows took,
    My God for sinners crucified,
    To Thee I for salvation look
    And while I in thy cross confide,
    Thy passion's fruit with faith receive,
    And quicken'd by thy death I live.

2. Sav'd from the death of sin & hell
    Thro' thine atoning sacrifice,
    I wait, till Thou the life reveal
    Reserv'd for me above the skies,
    Purchas'd with all thy precious blood,
    The rapturous, endless life of God. (p. 39)

Jn. 3:17, *God sent not His Son into the world to, &c.*

1. Thou didst not send thy Son
    To aggravate our guilt,
    But for the sins of all t'atone
    His precious blood was spilt:
    Not as our Judge he came,
    But our Redeemer kind,
    That all believing in his name,
    May life & pardon find.

2. Thou didst Thy Son bestow
    Thy truth of grace to prove,
    And Jesus did by dying show
    Sincerity of love:
    He suffer'd in our place
    By mercy's sole decree:
    Know every child of Adam's race
    Thy Saviour died for thee! (p. 41)[10]

---

10. [Verse 2 appears in *Poet. Works*, XI, p. 346.]

Jn. 3:18, *He that believeth not is condemned already, because he hath not believed in the name, etc.*

1. Who doth not in the Son believe
    Condemn'd he in his sins remains,
   But death-devoted, a reprieve
    Thro' Jesus' intercession gains:
   Yet O, the sentence must take place,
    If still his Saviour he denies,
   And scorning all his proffer'd grace
    A wilful unbeliever dies.

2. Shut up by unbelief, within
    The tempter's power a while he dwells,
   Under the guilt of reigning sin
    Its cruel tyranny he feels;
   He might thro' Jesus' name receive
    The power which all believers know,
   But will not come to Christ, and live,
    But will not lose his place below. (p. 42)

Jn. 3:19, *This is the condemnation, that light is come, &c.*

1. Poor sinful souls, diseas'd, and blind,
    Who will not thy salvation see,
   Their merciful Physician find,
    Or come for light, O Lord, to thee,
   Because they madly hug their chain,
    And with their sins refuse to part,
   Their sins and unbelief remain,
    And still the vail is on their heart.

2. All in their wretched selves alone
    The cause of their damnation lies,
   Lovers of sin, they hate and shun
    The light that pains their guilty eyes.

223

Who the dire deeds of darkness do
Abhorrence of the light they feel,
And the broad dreary path pursue
Which leads to the profoundest hell. (pp. 42–3)[11]

Jn. 3:21, *He that do[e]th truth cometh to the light, that his deeds may be manifest, that they are wrought in God.*

The truth who from their heart obey
Rejoice as children of the light,
To stand confess'd in open day
And blameless walk before thy sight:
Their lives with scrutiny severe
They by thy word & Spirit prove,
That all their actions may appear
Wrought in the light & power of love. (p. 43)

Jn. 3:28, *I am not the Christ, but I am sent before him.*

1. Th'ambassador of the Most High,
    Forerunner of his heavenly Lord
Himself can never magnify,
    But trembles to dispense the word,
Savour of life or death to deal,
And thus his awful charge fulfil.

2. He dares not arrogate or share
    The praise which all to God should pay,
Sent by instructions to prepare
    By penitence the Saviour's way,
And in himself the pattern give
How sinners should their Lord receive. (p. 45)

11. [Verse 2 appears in *Poet. Works*, XI, p. 347.]

Jn. 3:29, *He that hath the bride is the bridegroom: but the friend of the bridegroom rejoiceth greatly because of the bridegroom's voice: &c.*

1. Jesus is of his church possest
   And clasps her to his loving breast;
   He will not with his purchase part,
   He holds his consort in his heart:
   Who in Jesus' heart abide
   Faithful souls are all his bride.

2. My spirit doth in God rejoice
   Attentive to the Bridegroom's voice;
   He brings his kingdom from above,
   He fills me with the life of love,
   "Rise, my love, without delay,
   Rise, my fair, & come away!" (p. 45)

Jn. 3:34, *He whom God hath sent speaketh the words of God: for God giveth not the Spirit by measure unto him.*

1. Sent from the heavenly Father down,
   Thou cam'st to make the Godhead known,
   The mysteries divine t'impart,
   And speak his words into my heart:
   That Spirit I in measure feel
   Who doth the things of God reveal,
   Fathoms the depths of Deity,
   And dwells with all his grace in Thee.

2. The words Thou dost from God declare
   Pure life, and quickening Spirit are,
   Their own divinity they prove,
   Th'eternal Truth, and Power, and Love:

Our penetrated hearts agree
Never was man that spake like Thee,
God over all the Speaker own,
And seat Thee on Thy favourite throne. (p. 49)[12]

Jn. 4:4, *He must needs go through Samaria.*[13]

See the heavenly Shepherd's zeal,
    Saviour of the sinful kind,
Pity doth his heart compel
    A lost sheep to seek & find!
Love constrains him to draw near
    To the soul redeem'd of old,
Claims the thoughtless wanderer,
    Brings her back into his fold. (pp. 52–3)

Jn. 4:12, *Art thou greater than our father Jacob which gave us the well, and drank thereof himself,* etc.

Fulness of the Deity
    Resides in Christ the Lord:
Greater far than Jacob, Thee
    The patriarch ador'd:
Well of life, divinely deep,
Out of thy plenitude of grace
Water now thy lambs & sheep,
    And all the heaven-born race. (p. 55)

Jn. 4:14, *Whosoever drinketh of the water that I shall give him shall never thirst.*

1. The living water of thy grace
        On me, indulgent Lord, bestow,
    To quench my thirst of happiness,
        Vouchsafe that taste of heaven below:

12. [Verse 2 appears in *Poet. Works*, XI, p. 351.]
13. [Preceding the entries for chapter 4 in Wesley's shorthand is written: "D. 16" (December 16).]

When of thy love I freely take,
My wants are all in one supplied,
When in thy likeness I awake,
My soul is fill'd & satisfied.

2. My eager thirst of creature-bliss,
My earthly vain pursuits are o're,
The Lord my peace & Portion is,
Injoying Christ, I ask no more;
I drink the river from above,
The Spirit's pure, pellucid stream,
The Fount himself, the Life, the Love,
And all the joys of heaven in Him. (pp. 56–7)

Jn. 4:15, *Sir, give me this water, that I thirst not, neither come hither to draw.*

1. Thee, Saviour that I may
Thro' thy own Spirit know,
The willingness to pray,
The thirst of grace bestow,
The first imperfect wish inspire,
And then fulfil thine own desire.

2. Prevented by thy love,
Lord, if I now begin
To seek the things above,
The grace that saves from sin,
Do Thou the living water give,
Which makes my soul forever live.

3. The streams of holiness
Into my spirit pour,
And kept in perfect peace
I then shall thirst no more,
But seek my whole felicity,
But find it all compriz'd in Thee. (p. 58)

Jn. 4:19, *I perceive that Thou art a prophet.*

1. Lighten'd by a ray of grace,
   Christ, & sin I now perceive,
   Conscious of my wickedness,
   Jesus I my God believe;
   God supreme Thou surely art,
   God alone can search the heart.

2. Thee descended from the sky
   More than Prophet I embrace:
   Thine atoning blood apply,
   Then I shall my Priest confess:
   Fill me with thy Spirit's power,
   Then I shall my King adore. (p. 59)

Jn. 4:21, *Ye shall neither in this mountain, nor yet at Jerusalem, worship the Father.*

To no single sect confin'd,
   Or place, as heretofore,
God the Father of mankind
   We everywhere adore,
Coming to his gracious throne
Thro' Christ we all have free access,
   In the Spirit of his Son,
      The truth of holiness. (p. 60)

Jn. 4:22, *Ye worship ye know not what.*

God who out of Christ adore,
   Adore they know not what,
Serve him without faith or power
   For yet they know him not;
Blind, & void of filial fear
Till Christ their unbelief remove,
   Then they see, confess, revere,
      And praise the God they love. (p. 60)

Jn. 4:25, *I know that Messias cometh: when he is come, he will teach us all things.*

1. Come, thou Prophet of the Lord,
   Mighty both in deed & word,
   Prophet by thy Father seal'd,
   With his hallowing Spirit fill'd,
   Sent, anointed to proclaim
   His unutterable name,
   Come, Divine Interpreter,
   All his will to man declare.

2. Visible thro' faith I know,
   God thou dost to sinners show;
   Show us in thy Spirit's light
   How to worship Him aright;
   By the unction of thy grace
   Lead us into all thy ways:
   All our unbelief remove,
   Teach us everything in love. (p. 63)

Jn. 4:28–9, *The woman then left her waterpot, and went, &c.*

1. See a soul with pardon bless'd,
       Freely sav'd by grace alone!
   Knowing Christ, she cannot rest,
       Till she makes *her* Saviour known.
   Changed by one almighty word,
       Earthly things she leaves behind,
   This th'Apostle of the Lord,
       Lord of her, and all mankind.

2. Sinners, come by faith, and see
       A celestial Man unknown,
   One who hath reveal'd to me
       All I have in secret done:

Virtue doth from Him proceed;
    All my life & heart he shew'd:
Is not this the Christ indeed?
    Is not this th'omniscient God? (p. 64)[14]

Jn. 4:32, *I have meat to eat that ye know not of.*

But if thou the Father show,
    Manifest to me his love,
I that hidden meat shall know,
    I my Master's joy shall prove,
Gladly in thy labours share,
    Feast with thee on heavenly food,
Servant of thy church, declare,
    "Heaven on earth is serving God." (p. 65)[15]

Jn. 4:34, *My meat is to do the will of him that sent me, & to finish his work.*

Sent of God to do his will
    Every gospel-minister
Should his Father's work fulfil,
    Serve the heirs of glory here;
All his business & delight,
    Souls to win thro' Jesus' love,
Till he joins the saints in light,
    Banquets with his Lord above. (p. 66)

Jn. 4:35, *Lift up your eyes, and look on the fields, &c.*

1. Jesus, we now with pure delight
    Lift up our eyes and see
The gospel fields to harvest white,
    The crowds that flock to Thee:
Call'd by Thy ministers they run,
    With eager haste to find
The promised Christ, the God unknown,
    The Saviour of mankind.

14. [Verse 1 appears in *Poet. Works*, XI, p. 359.]
15. [This verse appears in *Poet. Works*, XI, p. 360, and *Short Hymns*, II, p. 244 as a six-lined poem. Wesley has expanded the poem adding lines five and seven above.]

2. Ready our record to receive
    From every side they press,
Made willing to repent, believe,
    And live thy witnesses:
O thou who hast their hearts prepar'd,
    Display thy pardning love,
And qualify for their reward,
    And lodge them safe above. (p. 66)[16]

Jn. 4:37–8, *Herein is that saying true, One soweth, and, &c.*

1. The prophets spake of Jesus' grace,
    The seed immortal sow'd;
Th'Apostles reap'd the ransom'd race,
    And brought a world to God:
The Prophets and Apostles too
    For us the way prepar'd,
And if their footsteps we pursue
    We share their full reward.

2. Enter'd into their labours we,
    And prosper'd in our deed,
Avail us of their ministry,
    And thro' their toil succeed;
We preach the Lord our righteousness,
    The world thro' Christ forgiven,
And God, to seal his word of grace,
    Reveals his Son from heaven. (p. 68)[17]

Jn. 4:40, *So when the Samaritans were come unto him, they besought him that he would tarry with them, etc.*

Convinc'd to Thee, O Lord, we come
    And instant in thy Spirit pray,
Enter, & make our hearts thy home,
    With poor converted heathens stay,
Thro' life's short day our Teacher be,
Our God thro' all eternity. (p. 69)

16. [Verse 1 appears in *Poet. Works*, XI, p. 360.]
17. [Verse 1 appears in *Poet. Works*, XI, p. 361.]

Jn. 4:42, *Now we believe, not because of thy saying, &c.*

1. This is the faith we humbly seek,
       The faith which with Thyself we find:
   Speak to our souls, in mercy speak,
       Thou Friend & Saviour of mankind,
   Messiah, sent us from above
   To teach the world, that God is Love.

2. Call'd by thy gospel messenger
       We gladly his report believe,
   But when of thine own mouth we hear
       The truth we savingly receive,
   And partners of thy Spirit know
   That God is manifest below.

3. By that unspoken word of thine
       Thou dost thy Deity reveal,
   The Saviour of the world is mine,
       Sav'd from my sins I surely feel
   The real Christ of God Thou art,
   Thy unction speaks it in my heart. (p. 69)[18]

Jn. 4:48, *Except ye see signs & wonders, ye will not believe.*

Oft have I heard, O Lord, and read
    Thy wondrous works perform'd of old,
Yet unconvinc'd by work or deed,
    My free & full assent with-hold:
Such is my stubbornness of will,
    Help'd by preventing grace in vain,
Unless I see thy power & feel,
    I still an infidel remain. (p. 70)

18. [Verses 2 and 3 appear in *Poet. Works*, XI, p. 362.]

Jn. 4:49, *Come down, ere my child die.*

> 'Tis not confin'd to time or place,
> The virtue of thy saving grace;
> Whene'er our wants to Thee we tell,
> Thy power is present, Lord, to heal:
> Ev'n now thou seest with pitying eye
> A sinner sick, & doom'd to die:
> But if thou speak the word, my soul
> Is at the point of death made whole. (p. 71)

Jn. 4:50, *Jesus saith, . . . Go thy way; thy son liveth, &c.*

> 1. He spake, and Jesus' word alone
>   Effects the double miracle;
>   The distant body of the son,
>   The father's heart, a word can heal;
>   Credence to God the father gives
>   Heal'd of his incredulity,
>   His son restor'd to health believes,
>   Believes the cure he doth not see.

> 2. This is the miracle I need,
>   Saviour of souls, for this I pray,
>   Let virtue out of Thee proceed,
>   And take the plague of sin away:
>   The fever of fierce passion chide,
>   Command it, Jesus, to depart,
>   The fever of desire & pride,
>   And cure my unbelieving heart. (p. 71)[19]

Jn. 4:54, *This is again the second miracle that Jesus did, when he was come out of Judea into Galilee.*

> The first effect of grace Divine
>   Is at the soul's espousals shew'd,
> It changes water into wine,
>   And gives our faith a taste of God:

---

19. [Verse 1 appears in *Poet. Works*, XI, p. 362.]

The second sign to life restores
The soul that Jesus' word receives,
And man th'eternal God adores,
And God in man eternal lives. (p. 73)

Jn. 5:5, *A certain man was there, which had an infirmity thirty and eight years.*[20]

For half a mournful century
I have afflicted been
And groan'd beneath the tyranny
Of my own bosom-sin:
Th'inveterate, obstinate disease
I struggled with in vain;
And hardly now at last confess
There is no help in man. (pp. 74–5)

Jn. 5:7, *The impotent man answered him, Sir, I have no man, when the water is troubled, etc.*

1. An impotent desire I feel
    At times to be made whole,
    But who shall undertake to heal
    My long-distemper'd soul?
    Not one of all our sinful race,
    When Christ his grace would give,
    Can help me to accept his grace,
    Can help me to believe.

2. While tortur'd here with lingring pains
    I languish for my cure,
    Another & another gains
    And feels his pardon sure:

---

20. [Preceding the entries for chapter 5 in Wesley's shorthand is written: "D. 25" (December 25).]

Pardon may all the world receive
Of their transgressions past,
But let me, Lord, at last believe,
Let me be sav'd at last. (p. 76)[21]

Jn. 5:13, *Jesus had conveyed himself away, a multitude being in that place.*

Jesus conveys himself away,
　　That ministers applause may shun;
If Christ by them his power display,
　　Or make his great salvation known,
The instruments themselves should hide,
And God alone be glorified. (p. 78)

Jn. 5:16, *Therefore did the Jews persecute Jesus, & sought to slay him.*

And shall we think it strange, or new,
　　That wicked men revile the good,
With cruel enmity pursue,
　　And thirst to drink the martyrs' blood?
Who most possess of Jesus' mind,
　　And truth, & meek benev'lent love,
Shall most of Jesus' treatment find,
　　And gain the brightest crown above. (p. 80)

Jn. 5:24, *He that . . . believeth . . . hath everlasting life.*

1.　If blest with faith that works by love,
　　　Blest with eternal life Thou art,
　　Thou hast the life of those above,
　　　The seed of glory in thy heart:

21. [In *Short Hymns*, II, pp. 244–5 and *Poet. Works*, XI, p. 365, there is a one verse poem on John 5:6, but only lines one and two appear here. In the margin in shorthand is an alternative to the last two lines:
　　　But me, O Lord, at last forgive,
　　　But save ev'n me at last.
Wesley mistakenly cited the biblical verse as 5:6 in MS John.]

For God in Christ is Love to man,
And when to the believer given,
The soul doth in itself contain
The pure essential bliss of heaven.

2. Wou'dst thou increase of faith receive?
The Saviour's word persist to hear,
Injoy thy priviledge, & live
From every charge of conscience clear;
Believing Him who sent his Son,
And pass'd from death to life divine,
Thou knowst the quickning Three in One,
Father, & Son, & Spirit thine. (pp. 83–4)[22]

Jn. 5:25, *The hour is coming, and now is, when the, &c.*

1. When Jesus first pronounc'd the word,
They found the Resurrection come,
Dead bodies heard their quickening Lord,
And Lazarus forsook the tomb;
Dead souls He every day doth raise:
They hear His voice, and faith receive,
And live the sinless life of grace,
And soon the life of heaven shall live.

2. Jesus, the only God and true,
The Father's co-eternal Son,
Life mortal, & immortal too
Thy gift unspeakable we own:
The Word of life, the Life reveal'd
And manifest to man Thou art;
And conscious of my pardon seal'd,
I find Thee in my faithful heart. (pp. 84–5)[23]

22. [Verse 1 appears in *Short Hymns*, II, p. 245 and *Poet. Works*, XI, p. 371, with lines one and eight varied.]
23. [Verse 1 appears in *Poet. Works*, XI, pp. 371-2.]

Jn. 5:26–7, *For as the Father hath life in himself, &c.*

Pure, independent life divine
    Thy Sire doth in himself possess:
Pure, independent life is thine,
    Who judgest all in righteousness:
Thou dost or life or death ordain,
    Such is thy Father's high decree,
And (for Thou art the Son of man)
    Mankind receive their doom from Thee. (p. 85)

Jn. 5:28–9, *Marvel not at this: for the hour is coming, &c.*

1. I cannot doubt the power Divine
    Dead souls, or bodies dead to save;
  Death oft hath heard that voice of Thine,
    Heard from the bed, the bier, the grave:
  That voice our mouldering dust again
    Shall from earth's lowest centre hear,
  And ocean pay its debt of man,
    And all before thy throne appear.

2. Whose works, & lives, & hearts were good
    They shall with joy & triumph rise,
  Obtain the crown by grace bestow'd,
    The life with Christ above the skies:
  But who on earth have evil done
    The day shall all their deeds reveal,
  Their righteous doom they cannot shun,
    But rise, to be thrust down to hell. (p. 85)[24]

---

24. [Verse 1 appears in *Poet. Works*, XI, p. 372.]

Jn. 5:30, *My judgment is just; because I seek not mine own will, but the will of my Father.*

O may I never seek my own,
    But thy most acceptable will,
So shalt thou make thy counsel known,
    Thy mind concerning me reveal,
My heart to all thy ways incline,
And make thy righteous judgment mine. (p. 86)

Jn. 6:5, *He saith unto Philip, Whence shall we buy bread, that these may eat?*[25]

Faithless & ungrateful men,
    Why should ye distrust your God?
Can He not his own sustain,
    He who fills the world with food?
Souls, & bodies too to feed
    Still his love is always near:
And if miracles ye *need*,
    Miracles again appear. (p. 91)

Jn. 6:15, *When Jesus perceived that they would come and take him by force to make him a king, etc.*

How few by his example led,
    Jesus' obscurity desire,
Its proffer'd pomp & grandeur dread,
    And gladly from the world retire!
Join'd to the poor inglorious few
    Fain would I, Lord, the people shun,
Thee to the sacred mount pursue,
    And live conceal'd with Thee alone. (p. 95)

25. [Preceding the entries for chapter 6 in Wesley's shorthand is written: "J. 1" (January 1).]

Jn. 6:18–19, *The sea arose, by reason of a great wind that blew.*

1.   Horribly the waves and wind
      Of fierce temptation roar,
    When our Lord we cannot find
      In present peace & power;
    When we mourn his help delay'd,
    The darkness of his absence feel,
      Wrapt in sin's profoundest shade
      As in the gloom of hell.

2.   Oft, alas, the penal night
      Doth from his wrath proceed;
    Oft his grace withdraws the light
      And fills our hearts with dread;
    Storms without, & fears within
    He lets arise, our faith to prove,
    Leaves us in th'abyss of sin
      The objects of his love. (p. 96)

Jn. 6:24, *When the people saw that Jesus was not there, they came to Capernaum, seeking for Jesus.*

1.   Come, let us anew
    Our Saviour pursue,
    Though now out of sight
We shall find him again, if we seek him aright.
    Us who often hath fed
    With spiritual bread,
    Will his comforts restore
And his kingdom bring in to the diligent poor.

2.   Invisibly near,
    He will quickly appear,
    No more to depart,
In his Spirit he comes to abide in our heart;
    Then united in love
    His fulness we prove,
    In his presence remain,
And never lose sight of our Saviour again. (pp. 97–8)

Jn. 6:26, *Ye seek me, not because ye saw the miracles, but because ye did eat of the loaves, and were filled.*

> Nature thy gifts requires
> With fond voluptuous aim,
> To satisfy its own desires,
> Not to exalt thy name:
> Drawn by the sweets of grace,
> Saviour, we follow on;
> But few are found who seek thy face
> For thy own sake alone. (p. 98)

Jn. 6:67, *Will ye also go away?*

> Yes; unless Thou hold me fast,
> After all thy love to me,
> I shall faithless prove at last,
> Treacherously depart from Thee:
> That from Thee I may not go,
> Leave me not to my own will;
> My Companion here below,
> Guide me to thy heavenly hill. (p. 114)[26]

Jn. 7:31, *Many of the people believed on him.*[27]

> God hath chose the simple poor,
> As followers of his Son,
> Rich in faith, of glory sure,
> To win the heavenly crown:
> Him the vulgar still embrace
> By the great & learned denied,
> Scorn'd by all the foes of grace,
> And daily crucified. (p. 129)

26. [The first four lines and two others appear as a six-lined poem in *Short Hymns*, II, p. 250, and *Poet. Works*, XI, pp. 393–4.]

27. [Preceding the entries for chapter 7 in Wesley's shorthand is written: "J. 5" (January 5).]

Jn. 7:31, *They said, When Christ cometh, will he do more miracles than these which this man hath done?*

All the world's disputers vain
Refuse the truth to know,
Slight the argument so plain,
Of God reveal'd below:
Who his gracious wonders see,
The humble, unopposing croud
Hence conclude that this is He,
The Christ, th'eternal God! (p. 129)

Jn. 7:38, *He that believeth on me, as the scripture hath said, out of his belly shall flow rivers, etc.*

1. The sinner that hath, O Jesus, from Thee
That scriptural faith, Thy vessel shall be,
Peace, mercy & blessing To others impart
And joy never ceasing, Which springs from his heart.

2. Pour'd out from above, Thy Spirit in him
In rivers of love To sinners shall stream:
With spiritual graces, Which ever o'reflow,
The world he refreshes, The desart below. (pp. 132–3)

Jn. 8:5, *Now Moses in the law commanded us, that such should be stoned: but what sayst thou?*[28]

1. In vain would Christ's insidious foes
The servant to the Lord oppose:
   The law to satisfy,
Not to destroy, from heaven He came,
That I, believing on his Name,
   Might live, & never die.

28. [No date is indicated preceding the entries for chapter 8.]

2. Moses may frown, if Jesus smiles;
      Justice & grace He reconciles;
        His yearning bowels move
      To sinners who their sins confess,
      He cloathes them with his righteousness,
        He saves them by his love. (p. 141)

Jn. 8:32, *And ye shall know the truth, & the truth shall make you free.*

      Then shall I in the Word abide,
        Establish'd & confirm'd in grace,
      Thy promise to the utmost tried
        With firm fidelity embrace,
      And know the Truth, as I am known,
      With God most intimately one. (p. 155)

Jn. 8:55, *Yet ye have not known him; but I know him, & if I should say, I know him not, etc.*

      Every real worshipper
        Who serves the God he loves,
      Thus attests his grace sincere,
        And by his actions proves:
      Faith by works itself will show:
      But liars are they all who say
        God they for their Father know,
          The God they disobey. (p. 165)

Jn. 8:59, *Then took they up stones to cast at him.*

1. Jesus, the Man Divine Thou art!
      Before created things begun,
    Thou dost thy Deity assert
      Jehovah's Fellow & his Son,
    Th'incomprehensible I AM,
    With God eternally the same.

2. Equal to the great God supreme,
   Thyself Thou dost with justice make:
   They sacrilegiously blaspheme,
   Thro' stubborn hellish pride mistake,
   Who thy Divinity disown,
   And wish to drag thee from thy throne. (p. 167)

Jn. 10:1, *Verily, verily, I say unto you, He that entreth not by the door into the sheepfold, etc.*[29]

1. Ye reverend thieves & robbers hear,
   Who steal into the church's fold,
   Usurp the sacred character
   Thro' love of ease, or lust of gold,
   Or hire yourselves, the flock to feed,
   And basely minister for bread!

2. Not by the Door ye enter in,
   Who seek your family to raise,
   Or introduc'd by *Simon's*[30] sin
   Hard labour — for the highest place:
   Ambition climbs that other way,
   And all the slaves who serve for pay. (p. 189)

Jn. 10:10, *The thief cometh not, but to steal and to kill, and to destroy.*

1. Lo, the ruthless felon comes,
   Hallow'd by unhallow'd hands,
   Honour to himself assumes,
   Bold the church's goods demands,
   From the poor their right he takes,
   Havock of the needy makes!

29. [Preceding the entries for chapter 9 in Wesley's shorthand is written: "J. 18" (January 18), and before chapter 10: "J. 22" (January 22).]
30. [Wesley refers to the sin of simony, the buying and selling of spiritual or ecclesiastical benefits, *cf.* Acts 8:18ff.]

2. The old thief and murderer
      Comes unseen to seize his prey,
   In his trusty agent here
      Comes, immortal souls to slay,
   By their wicked pastor's zeal
   Drags the wandering sheep to hell. (p. 195)

Jn. 10:11, *I am the good Shepherd: the good Shepherd giveth his life for the sheep.*

The Shepherd good indeed Thou art,
I feel Thy goodness at my heart;
No goodness out of Christ I see;
Goodness himself has died for me!
For me, and all the stragling kind
Thou didst the costly ransom find;
Thy life was the stupendous price,
And bought my peace, my paradise. (p. 196)[31]

Jn. 10:12, *But he that is an hireling, and not the shepherd, etc.*

1. The workman's worthy of his food;
   But if with eagerness pursued
      He *loves* his wages here,
   Labouring for filthy lucre's sake,
   He justly to himself must take
      The hireling's character.

2. The man whom covetous desire
   Impels to minister for hire
      We mercenary call:
   But O, what title shall we give
   A wretch who dares the hire receive,
      And never works at all?

31. [The first four lines appear in *Short Hymns*, II, p. 253, and *Poet. Works*, XI, p. 459.]

3. If want, or pestilence be near,
   If danger & the wolf appear,
     Or persecution rise,
   Aghast the lowring storm he sees,
   And proving that they are not his,
     Deserts the sheep, & flies. (p. 196)[32]

Jn. 10:13, *The hireling fleeth, because he is an hireling, and careth not for the sheep.*

The hire more than the sheep he loves,
And basely from his post removes,
  While their own shepherd stays,
He hides himself, requir'd t'appear
Their advocate, & dumb thro' fear
  The little flock betrays. (p. 197)

Jn. 10:29–30, *My Father who gave them me, is greater than all: & none is able to pluck them out of my Father's hand, etc.*

1. God over all in power supream,
     Thy Father doth thy sheep defend,
   They never can be forc'd from Him,
     Who loves thy members to the end,
   Who keeps the souls on Thee bestow'd
   Th'irrevocable gift of God.

2. Saviour, I in thy word confide,
     Nothing throughout eternity
   The Head and body shall divide,
     Or tear my faithful soul from Thee,
   Whom, by thy Spirit taught, I own
   Forever with thy Father One.

3. One God in essence and in power
     Mine utmost Saviour I proclaim,
   The Father and the Son adore
     From all eternity the same,
   That I may one in spirit be
   With God to all eternity. (pp. 203–4)

32. [Verse 2 appears in *Poet. Works*, XI, p. 459.]

Jn. 10:37, *If I do not the works of my Father, believe me not.*

> Christ himself, unless he wrought
> His Father's works alone,
> Willing was not to be thought
> The great Jehovah's Son:
> And would we be own'd untried?
> Believ'd, before the proofs are shew'd?
> No; let works the doubt decide,
> And speak us born of God. (pp. 205–6)

Jn. 10:39–40, *Therefore they sought again to take him; but he escaped out of their hands, etc.*

> When the wicked seek to slay
> Who Jesus testify,
> Following Him, we 'scape away,
> And from their violence fly,
> Faithfully the truth commend,
> And people to his guardian care,
> Calmly on our Lord attend
> In solitude & prayer. (pp. 206–7)

Jn. 11:5, *Now Jesus loved Martha, and her sister, and Lazarus.*[33]

> The suffering I this moment prove
> Is a fresh token of his love:
> I hear the rod, by Jesus sent,
> Which cries, "Be zealous, & repent!"
> Because Thou lov'st, Thou dost chastise;
> And quicken'd by the scourge I rise,
> And yield, when all th'affliction's past,
> That fruit which shall forever last. (p. 210)

---

33. [Preceding the entries for chapter 11 in Wesley's shorthand is written: "J. 27" (January 27).]

Jn. 11:6, *When He had heard therefore that he was sick, &c.*

1. He waits; to manifest His grace,
    To help His dying friend, delays,
    The sickness lingers to remove,
    But not through want of power or love.
    Thus our Physician from the sky
    Lets a beloved patient die,
    And then exerts His power to save
    And lifts the sinner from the grave.

2. Jesus, if such thy love's design
    Toward this weak, sinsick soul of mine,
    If still thou dost thine aid forbear
    To sink me down in just despair:
    I'll suffer all the mortal pain,
    And dead to God, in death remain,
    Till my almighty Saviour come,
    And call my soul out of its tomb. (p. 210)[34]

Jn. 11:32, *When Mary saw him, she fell down at his feet, saying unto him, Lord, if thou hadst, etc.*

Jesus' feet her refuge are:
    There accustom'd to complain,
Mary breathes her mournful prayer,
    Washes them with tears again;
Cries, in humble faith sincere,
    "Death could not with life abide;
"Life itself, hadst Thou been here,
    "Lord, my brother had not died." (p. 218)

Jn. 11:33, *When Jesus therefore saw them weeping, he groaned in the spirit.*

1. Jesus in the spirit groans
        Human wretchedness to see,
    Sin's severe effects bemoans,
        Sorrow and mortality;

---

34. [Verse 1 appears in *Poet. Works*, XI, pp. 468–9.]

Takes upon himself our pains,
Groans, & weeps, & prays, & cries,
All our wickedness sustains,
All our sufferings sanctifies.

2. When his troubled members feel
All the bitterness of sin,
Still with groans unspeakable
Groans the Comforter within!
By a load of woes opprest,
Woes too great for life to bear,
Still the sinner smites his breast,
Smites his breast — and God is there! (pp. 218–19)

Jn. 11:34, *He said, Where have ye laid him? they say unto him,*
Lord, come and see.

Where have ye the sinner laid?
In his Maker's hands no more,
Till the Quickner of the dead
Doth to second life restore:
In corruption's pit he lies:
Jesus, come, with pity see,
Speak, & bid the soul arise,
Call him forth to live for Thee. (pp. 219–20)

Jn. 11:35, *Jesus wept.*

1. Jesus weeps for sinners blind,
Mourns the death of all mankind;
Blesses us with sacred showers,
Sheds His tears to hallow ours:
Weeps, to make our case his own,
For our guilty joys t'atone,
Wipes at last the mourner's eyes,
Sorrow's source for ever dries!

2. Till that happy day I see,
Lord, I would lament with Thee,
Griev'd along the valley go,
Griev'd, but not for things below:

This my only burthen prove,
I have lost the life of love,
Never can myself forgive,
Till with Thee in heaven I live. (p. 220)[35]

Jn. 11:43, *Lazarus, come forth!*

1. Jesus, quickning Spirit, come,
   Call my soul out of its tomb;
   Dead in sins & trespasses,
   Thou art able to release,
   Canst the life of grace restore,
   Raise me up to sin no more.

2. That almighty word of thine
   Fills the dead with life divine:
   Speak again, & bid me go,
   Perfect liberty bestow;
   O repeat my sins forgiven,
   Loose, & lift me up to heaven. (pp. 225–6)[36]

Jn. 11:47, *Then gathered the chief priests & the Pharisees a council, & said, What do we? etc.*

What should ye do, who see
The wonders of his grace?
Believe in his Divinity
   And Christ your Lord embrace;
The signs & tokens know,
   While God his arm reveals,
And proves his work reviv'd below
   By twice ten thousand seals. (p. 227)

35. [Verse 1 appears in *Poet. Works*, XI, pp. 475–6 as verse 2 of a two-verse hymn.]
36. [This is an amplification of a poem of eight lines in *Short Hymns*, II, p. 254 and *Poet. Works*, XI, p. 480.]

Jn. 11:54, *Jesus therefore walked no more openly among the Jews, but went thence into a country, etc.*

[I]

By the ordinance divine,
    And not thro' servile fear,
Persecution we decline
    Till call'd of God t'appear:
Issuing then from our retreat
We openly maintain thy cause,
    Dauntless, Lord, thy murtherers meet,
    And suffer on thy cross.

II

Happy place that could afford
    A safe retreat to Thee,
Screen my persecuted Lord
    From hellish cruelty!
Hunted still by zealots blind,
Abhor'd by fiends & man Thou art:
    Shelter here vouchsafe to find
    Within my happy heart. (pp. 230–1)

Jn. 12:2–3, *Then they made him a supper, & Martha served, &c.*[37]

1. The church which keeps its Lord's commands,
    The house of true obedience,[38] stands,
        And Jesus entertains:
    'Tis there He kindly condescends
    To sup with his believing friends,
        And in their hearts remains.

37. [Preceding the entries for chapter 12 in Wesley's shorthand is written: "Fb. 1" (February 1).]

38. Bethany, i.e., The house of obedience; but modern scholars interpret "house of dates, or figs."

2. Martha renews her pious care,
    Attends him in his members there
        And furnishes the treat;
    Sinners to gracious life restor'd
    Enjoy the presence of their Lord,
        And at his table sit.

3. Mary, devoted Mary, lies
    Low at his feet with flowing eyes,
        And loose, dishevel'd hair;
    On him whom more than life she loves
    Pours out the faith which God approves,
        And all her soul in prayer. (pp. 232–3)

Jn. 12:3, *She wiped his feet with her hair: & the house was filled with the odour of the ointment.*

1. His Love the pardon'd sinner shows,
    And freely on the poor bestows
        What freely he receives;
    He clasps them with a kind embrace,
    Wipes off the sorrow from their face,
        And all their wants relieves.

2. Riches, as fast as they increase,
    Not as an ornamental dress,
        But a superfluous load
    He uses for the noblest ends,
    On Jesus in his saints expends,
        And serves the church of God.

3. The ointment's on the members spill'd,
    The house is with its odour fill'd,
        And prayers & praises rise,
    Grateful to his dear Lord above;
    And God in Christ with smiles of love
        Accepts the sacrifice. (p. 233)

Jn. 12:7, *Against the day of My burying hath she kept this.*

> The things we most affect and prize
> We offer Christ in sacrifice,
> His costliest gifts to Him restore,
> And wish our utmost all were more;
> Our Lord as for his tomb prepare,
> Languish to rest with Jesus there,
> And weeping, till his face appears,
> We still embalm him with our tears. (p. 234)[39]

Jn. 12:9, *They came not for Jesus' sake only, &c.*

> 1.   Ye who curiously desire
>   The works of Christ to see,
>   Come; but farther grace require,
>   And His disciples be:
> Him who rais'd *us* from the dead,
> Expect your sinful souls to raise;
>   Feel the Spirit of our Head,
>   And live to Jesus' praise.

> 2.   Burst the barriers of the tomb
>   Thro' his almighty word:
> All mankind to Him may come,
>   And glorify the Lord:
> Ye who sleep in death awake,
> While Christ his quickning power exerts,
>   Seek him for his own dear sake,
>   And find him in your hearts. (pp. 235–6)[40]

Jn. 12:10–11, *The chief priests consulted, that they might put Lazarus also to death; etc.*

> 1.   Impious priests in every age
>   Thy servants' death contrive,
> Persecute with cruel rage
>   Whom Thou hast made alive,

---

39. [The first four lines appear in *Poet. Works*, XI, pp. 484–5.]
40. [Verse 1 appears in *Poet. Works*, XI, p. 485.]

Hate thy faithful witnesses;
While crouds our resurrection see,
Wonder at our life of grace,
And turn themselves to Thee.

2.   O that more might see us live,
As risen from the grave,
Gladly our report receive,
And prove thy power to save!
Let them, Lord, the world desert,
Thyself that quickning Spirit own,
Give thee all their loving heart,
And live for Thee alone! (p. 236)

Jn. 12:17–18, *The people that was with him when he called Lazarus out of his grave, & raised him, etc.*

1.   We, Jesus, have heard Thy wonderful fame,
The power of thy word To sinners proclaim,
With hearty thanksgiving Acknowledge thy grace,
The living, the living Should publish thy praise.

2.   Our spirits were dead And buried in sin;
But waken'd & freed From death we have been;
The true Resurrection We found in our graves:
And Jesus' affection Whole multitudes saves.

3.   Come then at his call Our Jesus to meet!
His wonders on all He waits to repeat:
The proofs of his favour Ye all shall receive,
And friends of your Saviour And witnesses live.
(pp. 239–40)

Jn. 12:19, *The Pharisees therefore said among themselves, Perceive ye how ye prevail nothing? etc.*

1.   Who with hate implacable
The Lord of life oppose,
Pharisees against their will,
Their own foul hearts disclose:

Men who would the world engage
Their own blind followers to be,
Lo, the world, with envious rage,
Gone after Christ they see!

2.   Who with envy now behold
His messengers' success,
(Like your predecessors old)
Your baffled pride confess;
Ye that love the praise of men
Must surely forfeit their esteem,
If the love of Jesus reign,
And all go after Him. (p. 240)

Jn. 12:24, *Except a corn of wheat fall into the ground,*[41] *& die, it abideth alone, etc.*

1.   The members must their Head pursue,
One with Him they suffer too,
Or barren still abide:
Dies every consecrated grain,
Dies every re-begotten man
With Jesus crucified.

2.   As banish'd long from human thought,
Lord, thy follower is forgot,
Is buried out of sight,
Till Thou his dear Redeemer come,
And call his soul out of thy tomb,
And bring him forth to light.

3.   Who now participates thy death,
Shall thy living Spirit breathe,
Bring forth the fruits of grace,
Thy gifts abundantly improve,
Attaining in the fear of love
The perfect holiness. (p. 243)

---

41. [Wesley has added in square brackets after "ground:" "Gr. Earth." Gr. = Greek.]

Jn. 12:25, *He that loveth his life shall lose it.*

Th'inordinate, excessive love
    Of life, & the vain things below,
Damps the belief of joys above,
    Of joys which few desire to know;
Regardless of that bliss unseen
    Their portion here the worldlings chuse,
And for a moment's pleasure mean
    Consent th'eternal life to lose. (p. 243)

Jn. 12:25, *He that hateth his life in this world shall keep it unto life eternal.*

Saviour, to Thee our hearts we give,
    While here our short abode we make,
Submit the present life to live
    Not for its own, but thy dear sake;
Ready we would each moment be
    At thy command to lay it down,
And bear on earth thy cross with Thee,
    With Thee to share thy heavenly crown. (p. 244)

Jn. 12:26, *If any man serve me, let him follow me.*

Thy servant, Lord, I fain would be,
    Would fain thy faithful follower prove,
Abhor the things abhor'd by Thee,
    Love all the objects of thy love,
Myself renounce, my life despise,
To gain thy life which never dies. (p. 244)

Jn. 12:34, *And how sayest thou, The Son of Man must, &c.*

1. Seeming contrarieties
    Faith with readiness receives:
Lifted up from earth He is,
    Dies, and yet for ever lives!

Thus His suffering saints beneath
   Shame their way to glory see,
Find in the cold arms of death,
   Death is immortality.

2. Can we, Lord, the path decline
    Which Thou didst vouchsafe to tread,
  Followers of the Lamb Divine
    Members of our patient Head?
  No: our Master's joy to win,
    Bear we now the lingring pain,
  After Thee we enter in
    Endless life thro' death obtain. (pp. 248–9)[42]

Jn. 12:35, *He that walketh in darkness knoweth not whither he goeth*

Void of Christ, the real Light,
   God who neither fears nor loves,
Wanders on, a child of night
   In the paths of ruin roves;
On the brink of hell he stands,
   Down the threatning precipice
Tumbles into Satan's hands,
   Falls into the dark abyss. (p. 249)

Jn. 12:36, *While ye have the light, believe in the light, that ye may be the children of light.*

While with us His Spirit stays,
   Jesus would salvation give,
Doth not mock our helpless race,
   While he bids us all believe:
All the saving light may see,
   Cast away the works of night,
Rise from sin's obscurity,
   Rise the children of the light. (p. 250)

---

42. [Verse 1 appears in *Poet. Works*, XI, p. 494.]

Jn. 12:41, *These things said Isaiah, when he saw his glory.*

> Jesus, the everlasting Son,
> Thou reign'st above the sky,
> Jehovah sitting on thy throne
> The Lord & God most high!
> Thee very God, & very Man
> We see to sinners given:
> And soon the glories of thy train
> Shall fill both earth & heaven. (p. 252)

Jn. 13:2, *The devil having now put it into the heart of Judas to betray him.*[43]

1. Judas did first himself betray,
> Or with his utmost power & art
> Satan had never forc'd his way
> Into the perjur'd traitor's heart:
> The miser sold himself to sin,
> And avarice let the murtherer in.

2. Money! the direful love of thee,
> The root of every evil still,
> Springs up in deeds of perfidy;
> For thee we fawn, betray, & kill,
> And churchmen sell, like him of old,
> Their Master & their souls for gold. (pp. 257–8)

Jn. 13:14, *If I then, your Lord & Master, have washed your feet, ye also ought to wash one another's feet.*

1. No; the letter profits nought
> And few could that fulfil;
> But we all by Jesus taught
> May know and do His will;

---

43. [Preceding the entries for chapter 13 in Wesley's shorthand is written: "Fb. 8" (February 8).]

All to all may helpful prove,
To meanest offices submit:
Thus we humbly serve in love,
And wash each other's feet.

2.   Chiefly we thy word should keep,
Thy labouring messengers,
O're polluted sinners weep
And wash them with our tears:
But our tears must flow in vain
Unless we pray them back to God:
Jesus, stoop to worms again,
And wash them in thy blood. (p. 263)[44]

Jn. 13:16, *The servant is not greater than his Lord, neither he that is sent, greater than he that sent him.*

Ye who minister the word
You did from Christ receive,
More respected than your Lord
Can you desire to live?
Sent by him, with humble grace
The portion of your Master meet,
Find with joy your highest place
At every sinner's feet. (p. 264)

Jn. 13:17, *If ye know these things, happy are ye if ye do them.*

What avails it, Lord, to know,
And not to do thy will?
This my chief delight below
Thy pleasure to fulfil;
Till I join the church above,
This only happiness be mine,
Thee with all my heart to love,
And have no will but thine. (p. 264)[45]

44. [Verse 1 appears in *Poet. Works*, XI, p. 504. Wesley mistakenly cited the verse as Jn. 13:13 in MS John.]

45. [A similar poem appears in *Short Hymns*, II, p. 256 and *Poet. Works*, XI, p. 505. The verse in MS John appears to be a rewriting.]

Jn. 13:18, *I speak not of you all; I know whom I have chosen; but that the scripture may be fulfilled, etc.*

1. With such tranquillity of mind,
   So mild, dispassionate, & meek,
   So calm, & perfectly resign'd
   I would of my betrayers speak:
   And what Thou in thyself hast done,
   Thou wilt repeat in all thy own.

2. Thou David after God's own heart,
   Strengthen me with thy Spirit's aid,
   Thy lowliness of love impart,
   And lo, by bosom-friends betray'd,
   I come, thy portion here to find
   Rejected, spurn'd by all mankind. (p. 265)

Jn. 13:27, *And after the sop Satan entred into him.*

1. The wretch profane who without dread
   That sacred, sacramental bread
   Unworthily receives,
   Constrains the Saviour to depart,
   And full possession of his heart
   To the destroyer gives.

2. The slaves of lust & avarice
   Satan demands as lawful prize,
   The god whom they adore,
   Invited by the world & sin,
   After the sop he enters in,
   And *never leaves them more.*[46] (p. 269)

---

46. [Wesley wrote an alternative in the margin: "quits his house no more."]

Jn. 13:27, *Then said Jesus unto him, That thou doest, &c.*

1. How hopeless is a sinner's case,
    No more restrain'd by Jesus' grace
      Left to the fiend alone,
    The reprobate by God abhor'd
    The slave with his indwelling lord
      Is now forever one!

2. Conscience, & fear, & shame are o're,
    Obstructed in his sins no more,
      The soul insensible
    His tyrant's last commands fulfils,
    In haste his own damnation seals,
      And rushes into hell.

3. Least this my dreadful end should be,
    My Saviour, go not far from me;
      Who hast my rescue been,
    Still with Thy tempted servant stay,
    And hedge about with thorns my way,
      And hold me back from sin.

4. I know, if Thou thy hand withdraw,
    Without restraint, remorse, or awe,
      I into sin shall run,
    Caught in the hellish fowler's snare,
    Abandon'd to extreme despair
      Eternally undone. (pp. 269–70)[47]

Jn. 13:30, *He then having received the sop went, &c.*

1. Who hears His warnings with disdain,
    And Jesus' gifts receives in vain,
      Must fall from sin to sin:
    No time in Satan's service lose,
    No hellish drudgery refuse,
      Till Tophet takes him in.

---

47. [Verses 1 and 3 appear in *Poet. Works*, XI, p. 508.]

2. Satan admits of no delay,
   But governs with despotic sway
      Whoe'er his yoke receives,
   His slave he drives, & urges on,
   But never ventures him alone,
      Or time for thinking gives.

3. But O! how desperate he & blind
   Who Jesus leaves so good & kind,
      For an infernal lord!
   The frantic, base, ungrateful fool
   Plung'd headlong in the burning pool
      Must share the fiend's reward. (p. 271)[48]

Jn. 13:32, *If God be glorified in him, God shall also glorify him with himself, & shall, etc.*[49]

   Who gave his life mankind to save,
      And the great God to glorify,
   In forty hours he left the grave,
      In forty days regain'd the sky;
   When Jesus from the dead He rais'd,
      The Father glorified the Son,
   Jehovah by Jehovah plac'd,
      Th'eternal Partner of his throne! (p. 273)

Jn. 13:33, *Little children, yet a little while I am with you: Ye shall seek me: & as I said unto the Jews, etc.*

1. O the strength of Jesus' zeal!
      What is ours, compar'd to thine?
   What can fondest mothers feel
      Like that tenderness Divine?
   Yet, unless our Lord depart,
      Wean'd, alas, we cannot be:
   When the loss hath broke my heart,
      Draw my broken heart to Thee.

48. [Verse 1 appears in *Poet. Works*, XI, p. 509.]
49. [The AV reads: "in himself." Wesley has presumably followed his brother John's reading in *Notes* and later in his translation of the New Testament.]

2. Jesus, vanish'd from my sight,
    Of thine absence I complain,
Seek that sensible delight
    That extatic joy in vain:
Where Thou art, I cannot come;
    Yet I after Thee shall rise,
Soon emerging from the tomb,
    Meet my Saviour in the skies. (p. 274)

Jn. 13:36, *Whither I go, thou canst not follow me now, but thou shalt follow me afterwards.*

The times & seasons when to give
    His grace, are in my Saviour's power;
And what I cannot now receive,
    I shall, in his appointed hour:
His great salvation is for me,
    The moment when I need not know;
Suffice that I my Lord shall see,
    And walk as Jesus walk'd below. (p. 276)

Jn. 13:37, *Lord, why cannot I follow thee now? I will lay down my life for thy sake.*

1. He cannot now his Pattern trace,
    Because he fondly thinks he can,
Nor knows the desperate wickedness,
    The evil heart that is in man:
He should to Jesus' word submit,
    But doth on his own strength rely;
He cannot his own judgment quit,
    Yet promises for Christ to die.

2. A fancied strength presumption gives,
    And stops our praying for the true:
But who his own weak heart believes,
    His foolish confidence shall rue:
Full of himself, the swelling worm
    Is of a martyr's zeal possest,
Can mighty things for God perform,
    Yet fails, & stumbles in the least. (pp. 276–7)

Jn. 14:15, *If ye love me, keep my commandments.*[50]

1.   But if I love Thee not,
How can I, Lord, obey?
Who hast my soul so dearly bought,
Thy pretious blood display:
O let thy wounds impart
To me the loving power,
And I shall serve with all my heart,
And never grieve thee more.

2.   Inspire me with the grace,
And lo, my grateful love,
By walking in thy righteous ways,
I gladly come to prove,
Thy counsel to fulfil,
To live for God alone,
And do on earth thy blisful will,
Like those around thy throne. (p. 288)

Jn. 14:28, *Ye have heard how I said unto you, I go away, & come again unto you. If ye loved me, etc.*

This is our rejoicing here,
    That Thou to heaven art gone,
Dost at God's right hand appear,
    And seated on his throne:
Object of our faithful love
Thou wilt, who hast for sinners died,
    Leave again thy place above,
    And come to fetch thy bride. (p. 298)

Jn. 14:30, *The prince of this world cometh.*

Ye who madly love your sins,
    By the worldly spirit led,
Know that Satan is your prince,
    Know the devil is your head:

---

50. [Preceding the entries for chapter 14 in Wesley's shorthand is written: "Fb. 13" (February 13).]

Ye that your own will pursue,
    Only move as he inspires,
His designs ye blindly do,
    Gratify the fiend's desires. (p. 299)

Jn. 15:16, *Ye have not chosen Me, but I have chosen you.*[51]

Thee we never could have chose,
    Dead in sins and trespasses:
But Thou hast redeem'd thy foes,
    Bought the universal peace,
That our whole apostate kind,
    Might receive Thee from above,
Call'd our common Lord to find,
    Sav'd by free, electing love. (p. 313)[52]

Jn. 16:33, *These things I have spoken unto you, that, &c.*[53]

1. Yes, the promis'd tribulation,
    Saviour, in the world we find,
Find the pledge of sure salvation
    In a patient, chearful mind;
Thou the gracious word hast spoken;
    Thy companions in distress,
Thankful we accept the token
    Of our everlasting peace.

2. Peace surpassing all expression,
    Heavenly bliss begun below,
Now, ev'n now in the possession
    Of our loving Lord we know;
Peace, the seal of sins forgiven,
    Peace which Thou *my* Saviour art,
Fills with antedated heaven
    Mine, & every faithful heart.

---

51. [Preceding the entries for chapter 15 in Wesley's shorthand is written: "Fb. 18" (February 18).]

52. [A six-lined form of this verse appears in *Short Hymns*, II, p. 261, *Poet. Works*, XII, pp. 27–8, and *Rep. Verse*, No. 177, p. 219. In that version, however, only the first four lines are identical with the above poem.]

53. [Preceding the entries for chapter 16 in Wesley's shorthand is written: "Fb. 22" (February 22).]

3. With an hostile world surrounded
   Us Thou dost at parting chear:
   We shall never be confounded,
   Conscious that Thou still art here;
   We on all our foes shall trample,
   Sharers of thy victory,
   Followers of thy great example,
   Conquerors of the world thro' Thee. (p. 349)[54]

Jn. 18:15, *Simon Peter followed Jesus.*[55]

[I]

With nature for his guide
The self-presuming man,
Who follows in the strength of pride,
He follows Christ in vain:
He cannot persevere,
Or stand a threatning word,
But struck with misbelieving fear
Basely disowns his Lord.

II

"Let my disciples go,"
The warning Saviour said;
But Peter must his courage show,
And stay, while others fled;
Single in Jesus' cause
He dares a troop defy,
But dares not follow to the cross,
Or with his Master die.

---

54. [The first four lines of verse 1 and the last four lines of verse 3 appear in *Short Hymns*, II, pp. 263–4 and *Poet. Works*, XII, p. 46.]
55. [Preceding the entries for chapter 17 in Wesley's shorthand is written: "M. 1" (March 1), and before chapter 18: "M. 14" (March 14).]

III

Trusting his own weak heart
He could not God believe,
Who vow'd, though all beside depart,
He will to Jesus cleave:
"Thy persecuted Lord
Thou canst not now pursue":
He tries, but finds the slighted word
By sad experience true. (pp. 380–1)

Jn. 18:15, *That disciple went in with Jesus into the palace of the high priest.*

Occasions sure to meet
Of sin & sad disgrace,
To the proud mansions of the great
Our Lord we will not trace:
The houses of his foes
Unfit for Christians are;
And Jesus by compulsion goes,
Goes to be humbled there. (pp. 381–2)

Jn. 18:16, *Then went out that other disciple, and brought in Peter.*

Thou never wilt forget
His fatal courtesy
Who to the houses of the great
Admittance gains for thee:
Expos'd to shame & pain,
Thou must take up thy cross,
Or suffer, if the world thou gain,
Thy soul's eternal loss. (p. 382)

Jn. 18:17, *Then said the damsel, Art thou also one of this man's disciples? He saith, I am not.*

[I]

The man that on himself relies
  By blind presumption led,
Strong as a rock in his own eyes,
  Is weaker than a reed:
With fainting heart & feeble mind
  He fears his Lord to own:
And lo, by the first breath of wind
  The pillar is o'rethrown!

II

Urg'd by the hostile world, unless
  The truth I testify,
And one of his myself confess,
  My Master I deny:
I still renounce my Lord in deed,
  Unless I serve his will,
Obedient in his footsteps tread,
  And all his mind fulfil. (pp. 382–3)

Jn. 18:18, *And Peter stood with them, & warmed himself.*

1. The weak with prudent fear should shun
      Th'inquisitive & idle croud,
    Far from th'infectious converse run
      Of men who blush to mention God,
    Assemblies where the fiend presides,
    And all their tongues & counsels guides.

2. The fools' companion is not wise,
      Nor can his innocence maintain
    His virtue with the slaves of vice,
      Or touch the world without a stain;
    That pitch which makes the conscience foul,
    And ruins, & destroys the soul. (p. 383)

Jn. 18:20, *In secret have I said nothing.*

1. O might I, like Jesus, be
Foe to guile & secrecy,
Walk as always in his sight,
Free & open as the light,
Boldly to mankind appeal,
All the truth of God reveal!

2. Lord, that I to friend & foe
May thy utmost counsel show,
To thy messenger impart
The true nobleness of heart,
The unfeign'd simplicity
The pure mind, which was in Thee. (p. 384)[56]

Jn. 18:25, *Art thou one of his disciples? He denied, and said, I am not.*

See the strength that is in man!
Peter by a word o'rethrown
Checks our self-presumption vain,
Makes our utter weakness known:
Thus we feel our helplessness,
Tremble at temptation nigh,
Own our constant need of grace,
From ourselves to Jesus fly. (pp. 386–7)

Jn. 18:27, *Peter then denied again, & immediately the cock crew.*

1. Saviour, till thine eye recalls,
Till thou dost thy work begin,
Lower still the sinner falls,
Harden'd falls from sin to sin:

56. [The first four lines of verse 1 and the last four lines of verse 2 appear as a one-verse poem in *Short Hymns*, II, p. 264, and *Poet. Works*, XII, p. 71; however, line three of verse 2 is varied in that version.]

O that now the cock might crow!
Griev'd at my apostasy,
Jesus, thy compassion show,
Turn, & look me back to Thee.

2. Though I have thy Spirit griev'd,
Have so oft relaps'd again,
In thy mercy's arms receiv'd,
Favour I may still obtain:
Peter gives me back my hope;
After frequent falls restor'd,
I shall soon be lifted up,
Praise again my pardning Lord. (pp. 387–8)

Jn. 18:39, *But ye have a custom that I should release unto you one at the passover: will ye therefore, etc.*

1. Father, how great thy love to man,
Love inconceivable, unknown!
Thy bowels toward thy foes restrain
Their bowels toward thy fav'rite Son:
Had Jesus been from sufferings freed,
Releas'd we never could have been:
But dying in the sinner's stead,
He saves a world from death, & sin.

2. The criminal prefer'd to Thee,
Saviour, myself amaz'd I find!
At the true Passover set free
The criminal is all mankind:
Deliver'd by the Paschal Lamb
We all our pardon may receive:
And lo, a sinner sav'd I am,
And ransom'd by thy death I live! (p. 394)

Jn. 18:40, *Then cried they all again, saying, Not this, &c.*

1. Who blame the sin of Jews abhor'd,
   Of Jews, that once renounc'd their Lord,
      We blindly every day
   Our own corrupt desires fulfil,
   To save the life of nature's will,
      The life of Jesus slay.

2. Our carnal joys & pleasures here
   We to this Man of grief prefer,
      This self-denying Man:
   We will not suffer in his cause,
   But hate his poverty & cross,
      The scandal & the pain.

3. By wild impetuous passion led
   We still repeat the direful deed,
      With one consent we cry
   (While to the world our hearts we give)
   In us let the first Adam live,
      And let the Second die.

4. But let the season past suffice;
   Jesus, we now unite our cries
      And ask the death of sin;
   Nail this Barabbas to the tree,
   These lusts which steal our hearts from Thee;
      And spread thy life within.

5. The cruel murderers of our God,
   Which shed so oft thy precious blood
      No longer, Lord, reprieve,
   But slay them by the Spirit of grace,
   And with thy vital holiness
      In all thy members live. (pp. 394–5)[57]

57. [Verses 3–5 appear in *Poet. Works*, XII, p. 78.]

Jn. 19:1, *Then Pilate therefore took Jesus and scourged, &c.*[58]

1. The Man of griefs, by all despis'd,
    Loaded with pain and infamy,
    Like a rebellious slave chastiz'd,
    We mourn, but wonder not, to see:
    He stands in the first Adam's place
    Beneath our penalties and pains,
    Of all our disobedient race
    The sin and chastisement sustains.

2. His sacred flesh the scourges tear,
    While to the bloody pillar bound,
    The ploughers make long furrows there,
    Till all his body is one wound:
    The sins we in our flesh have done
    For these He doth the torture feel,
    He sheds his blood for these t'atone,
    And by his stripes our souls to heal. (p. 396)

Jn. 19:3, *And said, Hail, King of the Jews: and they smote him with their hands.*

1.   They crown with prickly thorn,
        With purple rags adorn,
    Mock him in his tatter'd robe,
        Smite with sacrilegious hands,
    Him whose power supports the globe,
        Him who earth & heaven commands.

2.   But Thee thy saints revere
        With loyalty sincere:
    Dignified by thy disgrace,
        Hail, derided Majesty!
    Every tongue shall soon confess,
        Every soul bow down to Thee.

---

58. [Preceding the entries for chapter 19 in Wesley's shorthand is written: "M. 26" (March 26). The first four lines of verse 2 are quoted from Charles Wesley's poem, "Ye that pass by, behold, the Man" in *Hymns and Sacred Poems*, 1742, pp. 22–4. Verse 1 appears in *Poet. Works*, XII, p. 79.]

3.   Omnipotently great
Ev'n in thy low estate,
Cloth'd again with all thy power
Israel's King, thy sway we own;
Prostrate Seraphim adore,
Cast their crowns before thy throne.

4.   Yet still thy saints attend
To see their King descend:
Hasten, Lord, the destin'd time,
Sovereign Potentate, appear,
On thy cloudy car sublime,
Come, & fix thy kingdom here. (pp. 397–8)

Jn 19:4, *Behold, I bring him forth to you, that ye may know that I find no fault in him.*

1. If the just God himself consent
    That thou shou'dst be entreated so,
Thou must deserve the punishment
    For crimes which Pilate doth not know,
The crimes which only God can find,
The crimes of me, & all mankind.

2. Thee, innocent in deed & thought,
    Th'unrighteous judge is forc'd to clear;
Yet burthen'd with another's fault
    Thou bear'st the sinner's character,
And suffer'st, guiltless, on the tree,
That God may find no fault in me. (p. 398)[59]

Jn. 19:6, *They cried out, saying, Crucify him, crucify him.*

1. Angry at th'ungrateful Jews
    Them we ignorantly blame,
Them who did their King refuse,
    Every day we do the same,
Still, Away with him, we cry,
Still require that He should die!

59. [*Rep. Verse*, No. 179, p. 220.]

2. Sin for vengeance calls aloud,
   'Gainst his innocence prevails,
   Clamouring for his guiltless blood,
   Jesus to the cross it nails;
   Sin which I alas, have done,
   Murthering God's eternal Son. (pp. 399–400)

Jn 19:9, *And saith unto Jesus, Whence art Thou? &c.*

[I]

1. When He could Himself defend,
   The Saviour holds His peace,
   Our apologies to end,
   And clamours to suppress:
   Hear we then the speechless Lamb
   Who doth our eagerness reprove,
   Silence and for ever shame
   Our self-excusing love.

2. Charg'd with crimes we never knew
   Answer we not a word,
   Quietly the steps pursue
   Of our most patient Lord;
   Wrongs without emotion bear,
   Rest in thy humility:
   Whence, & whose, & what we are,
   Is known, O God, to Thee. (p. 401)[60]

60. [Verse 1 appears in *Poet. Works*, XII, p. 81. Line six of verse 2 is an example of Wesley's very rare error in metre. In verse 1 line six has eight syllables, but in verse 2 it has seven. It is the result of a half-made correction in the MS. He had seen that the line was wrong, put a new eight syllable line in the margin ("Inrapt in thy humility"), was not satisfied, and crossed it out, but did not find another substitute.]

II

Yes, thou silent Man of woe,
Thy mind we comprehend,
Thankfully rejoice to know
Thy love's mysterious end:
Death unmerited to shun,
Thyself if Thou hadst justified,
All mankind condemn'd, undone,
The second death had died. (p. 401)

Jn. 19:10, *Speakest thou not unto me? knowest thou not, that I have power to crucify thee, etc.*

[I]

By Pilate urg'd in vain to speak,
Jesus with all his humbled powers
In silence & submission meek
His Judge invisible adores;
Disposing all the acts of men
The sovereign Arbiter he sees;
And lo, the sinner's cause to gain,
His silence doth our guilt confess!

II

A righteous judge can never boast
Or glory in his boundless power,
Can never do a deed unjust,
Or let the wolf the lamb devour:
He only from above receives
A power to make the laws take place,
The laws whose minister he lives,
The laws he first himself obeys. (p. 402)

Jn. 19:16, *Then delivered he him therefore unto them to be crucified. And they took Jesus, etc.*

1. Who take at first the Saviour's side,
    Thro' cowardly regard to men,
    Thro' interest, or ambitious pride,
    We soon abandon him again,
    Or lead him to his cross away,
    And Jesus in his members slay.

2. Thee that we may no more deny,
    Appear as bleeding on the tree;
    Ourselves we then shall crucify,
    In close Divine conformity
    Our steady faithfulness approve
    And pay thee back thy dying love. (p. 405)

Jn. 19:17, *And he bearing his cross, went forth.*

1. Victim of an angry God,
    Devoted to the skies,
    Isaac-like he bears the wood
    Of his own sacrifice;
    Bears with strength invincible
    The arms which still the world o'rethrow,
    Daily conquer sin & hell
    And our last deadly foe.

2. King of saints, he meekly bears
    The sceptre of his cross,
    Thus his royal power declares,
    And executes his laws;
    Thus his government maintains,
    The virtue of his death exerts,
    By his bleeding passion reigns
    In all his people's hearts. (pp. 405–6)

Jn. 19:26–7, *Behold thy son: behold thy mother.*

We would thine aged followers give
The honour to a parent due,
We would the young with love receive,
Purer than nature ever knew:
Saviour, bestow th'intend'ring[61] grace,
Us in a new relation join,
So shall we all thy saints embrace,
And love them with a love like thine. (p. 412)[62]

Jn. 19:28, *I thirst.*

1. Expiring in the Sinners' stead,
    "I thirst," the Friend of Sinners cries,
    And feebly lifts his languid Head
    And breathes his Wishes to the Skies.

2. Not for the Vinegar they gave,
    For Life, or Liberty, or Ease,
    He thirsted — all the world to save,
    He only thirsted after this.

3. He thirsted for this Soul of mine,
    That I might His Salvation see,
    That I might in his Image shine;
    Dear Wounded Lamb, he long'd for me.

4. Willing that All his Truth should know,
    And feel the Virtue of his Blood,
    He thirsted to redeem his Foe,
    And reconcile a World to GOD.

---

61. [The *Oxford English Dictionary* quotes this as a variation of the obsolete verb "entender," "to soften, melt the heart." The last example quoted is contemporaneous with Wesley's use here.]

62. [Wesley has made use of some similar phrases in a longer poem in *Poet. Works*, XII, p. 96. The poem in MS John appears in *Short Hymns*, II, pp. 232–3, though not in *Poet. Works*, with one variation: line seven, "all mankind" in place of "all thy saints."]

5. And shall not we the same require,
   And languish to be sav'd from Sin!
   Yes, Lord, 'tis all our Soul's Desire;
   O wash, & make us pure within.

6. We thirst to drink thy healing blood,
   To wash us in the cleansing Tide,
   We only long for Thee our God,
   Our Jesus, and Thee crucified.

7. Be satisfied; We long for Thee,
   We add our strong Desires to Thine,
   See then, thy Soul's hard Travail see,
   And die, to make us All Divine.[63]

Jn. 19:28, *I thirst.*

He thirsted, to redeem his foe,
   And reconcile a world to God,
He long'd that all his love might know,
   Sav'd by the virtue of his blood!
Be satisfied; we thirst for thee,
   We add our strong desires to thine:
See then, thy soul's hard travail see,
   And die, to make us all divine. (p. 412)[64]

Jn. 19:30, *It is finish'd.*

1. 'Tis finish'd! the Messias dies,
   Cut off for Sins, but not his own!
   Accomplish'd is the Sacrifice,
   The great redeeming Work is done.

2. 'Tis finish'd! all the Debt is paid,
   Justice Divine is satisfied,
   The grand and full Atonement's made,
   GOD for a guilty World hath died.

---

63. [MS Thirty, pp. 190–1, Verses 1–5, 7 appear in *Poet. Works*, XII, p. 94. This poem is not included in MS John.]

64. [This verse is a variant of two verses of the poem, "Expiring in the sinner's stead," *supra*, and appeared in *Short Hymns*, II, p. 233, but was omitted in *Poet. Works*.]

3. The Veil is rent, the Way is shewn,
   The Living Way to Heaven is seen,
   The middle-Wall is broken down,
   And All mankind may enter in.

4. The Types and Figures are fulfill'd,
   Exacted is the legal Pain,
   The precious Promises are seal'd,
   The spotless Lamb of GOD is slain.

5. Finish'd the First Transgression is,
   And purg'd the Guilt of actual Sin,
   And Everlasting Righteousness
   Is now to all the World brought in.

6. The Reign of Sin and Death is or'e
   And all may live from Sin set free,
   Satan hath lost his mortal Power,
   'Tis swallow'd up in Victory.

7. 'Tis finish'd! All my Guilt & Pain,
   I want no Sacrifice beside;
   For me, for me, the Lamb is slain;
   'Tis finish'd! I am Justified!

8. Sav'd from the Legal Curse I am,
   My Saviour hangs on yonder Tree;
   See there the dear Expiring Lamb,
   'Tis finish'd! He expires for me.

9. Accepted in the well–belov'd
   And cloath'd in Righteousness Divine,
   I see the Bar to Heaven remov'd,
   And All thy Merits, Lord, are mine.

10. Death, Hell, & Sin are now subdued,
     All Grace is now to Sinners giv'n,
     And lo! I plead th'Atoning Blood,
     And in thy Right, demand thy Heaven.[65]

Jn. 20:19, *Peace be unto you.*[66]

1. The peace Thou didst to man bequeath
    So dearly purchas'd by thy death
       Thou freely dost bestow;
    Fruit of thy blessed lips, we feel
    The peace thy gracious words reveal,
       And all the comfort know.

2. We thus our legacy receive,
    And blest by the Testator, live
       A life of faith & love,
    A life, the sure effect of thine,
    The life of purity Divine
       Which angels live above. (p. 436)

Jn. 21:4, *But when the morning was now come, Jesus stood on the shore.*[67]

1. Absent from those whom most He loves,
    Jesus our faith & patience proves:
       And left a tedious while
    Thro' the long night of doubts & fears
    We labour, (till our Lord appears)
       With unsuccessful toil.

65. [MS Thirty, pp. 193–5. Verses 1–4, 6, 8–10 appear in *Poet. Works*, XII, pp. 99–100. Verses 1, 5, 7, 10 appear with slight variations in *Short Hymns*, II, p. 234, and in MS John, pp. 412–13.]
66. [Preceding the entries for chapter 20 in Wesley's shorthand is written: "A. 10" (April 10).]
67. [Above Jn. 21:1 in Wesley's shorthand is written: "A. 18" (April 18).]

2. But labouring on with fruitless pain
Resolv'd we in the ship remain,
   Till the expected morn:
And sure as day succeeds to night,
We see the soul-reviving Light,
   And joy with Christ return. (p. 442)

Jn. 21:15–16, [*Feed my lambs; feed my sheep.*]

II

1.   Words cannot prove
        That Thee I love,
My soul's eternal Lover;
        Actions must the doubt remove.
And all my soul discover.

2.   Fill'd may I be
        With charity,
And carry in my bosom
        The dear lambs redeem'd by thee,
And rather die than lose 'em.

3.   By pangs extreme
        Thou didst redeem
The flock of thine election:
        Let me give this proof supreme
Of my unfeign'd affection.

4.   By thee renew'd,
        Thou Shepherd good,
I can thy cross endure,
        Strive resisting unto blood
With love divinely pure.

5.   Arm'd with thy mind
        I come resign'd,
A rival of thy passion,
        Lose my life with joy, to find
The God of my salvation.

6.   Now, dearest Lord,
      Let fire or sword
My soul & body sever,
      Give me but that parting word,
"I love my God forever!" (pp.455–6)[68]

Jn. 21:18, *When thou wast young, thou girdedst thyself, & walkedst whither thou wouldest: but when, etc.*

1. When young & full of sanguine hope
     And warm in my first love,
My spirit's loins I girded up,
     And sought the things above;
Swift on the wings of active zeal
     With Jesus' message flew,
O'rejoy'd with all my heart & will
     My Master's work to do.

2. Freely, where'er I would, I went
     Thro' Wisdom's pleasant ways,
Happy to spend, & to be spent
     In ministring his grace;
I found no want of will, or power,
     In love's sweet task employ'd,
And put forth, every day & hour,
     My utmost strength for God.

3. As strong, & glorying in my might
     I drew the two-edg'd sword,
Valiant against a troop to fight
     The battles of the Lord:
I scorn'd the multitude to dread,
     Rush'd on with full career,
And aim'd at each opposer's head,
     And smote off many an ear.

68. [This poem appears in *Rep. Verse*, No. 182, p. 221. The first poem, numbered "i" in the MS, appears in *Poet. Works*, XII, p. 126.]

4. But now enervated by age
   I feel my fierceness gone,
And nature's powers no more engage
   To prop the Saviour's throne:
My total impotence I see,
   For help on Jesus call,
And stretch my feeble hands to Thee
   Who workest all in all.

5. Thy captive, Lord, myself I yield
   As purely-passive clay;
Thy holy will be all fulfill'd
   Constraining mine t'obey:
My passions by thy Spirit bind,
   And govern'd by thy word,
I'll suffer all the woes design'd
   To make me like my Lord.

6. Wholly at thy dispose I am,
   No longer at my own,
All self-activity disclaim,
   And move in God alone;
Transport, do what Thou wilt with me,
   A few more evil days,
But bear me safe thro' all to see
   My dear Redeemer's face. (pp. 461–2)[69]

69. [At the foot of the page in Wesley's shorthand is written: "Finished April 30, 1764."]

THE BOOK OF ACTS

THE BOOK OF ACTS
(MS Acts)[1]

Ac. 1:4, *He commanded them that they should not depart from Jerusalem, but wait for the promise of the Father, etc.*

1. Who wait in view of gospel-peace,
    Sum of all the promises,
        Thy Spirit to receive,
    Howe'er impatient nature fret,
    A time to God we will not set,
        Or teach Thee when to give.

2. Thou bid'st us patiently attend,
    Till the Comforter descend,
        Thy Father's Gift, & thine;
    And all, who for thy coming stay,
    Shall gain in that appointed day
        Th'abiding Guest Divine. (p. 2)

Ac. 1:8, *But ye shall receive power, the Holy Ghost being come upon you, and ye shall be witnesses to me, etc.*[2]

Sinners, the Promise is for you,
Whoe'er believe that God is true,
    And will to man his Spirit give:
Your day of Pentecost is near,
And while the joyful news ye hear,
    Ye shall the Holy Ghost receive;

1. [At the top of page 1 Charles Wesley has written: "N. 13. 1764" (i.e., November 13, 1764); the same style of dating used in MS John.]
2. [Charles followed the text of his brother John's *Notes* repeated later in his translation of the New Testament (1790), rather than the text of the AV.]

Impower'd of Christ to testify,
The Saviour-Prince, the Lord Most-high,
  The great omnipotent I AM,
The glorious God of truth and grace,
The Friend of all our pardon'd race,
  Ye shall in life and death proclaim. (p. 5)

Ac. 1:17, *He was numbred with us, and had obtained part of this*
ministry.

Th'unworthiest of thy ministers,
  O God, is truly thine,
The sacred character he bears,
  Th'authority divine:
Nor doth the sacramental grace
  On man, but Thee depend,
Who promisest thy church to bless
  And guide till time shall end. (p. 10)

Ac. 1:19, *And it was known to all the dwellers at Jerusalem.*

Be it known to all our race!
  The avaricious crime
Jesus to his foes betrays
  In every place & time;
Cherishing the vile desire,
Satan his instrument employs,
  Pays the wretch his sordid hire,
    And then his soul destroys. (pp. 10–11)

Ac. 1:[19], *That field is called the field of blood.*

Wo to Judas' successors
  Who rob the church of God,
Grasping for themselves & heirs
  Possessions bought with blood!
Curst the wealth they tear away,
The blood and substance of the poor:
God shall shew in that great day
  Their swift damnation sure. (p. 11)

Ac. **2:17,** *I will pour out of my Spirit upon all flesh.*

1.   Sinners, lift up your hearts
         The Promise to receive!
       Jesus himself imparts,
         He comes in man to live:
       The holy Ghost to man is given;
       Rejoice in God sent down from heaven.

2.   Jesus is glorified,
         And gives the Comforter,
       His Spirit, to reside
         In all his members here:
       The holy Ghost to man is given;
       Rejoice in God sent down from heaven.

3.   To make an end of sin,
         And Satan's works destroy,
       He brings his kingdom in,
         Peace, righteousness, and joy:
       The holy Ghost to man is given;
       Rejoice in God sent down from heaven.

4.   The cleansing blood t'apply,
         The heavenly life display,
       And wholly sanctify,
         And seal us to that day,
       The holy Ghost to man is given:
       Rejoice in God sent down from heaven.

5.   Sent down to make us meet
         To see his open face,
       And grant us each a seat
         In that thrice happy place,
       The holy Ghost to man is given:
       Rejoice in God sent down from heaven.

6. From heaven He shall once more
    Triumphantly descend,
    And all his saints restore
    To joys that never end:
    Then, then when all our joys are given,
    Rejoice in God, rejoice in heaven! (pp. 21–2)

Ac. 2:19–20, *I will shew wonders in heaven, &c.*

1. When the great God His Spirit pours
    Judgment attends in flaming showers,
    To plague the disobedient race,
    And vindicate His slighted grace.

2. His wrath He with His love reveals,
    The vessels of destruction fills,
    The bold despisers of His word,
    And pleads His cause with fire and sword.

3. He soon His prodigies will show
    In heaven above, and earth below,
    The heavenly powers shall melt & shake,
    The earth to its foundation quake.

4. The sun and moon eclips'd shall be
    With permanent obscurity,
    And then the day of general doom,
    And then the glorious Judge is come! (p. 23)[3]

Ac. 2:33, *Therefore being by the right-hand of God exalted, &c.*

He is indeed ascended,
    The God of our salvation!
    The tokens we
    Both hear & see
Of Jesus' exaltation:

3. [Verses 1–2 appear in *Poet. Works*, XII, p. 147.]

Our Spokesman with the Father
By his own proper merit
Hath bought the grace
For all our race,
Hath claim'd the promis'd Spirit. (pp. 27–8)

Ac. 2:33–5, *The Lord said unto my Lord, Sit thou on my right hand, Until I make thy foes thy footstool, &c.*

1. Jehovah to Jehovah,
    The Lord of earth & heaven
    To Christ my Lord
    Hath spoke the word,
    Hath full dominion given:
    At my right-hand exalted,
    Sit down with me in glory,
    In calm repose,
    Till all thy foes
    I force to bow before Thee.

2. Thy foes shall be thy footstool,
    The beast & the false prophet
    With death at last
    And Hades cast
    Into that fiery Tophet:
    Thee all shall then acknowledge
    Almighty to deliver,
    Who once wast slain,
    But liv'st again
    Our Lord and King forever! (pp. 28–9)

Ac. 2:44–5, *And sold their possessions and goods, &c.*

1. How happy the men
    Who born from above
    Were first to maintain
    The freedom of love;
    Who left an example
    Ourselves to forego,
    And taught us to trample
    On all things below.

2. Believers of old
     Who Jesus confess'd,
   Lands, houses they sold
     With all they possess'd;
   The miserly pleasure
     They dared to despise,
   And laid up their treasure
     And hearts in the skies.

3. Affection unfeign'd
     The members inclin'd,
   And sweetly constrain'd
     Each other to mind;
   As sisters & brothers
     The faithful were one,
   The souls of all others
     Each lov'd as his own.

4. The deed we commend
     For ages is past;
   Yet God did intend
     The usage to last:
   And could we inherit
     That primitive Flame,
   The fruit of that Spirit
     Would now be the same. (p. 34)[4]

Ac. 3:12, *Why look ye so earnestly on us, as though by our own power or holiness we had made this man to walk?*

1. Why should the fond admiring throng
     On feeble creatures gaze,
   If God pronounce a sinner strong
     Thro' his almighty grace?
   Not all our holiness or power
     Can make the spirit rise,
   God only doth to health restore,
     And freely justifies.

4. [Verses 1 and 2 appear in *Poet. Works*, XII, p. 155.]

2. Jehovah sends by whom he will
   As sovereign Lord of all,
   His mercy's counsel to fulfil,
   And raise us from our fall:
   He oft employs the words of man,
   But bids us humbly own
   He doth the help on earth ordain,
   The work he works alone. (p. 44)

Ac. 3:13, *The God of our fathers hath glorified his Son Jesus,*
whom ye delivered, &c.

The Patriarchal God,
To our forefathers known,
Hath gracious signs & wonders show'd
In honour of his Son,
Hath fallen spirits rais'd,
Hath guilty souls forgiven,
That Jesus may be own'd, & prais'd
By all in earth & heaven:
Jesus deliver'd o're
To suffer in our stead,
By his eternal Spirit's power
Is risen from the dead;
The just & holy One
By sinful men denied,
Again He fills his Father's throne,
And triumphs at his side. (pp. 44–5)

Ac. 3:14–15, *Ye desired a murtherer to be granted unto you: And*
killed the Prince of life, etc.

Ye who your sin have spar'd
And cherish'd in your breast,
A thief & murtherer prefer'd
To God forever blest;
The Prince of life & peace
Ye wickedly have slain,
Renew'd his dying agonies,
And tortur'd him again:

But God hath him restor'd,
No more to mourn or die:
He lives, He lives, our glorious Lord,
He reigns above the sky!
His witnesses and friends
Throughout the world proclaim
The kingdom come that never ends,
The powers of Jesus' Name. (pp. 45–6)

Ac. 3:25–6, *Ye are the children of the prophets, &c.*

1. Heirs of the prophecies are we,
    Jesus, who depend on Thee,
        By Love Paternal given,
    Thou Covenant made with all our race,
    Who trust thy death for pardning grace,
        For purity, and heaven.

2. Who in the steps of Abraham tread,
    Thee we claim the promis'd Seed,
        On the whole earth bestow'd,
    Embrace the Saviour of mankind,
    And blest in Thee, exult to find
        Redemption thro' thy blood.

3. We taste that God is good, and see
    The divine felicity
        To all thy people known,
    Assur'd the Father of our Head
    Hath rais'd our Raiser from the dead,
        And glorified his Son.

4. Accomplishing his kind intent,
    God into our hearts hath sent
        The Spirit of thy love,
    Our blood-bought pardon to reveal,
    And mark us by his hallowing seal
        For thrones prepar'd above.

5. Peace, joy, & righteousness brought in,
    Perfect liberty from sin,
        Our happiness maintain,
    Till Thou receive Thy spotless bride,
    To sit illustrious at thy side,
        And in thy presence reign. (pp. 53–4)

Ac. 4:8, *Then Peter filled with the holy Ghost, said unto them.*

    Peter with himself compare!
    Lately he his Lord foreswore;
    Now at man's unrighteous bar
        Stands th'undaunted confessor,
    Bold in presence of his foes,
        Peter out of weakness strong,
    Fill'd with faith's assurance, shows
    Power doth all to God belong! (pp. 58–9)

Ac. 4:11, *This is the stone which was set at nought of you
builders, which is become, etc.*

1. Christ is the head, the corner stone,
    The Basis firm is Christ alone!
    But you who o're his church preside,
    Have always scorn'd the Crucified,
    Have Jesus for your King refus'd,
    And in his dearest saints abus'd.

2. His members, one in heart & mind,
    Most strictly each to other join'd,
    Who constitute his church below,
    And closest in his footsteps go,
    Ye hate, & spitefully reject,
    And brand them as a separate sect. (p. 60)

Ac. 4:16, *What shall we do to these men? for that, &c.*

1. Still at a loss, ye know not how
       With these wild vagabonds to deal:
   Shall priests Irregulars allow,
       Or stop by force the growing ill?
   But, should ye crush by open force,
   Ye fear to make the mischief worse.

2. Perplex'd, ye know not what to do:
       Ye neither can destroy, nor praise
   The men, who prove their mission true
       By wonders of converting grace,
   Who spread the news of sin forgiven,
   Confirm'd by daily signs from heaven.

3. The glaring fact to all appears,
       The grace on multitudes bestow'd:
   Jesus hath bless'd his messengers,
       Thousands are truly turn'd to God:
   The fact yourselves are forc'd to own,
   "The men undoubted good have done."

4. Yet harden'd still ye will not yield
       To truth which ye cannot deny;
   The instruments rais'd up & seal'd
       Your lack of service to supply,
   To countenance ye dare not seem,
   Ye dare not yet to death condemn. (pp. 76, 64–5)[5]

Ac. 4:17, *But that it spread no farther among the people, let us straitly threaten them, that, etc.*

1. Pure, inward, genuin piety
       External Christians dread,
   With consternation struck to see
       The loathsome gangreen spread!

5. [Verse 1 appears in *Poet. Works*, XII, p. 175.]

A few, they say, may multiply,
And the whole croud infect;
And every hellish means they try
To stop the growing sect.

2. But all your policy is blind,
   Your threatnings too are vain;
   The word of God ye cannot bind,
   The Spirit's course restrain:
   In Jesus' name we must speak on,
   And testify his grace,
   And make his pardning mercy known
   To all the ransom'd race. (p. 65)

Ac. 4:32, *The multitude of them that believed, were of one heart, and one soul: neither said any of them, that aught of the things which he possessed, was his own, but they had all things common. Neither was there any among them that lacked.*

1. Happy the multitude
   (But far above our sphere)
   Redeem'd by Jesus' blood
   From all we covet here!
   To Him, & to each other join'd,
   They all were of one heart and mind.

2. His blood the cement was
   Who died on Calvary,
   And fasten'd to his cross
   They could not disagree:
   One soul did all the members move,
   The soul of harmony & love.

3. Their goods were free for all,
   Appropriated to none,
   While none presum'd to call
   What he possess'd his own;
   The difference base of *thine* & *mine*
   Was lost in charity Divine.

4.   No overplus, or need,
      No rich or poor were there,
    Content with daily bread
      Where each injoy'd his share;
  With every common blessing bless'd
  They nothing had, yet all possess'd. (pp. 71–2)[6]

Ac. 4:33, *And with great power gave the Apostles witness of the resurrection of the Lord Jesus.*

1.   Where is that ancient power
      Which did the Lord reveal,
  And spake him more than conqueror
      Or'e death, & earth, & hell!
      While men by Jesus chose
      Were bold to testify
  He died to pay our debts, and rose
      To fit us for the sky:
      He rose himself, to raise
      His creatures from their fall,
  He sits at God's right hand, & prays,
      Demanding life for all:
      The Spirit of life he gives
      In sinners' hearts to dwell;
  And still who hears with faith, receives
      The Gift unspeakable.

2.   Our record is the same,
      Our testimony's sure,
  The gospel we today proclaim
      Shall evermore endure:
      Who minister the word
      Are Jesus' witnesses,
  And still we preach our risen Lord,
      The Prince of life & peace:

---

6. [Verses 1–2 appear in *Poet. Works*, XII, p. 180, together with verses 3 and 4 of the poem on Acts 4:3–5, *infra*.]

High on his Father's throne
Forgiveness to confer,
He sends the promis'd Blessing down,
Th'abiding Comforter!
His power, & peace, & love
Our cancel'd sin attest,
And heaven is open'd from above
In every faithful breast. (pp. 72–3)[7]

Ac. **4:33**, *Great grace was upon them all.*

Abundant grace indeed
On the first saints bestow'd!
From every selfish temper freed
Their hearts with love o'reflow'd:
Who suffer'd none to lack;
Their fruits of grace were shown,
Their mutual love for Jesus' sake
Declar'd they all were one.
By the same strength of grace
And cordial charity,
Produc'd in every age & place
The same effects must be:
And thus, ye sons of light,
Thus only can ye *prove*
The length, & breadth, & depth, & height
Of truly perfect love. (pp. 73–4)

Ac. **4:34–5**, *As many as were possessors of lands, or houses sold them, & brought the prices of, &c.*

1.   Which of the Christians now
Would his possessions sell?
The fact ye scarce allow,
The truth incredible,
That men of old so weak should prove,
And as themselves their neighbour love.

7. [*Rep. Verse*, No. 186, pp. 224–5.]

2.   Of your redundant store
       Ye may a few relieve,
    But all to feed the poor
       Ye cannot, cannot give,
Houses & lands for Christ forego,
Or live as Jesus liv'd below.

3.   Jesus, thy church inspire
       With Apostolic love,
    Infuse the one desire
       T'insure our wealth above,
Freely with earthly goods to part,
And joyfully sell all in heart.

4.   With thy pure Spirit fill'd,
       And loving Thee alone,
    We shall our substance yield,
       Call nothing here our own,
Whate'er we have or are submit
And lie, as beggars, at thy feet. (pp. 74–5)[8]

Ac. 4:36, *Barnabas . . . (The son of consolation), a Levite, &c.*

1. Ye Levites hir'd who undertake
      The awful ministry,
  For lucre or ambition's sake,
      A nobler pattern see!
Who greedily your pay receive,
      And adding cure to cure,
In splendid ease and pleasures live,
      By pillaging the poor:

2. See here an Apostolic priest,
      Commission'd from the sky,
  Who dares of all himself divest,
      The needy to supply!

---

8. [Verses 3 and 4 appear in *Poet. Works*, XII, p. 181; *cf.* footnote to Acts 4:32, *supra*.]

A primitive example rare
    Of gospel-poverty,
To feed the flock his only care,
    And like his Lord to be.

3. Jesus, to us apostles raise,
        Like-minded pastors give
    Who freely may dispence Thy grace
        As freely they receive;
    Who disengag'd from all below
        May earthly things despise,
    And every creature-good forego
        For treasure in the skies.

4. The sons of consolation these
        As sent by thee approve,
    Who nothing have, yet all possess
        In their Redeemer's love:
    The mourners for Thyself to chear,
        Thy ministers employ,
    With tidings glad of pardon here,
        And heaven's eternal joy. (p. 75)[9]

Ac. 5:8, *She said, Yea, for so much.*

The ground of every heart is known
With every thought, to Him alone
    Who doth in secret see:
O may I always bear in mind
The Eye which looks thro' all mankind
    Is now intent on me! (p. 78)

9. [Verses 2–3 appear in *Poet. Works*, XII, p. 181.]

Ac. 5:21, *And when they heard that, they entred into the temple early in the morning, & taught, &c.*

> A gospel-minister disdains
>> Dangers, or bonds, or death to fear;
> Jesus, he knows, the cause maintains,
>> And, conscious that his call is clear,
> Prevents the morning-ray, & flies
> To preach the life that never dies. (p. 86)

Ac. 5:21, *But the high-priest came, and called the council together, & sent to the prison to have them brought.*

> God laughs at the designs of men
>> Against the work & will Divine:
> Though zealous priests conspire again
>> And hand in hand the wicked join,
> The counsel of our Lord shall stand
> And spread his love throughout the land. (p. 86)

Ac. 5:23, *The prison truly found we shut with all safety, and the keepers standing without before the doors, etc.*

> Who can defeat the Saviour's plan,
>> Or traverse his designs of love?
> The surest means employ'd by man
>> Shall vain & unsucces[s]ful prove,
> That all his baffled foes may own
> Wisdom and Power is Christ alone. (pp. 86–7)

Ac. 5:31, *Him hath God exalted to give repentance.*

> 1. Saviour & Prince, I lift
>> To Thee my flinty heart,
> Who only dost the precious gift
>> Of penitence impart,
> Cloath'd with omnipotence,
>> Thou canst the stone remove,
> Thou wilt bestow the contrite sense,
>> For thou, O God, art Love.

2.   I wait the powerful look
Of tenderness divine,
The Sight which many an heart hath broke
Almost as hard as mine;
The piteous spectacle
Of Jesus on the tree,
Which bids my wounded spirit feel
The death he bore for me.

3.   Soon as thy cross appears,
The rocks again are rent,
Sinners dissolve in gracious tears,
And I, their chief, repent!
I weep, & still weep on,
Tho' Thou my sins remove,
Lamenting with my latest groan
That e'er I griev'd thy love. (p. 92a)

Ac. 5:31, *Him hath God exalted to be a Prince & a Saviour, to give repentance.*

1.   Giver of repentance, Thee
My Lord I long to prove,
O vouchsafe the grace to me,
The grief of contrite love:
Sunk in sin, to Thee I pray
Exalted on thy glorious throne,
Saviour, Prince, thy power display,
And break my heart of stone.

2.   Waits my heart insensible
Thy mercy's power to know,
Cast the pitying look, & fill
My soul with sacred woe:
Then I to my Lord shall turn,
And conscious of the blood applied,
Look on Him I pierc'd, & mourn,
With Jesus crucified.

3.   Thus my few remaining days
       I would in sorrow spend,
    Trampler on the God of grace,
       And murtherer of my Friend,
    Weeping, till my Friend appears,
  By Him but not myself forgiven,
    Till he wipes away my tears,
       And comforts me in heaven. (p. 92c)

Ac. 5:31, *Him hath God exalted, &c.*

1. Jesus, mighty Intercessor,
       Saviour, Prince enthroned on high,
    Plead the cause of a transgressor,
       Save a soul condemned to die:
    Second death's most righteous sentence
       While I in myself receive,
    Bless me with sincere repentance,
       Bid the gasping sinner live.

2. By thy passion's exhibition
       Into flesh the stony turn,
    Then I feel the true contrition
       Then I look on thee and mourn,
    Mourn with sorrow never-ceasing
       Till the pardon Thou impart,
    All my sins and fears dismissing,
       Binding up my broken heart.

3. Who is This that comes from Edom
       Glorious in his garments dyed?
    Comes to buy my life and freedom,
       Shews his bleeding hands and side!
    Jesus, mighty to deliver,
       Full of truth and full of grace
    Live, O King, and reign for ever,
       Theme of my eternal praise.

4. Thee let every ransomed Nation,
   Their divine Redeemer greet
   Shout the God of their Salvation,
   Cast their crowns before thy feet.[10]

Ac. 5:34, *Then stood there up one in the council, a Pharisee named Gamaliel, a doctor of law, had in, etc.*

1. Among the most corrupt of men
   Is oft reserv'd, for ends unseen,
       One prudent man & good,
   Design'd to stand in truth's defence,
   Appear for injur'd innocence,
       And stem the rising flood.

2. Ev'n now th'omniscient God perceives,
   But hid & unsuspected leaves
       His instrument unknown,
   In senate, court, or sanhedrim,
   The man whom still the world esteem,
       And count him all their own.

3. Rais'd up by an Almighty Hand,
   He shortly in the gap shall stand,
       The violent to repress;
   With heavenly Wisdom on his side
   Shall singly turn th'outrageous tide,
       And save the witnesses. (p. 93)

Ac. 5:35, *He said unto them, Ye men of Israel, take heed to yourselves, what ye intend to do, etc.*

The wise will not with rage oppose
Religion's fierce, impetuous foes,
    But first the storm allay,
Their passions calm, their reason clear,
And bend their willing souls to hear
    What truth & wisdom say. (pp. 93–4)

10. [MS CW III(a), p. 12. The poem is incomplete and is not included in MS Acts.]

Ac. 5:40, *And to him they agreed.*

1. Join'd to a sinful multitude,
    The man who singularly good
        Defends the poor opprest,
    Who speaks unmov'd, unterrified,
    May often to the righteous side
        Bring over all the rest.

2. Superior though he stands alone,
    His duty is the truth to own
        Of virtue in distress:
    His counsel to the croud he gives,
    His testimony bold, & leaves
        With God the whole success. (p. 95)

Ac. 5:41, *They departed from the council, rejoicing that they were counted worthy to suffer shame, &c.*

1. Who knows the joy we feel,
        Solid, and deep, and pure,
    Joy inconceivable
        Which always shall endure,
    When worthy deem'd to suffer shame,
    Accounted vile for Jesus' name?

2. Transported we receive
        The Apostolic grace,
    To Christ more closely cleave,
        And triumph in his praise,
    Honour the stripes for us he bore,
    And Jesus' bleeding wounds adore.

3. Th'ineffable delight
        To flesh and blood unknown,
    Doth all our souls unite
        With those around the throne;
    On us the heavenly Spirit rests,
    And glory fills our ravish'd breasts. (pp. 86–7)

Ac. 6:1, *And in those days . . . there arose a murmuring.*

1. See the first fatal step to part
   Men of one soul, and of one heart!
      Undue respect of man,
   Pride imperceptibly steals in,
   Begets the discontented sin,
      And mars the perfect plan.

2. Where are humility and peace?
   The root of envious bitterness
      Pride, only pride could prove:
   Envy unkind suspicion wakes,
   Suspicion all the murmurs makes
      And poisons social love.

3. Who can, O God, Thy counsels tell!
   Thy judgments are unsearchable!
      The pure and perfect way,
   Religion undefil'd and true
   Scarcely appear'd to mortal view,
      And vanish'd in a day!

4. But may we not expect to see
   The genuine pristine piety
      On this our earth restor'd;
   The heavenly life again made known,
   The Christians all in Spirit one,
      One Spirit with their Lord?

5. Surely Thou wilt from heaven descend,
   The dark apostacy to end,
      And re-collect thine own:
   These eyes our beauteous King shall view,
   Jesus creating all things new
      On his millennial throne!

6. Then shall thy church in Thee abide,
   Renew'd, & wholly sanctified
      And pure as those above;
   No power shall then impair our peace,
   Or break the bond of perfectness,
      The unity of love. (pp. 98–9)[11]

Ac. 6:3, *Wherefore, brethren, look ye out among you seven men of honest report, full of the holy Ghost, etc.*

1. O that with ancient harmony
      Pastors & flock might still combine,
   In choice of officers agree,
      Of servants for the work divine,
   Pursue the Apostolic plan;
   The church present, the priest ordain!

2. The people should look out & find
      Not children weak, but solid men,
   Whose judgment & experience join'd
      Throughout their spotless life is seen,
   Men from among themselves alone,
   Whose truth and ways to all are known.

3. Not of a blemish'd character
      The sacred candidates should be,
   But irreproachably sincere,
      Adorn'd with genuine piety,
   Fill'd by the Spirit of holiness,
   And led by him in all their ways.

4. But piety cannot suffice,
      Unless both gifts & graces meet;
   The deacons should be grave & wise,
      Prudent, deliberate, and discreet,
   Appointed, when their trial's past,
   By Apostolic hands at last.

---

11. [Verses 1–3 appear in *Poet. Works*, XII, p. 196.]

5. Ordain'd to long laborious pain,
   They then their one great work fulfil,
Tend the poor sinsick souls of men,
   Exert their utmost strength & skill,
   Themselves the least & meanest call,
   Servants & ministers of all. (pp. 100–1)[12]

Ac. **6:4**, *We will give ourselves continually to prayer, &c.*

1. Priests of the Lord, we stand between
   Jehovah & the sons of men,
      His awful will proclaim,
   And offering up the people's prayers,
   To them, as God's ambassadors,
      We speak in Jesus' name.

2. The Lamb before his Father's eyes,
   The emblem of his sacrifice
      We constantly present;
   For man with God we intercede,
   For God with guilty sinners plead,
      And urge them to repent.

3. We live to make the Saviour known,
   And bring His gifts and blessings down
      On those who Christ obey;
   Joyful in this to persevere,
   For all a pastor's business here
      Is but to preach and pray.

4. Still let us earthly matters leave,
   Ourselves to God entirely give
      And to His church below;
   Live out a life of prayer and love,
   And to our great reward above
      In Jesus' footsteps go. (pp. 101–2)[13]

12. [*Rep. Verse*, No. 88, p. 226.]
13. [Verses 3–4 appear in *Poet. Works*, XII, p. 197.]

Ac. 6:6, *Whom they set before the Apostles: and when they had prayed, they laid their hands on them.*

Each presents the officers,
And makes the choice his own;
All unite in faithful prayers
To bring the Spirit down:
Presbyters their hands impose,
The whole collected Church approve,
But the Grace Ordaining flows
From our High-priest above! (p. 103)[14]

Ac. 6:7, *And the word of God increased, etc.*

1. When the stumbling-block is gone,
Envy and contentious pride,
When the word doth swiftly run,
Then the church is multiplied;
When the Christians all agree
Priests themselves in troops submit,
Those that nail'd Him to the tree
Fall and kiss His bleeding feet.

2. O that crouds in this our day
Might the Crucified receive,
Priests the gospel-truth obey,
Humbly in their Lord believe!
Jesus, fill them with thy grace,
Thee thy church shall then adore,
With thy murtherers confess
Miracles are never o're.[15] (pp. 103–4)[16]

---

14. [*Rep Verse*, No. 189, p. 227.]
15. See the prayer for clergy. [Wesley's note refers to the "Prayer for the Clergy and People," towards the end of Morning and Evening Prayer in *The Book of Common Prayer* which begins, "Almighty and everlasting God, who alone workest great marvels."]
16. [Verse 1 appears in *Poet. Works*, XII, p. 198.]

Ac. 6:11–12, *Then they suborned men, . . . Which said, We, &c.*

1. Silenced, but not convinced, the foes
   Of Christ a surer method take,
   Violence and fraud to truth oppose,
   Slander and lies their refuge make,
   And rouse the sons of wickedness,
   The furious crowd, their prey to seize.

2. Whose words they can no more withstand
   They now their persons apprehend,
   Attended with a ruffian band
   Like ravenous wolves the sheep they rend,
   As guilty criminals entreat,
   And drag them to the judgment-seat.

3. Elders & scribes be sure are there,
   The hated witnesses condemn
   Who Jesus' pardning grace declare,
   "But Moses & his law blaspheme,
   "The merit of good works deny,
   "As God could freely justify.

4. "The wretched hereticks profane
   "Disown a local Deity
   "And dare ev'n in our ears maintain
   "No holiness in walls can be,
   "Our temples, rites, & forms shall fall,
   "And Christ, they say, be all in all." (pp. 105–6)[17]

Ac. 7:8, *He gave them the covenant of circumcision.*[18]

The covenant old in types conceal'd
Now in the gospel is reveal'd;
The gospel-covenant has took place,
And saves us not by works but grace:

---

17. [Verses 1–2 appear in *Poet. Works*, XII, pp. 199–200.]
18. [Above this poem in Wesley's shorthand is written "Dec. 16." The AV reads: "He gave him." Wesley mistakenly wrote "He gave them."]

The Lord his Spirit's seal applies,
His people all to circumcise,
And when our sins & us He parts,
Cuts off the foreskin of our hearts. (p. 111)

Ac. 7:13, *And at the second time Joseph was made known to his brethren; & Joseph's kindred was made, etc.*

1. Is there a second time for them,
   Who their own flesh refus'd to know,
The Man they did to death condemn?
   Will He again appear below
To Jacob's unbelieving race,
And shew the Jews his smiling face?

2. When all the Gentiles are brought in
   (In type by Pharaoh signified)
Jesus shall on the clouds be seen,
   By every human eye espied
And Israel's tribes to Him shall turn,
Behold the God they pierc'd, & mourn.

3. They all shall then their Saviour see,
   Their long-rejected Brother own,
In glorified humanity,
   Flesh of their flesh, bone of their bone,
And gain thro' one forgiving kiss
The fulness of eternal bliss. (p. 114)

Ac. 7:14, *Then sent Joseph, & called to him all his kindred.*

1. Stablish'd in his state above
      Of glorious endless rest,
   Christ shall call with yearning love
      His family distrest;
   All his needy people here
   With those after the flesh allied
   Shall before his face appear
      And banquet at his side.

2.   Taught by thy example, Lord,
      We will the worst pursue,
      Those who spurn'd the saving word
      Invite with proffers new;
      Deaf to all entreaties past
      The most obdurate may come in,
      Know their Friend, & yield at last
      To be redeem'd from sin. (p. 115)

Ac. 7:32, *I am the God of Abraham, and the God of Isaac, and the God of Jacob.*

1.   The God of Abraham we adore,
      Who faith did to our father give,[19]
      And rais'd him up to go before,
      The Guide to all that should believe;
      The God of hope in Isaac's God
      Receiv'd as from the dead we see,
      T'express the life on saints bestow'd,
      The glorious immortality.

2.   The God of love with cordial praise
      As Jacob's God we magnify,
      That model of paternal grace,
      Fruitful in Blessings from the sky!
      Blessings in death to his own seed
      He dealt; but Goodness unconfin'd
      Expir'd, when Jesus bow'd his head,
      And life bequeath'd to all mankind. (p. 122)

19. [The opening lines of this poem originally read:
      Let all the faithful God adore,
      Who faith to Abraham did give.]

Ac. 7:35, *This Moses whom they refused, &c.*

1. Jesus, refus'd by sinners,
   Thou, after thy rejection,
   Art stablished
   Thy church's Head,
   And Life & Resurrection;
   Thyself Jehovah's Angel,
   And Witness of his favor,
   Thy Father's love
   Sent from above,
   To be our Prince and Saviour.

2. By God's right-hand exalted,
   All power to Thee is given,
   And every knee
   Bows down to Thee
   In earth, & hell, & heaven!
   Sole Ruler of thine Israel,
   Almighty to deliver,
   Set up thy throne,
   And reign alone
   O're all thy saints forever. (p. 124)

Ac. 7:40, *As for this Moses, we know not what is become of him.*[20]

No matter what — if God be here,
And Jesus with his church abide;
Ye cannot *need* the minister
Whose Lord & Master is your Guide:
But if in man ye put your trust
Or idols of the creatures make,
Ye force the jealous God & just
His faithless people to forsake. (p. 127)

20. [With the words "we know not" Charles quoted the text of *Notes*. The AV reads: "we wot not."]

Ac. 7:42, *Have ye offer'd to me slain beasts and sacrifices?*

> Lord, from sinful worshippers
> Thou dost avert thine eyes,
> Man's abominable prayers
> And formal sacrifice
> Are no sacrifice to Thee,
> For Thou an holy Spirit art,
> Thou our sole Felicity
> Requirest all our heart. (pp. 128–9)

Ac. 7:44, *God spake unto Moses, that he should make it according to the fashion that he had seen.*

> Our God the true religion forms
> On earth by that above,
> And teaches highly favour'd worms
> To praise, adore, and love;
> The power to do his perfect will
> Is with the precept given,
> And we shall all his mind fulfil
> As angels do in heaven. (p. 129)

Ac. 7:51, *Ye do always resist the Holy Ghost.*

> 1. Who act the persecutor's part
> A stubborn, stiff-neck'd, Jewish race,
> Uncircumcis'd in ears and heart,
> Ye still resist the Spirit of grace,
> Harden your heart, and stop your ears,
> When God commands you to repent,
> And run upon the messengers,
> And stone the *Sender* in the *sent.*

2. Rebels, your iron-sinew'd neck
    Ye will not bow to God's own yoke,
    Your rocky hearts disdain to break;
      The word by all the prophets spoke,
    The word which offers Christ to all
      Ye have in every age withstood,
    Refus'd the Spirit's loudest call,
      And rush'd to shed the martyrs' blood. (pp. 131–2)[21]

Ac. 7:51, *As your fathers did, so do ye.*

      Your sires inflam'd with hellish zeal,
        Your Popish, Antichristian sires,
      Rejoic'd the saints of God to kill
        By gibbets, racks, or tort'ring fires:
      Their steps ye eagerly pursue,
        Severest menaces ye breathe
      'Gainst all the Lord's disciples true,
        And bonds, & banishment, & death. (p. 132)

Ac. 7:52, *Which of the prophets have not your fathers persecuted,
&c.*

1.   Which of the prophets old,
          Inspir'd, & sent by God,
        Who Jesus to the world foretold,
          Was not to death pursued?
        Is there a messenger,
          Who since proclaim'd his word,
        And was not persecuted here,
          And treated as his Lord?
        Ye men of high estate,
          Who bear unrighteous sway,
        Ungodly priests, who always hate,
          And Jesus Christ betray;
        Who on the servants fall,
          Ye have the Lord denied,
        And murtherers in your hearts, ye all
          Are stain'd with deicide.

21. [Verse 1 appears in *Poet. Works*, XII, p. 216.]

2.   Oft as the God of grace
His work on earth revives,
And pleads with the rebellious race,
And by his Spirit strives;
Born of the flesh alone
Ye persecute the just,
The Saviour's messengers disown,
And from your churches thrust.
When cast out of the pale,
As Schismaticks ye brand,
And then the Lollards never fail
To feel your bruising hand;
The sheep of Jesus' fold
Blacken'd with odious names,
(If He no more your rage with-hold)
Ye sentence to the flames. (pp. 133–4)

Ac. 7:53, *Who have received the law by the disposition of angels, and have not kept it.*

1.   Not by Angelic ministry
Ye did the law of Christ embrace:
Glad tidings of a pardon free
Himself proclaim'd to all our race,
Sent from Jehovah's throne above
To teach the world his Father's love.

2.   But ye his offers have withstood,
Deaf to his word & Spirit's cry;
Ye call yourselves the church of God,
The temple of the Lord Most-high,
His name & sacraments receive,
Yet Christians stil'd, as Heathens live. (p. 134)

Ac. 7:54, *When they heard these things, they were cut to the heart, & they gnashed on him with their teeth.*

Ye threaten us in vain,
And fiercely gnash your teeth,
The bridle doth your wrath restrain,
And respite us from death:

Ye may declare your will
By casting many a stone;
The witnesses ye cannot kill,
Till all our work is done:
Till then we persevere:
And lo, the gospel grows
Thro' men who neither scorn nor fear
Their irritated foes:
But when our toils are past,
We shall our lives lay down,
If Jesus count us meet at last
To win the martyr's crown. (pp. 134–5)

Ac. 7:57, *Then they cried out with a loud voice, and stopped their ears, and ran upon him with one accord.*

1. The proud & envious cannot bear
    God's gifts in other men to see,
    Incens'd by everything they are
    Mad with revenge & cruelty,
    They cannot wrong discern from right,
    Blasphemers from the sons of light.

2. Against the truth they stop their ears
    Raising the loud infernal cry,
    When Jesus to a saint appears,
    And shows his glory in the sky,
    The "daring wretch" who God hath seen
    They count not fit to live with men. (pp. 136–7)

Ac. 8:4, *Therefore they that were scattered abroad, went everywhere preaching the word.*

1. They did not run, in sudden fright,
    To save themselves alone,
    But fled, directed in their flight
    To gracious ends unknown:
    The preachers both by word & deed
    Did the glad news proclaim,
    The people's lives conspir'd to spread
    Their mighty Saviour's name.

2. Women, & men, & children too
   By powerful godliness
   The general observation drew,
   And shew'd the truth of grace.
   O that we all might preach & live,
   Like them, the gospel-word,
   And force the heathen to receive
   Our dear redeeming Lord!

3. Surely, if God permit our foes
   To scatter us abroad,
   (The men who now his work oppose,
   And hate th'atoning blood)
   We everywhere with Christ shall run
   And propagate the sect,
   And spread thro' distant lands unknown
   The grace which they reject. (pp. 142–3)

Ac. **8:5,** *Then Philip went down to the city of Samaria, and preached Christ unto them.*

Philip the Lord our Righteousness
Proclaims, & preaches in the place
    Where Christ had preach'd before;
Heathens to zealous Jews prefers:
And all the Saviour's messengers
    Evangelize the poor. (p. 143)

Ac. **8:6,** *And the people with one accord gave heed unto those things which Philip spoke, &c.*

1. They all with one consent give heed:
   And lo, the good celestial seed,
       Which God himself had sown,
   Brings forth the hundred-fold increase;
   And Philip owes his vast success
       To Jesus' word alone.

2.   Thou, Lord, dost still the fruit produce,
    When sinners listen to the news
      Of reconciling grace;
    Thou only dost prepare the heart,
    Doer of all the work Thou art,
      Worthy of all the praise. (pp. 143–4)

Ac. 8:7, *Many taken with palsies, and that were lame, were healed.*

    Nature's impotent condition
      Feels my paralytic soul,
    Finds in Christ a kind Physician,
      By the word of faith made whole;
    Joyful tidings of salvation
      Came, & spake my pardon sure,
    Faith in Jesus' bloody passion
      Minister'd the perfect cure. (p. 145)

Ac. 8:8, *And there was great joy in that city.*

1.   In the city or place,
      Where salvation by grace
      Poor sinners receive,
    There is joy above measure in all that believe;
      The redeem'd of the Lord,
      To his favor restor'd,
      We exult in his love,
    And with singing return to our country above.

2.   By faith we possess
      The unspeakable peace,
      Freely justified we,
    And rejoicing in hope our Redeemer to see:
      He gives us a taste
      Of that heavenly feast
      His Spirit imparts;
    And the earnest of glory is grace in our hearts! (p. 145)

Ac. 8:9, *There was a certain man, called Simon, which before time in the same city used sorcery, &c.*

1. A plain indisputable case!
   Once upon earth there witchcraft was,
   A compact with the hellish foe,
   "But seventeen hundred years ago,
   "In Asia, not in Europe, made;
   "The fiend hath here forgot his trade.

2. "The *Christian* world is wiser grown,
   "And lets his works & him alone;
   "Full license is indulg'd to all;
   "Both high & low, both great & small,
   "Who weakly thought his worship evil,
   "May safely now adore the devil!" (p. 146)[22]

Ac. 8:10, *To whom they all gave heed, saying, This man is the great power of God.*

An hellish sorcerer say seize
   Honors Divine, to charm the croud;
Of Christ alone his church confess,
   "*This* Man is the great Power of God!" (p. 146)

Ac. 8:14–15, *Now when the Apostles heard that Samaria had received the word of God, they sent unto them, &c.*

1. Who have the gospel truth believ'd
   And mercy from the Lord receiv'd,
      And known our sins forgiven,
   We surely need a farther grace,
   We want the Spirit of holiness,
      To seal us heirs of heaven.

22. [Verse 1 appears in *Poet. Works*, XII, p. 222.]

2. Our souls confirm'd by solemn prayer,
   Our hearts by grace establish'd are,
      And rooted fast in love;
   And when the Giver we receive,
   Fill'd with the Holy Ghost we live
      That sinless life above. (p. 148)

Ac. 8:17, *Then laid they their hands on them, and they received the Holy Ghost.*

The laying on of hands implies,
   That God asserts his lawful claim,
Possession takes, and sanctifies
   The men baptiz'd into his name;
Subjecting them to his commands,
   Uniting to himself, He still
Keeps them in his own gracious hands,
   To serve the counsels of his will. (p. 149)

Ac. 8:18–19, *He offered them money, saying, Give me also this power, &c.*

What multitudes have thought
   Like the magician old,
That ministerial powers were bought
   With perishable gold!
By proud ambition led,
   Or groveling avarice,
They have the sin of Simon made
   The sacerdotal vice. (p. 149)

Ac. 8:22, *Repent therefore of this thy wickedness, and pray God, if perhaps the thought of thine heart, etc.*

Repent, ye impious tribe, repent,
   And put away the priestly sin,
Before ye feel the punishment
   When hell is mov'd to take you in!
Renounce your secret wickedness,
   Your purchas'd stalls & livings leave,
And God perhaps, so rich in grace,
   May *Simonists* themselves forgive. (p. 151)

Ac. 8:24, *Then answered Simon, and said, Pray ye to the Lord for me, that none of these things, etc.*

1. An hypocrite will oft appear
    To tremble and relent,
    And destitute of godly fear
    Shrink from the punishment,
    As Pharaoh, in affliction, pray
    The judgment to remove,
    Or cry, Take all these plagues away,
    But not the sin I love.

2. He may his bosom-lust confess,
    While yet his heart is whole,
    Concern'd to save appearances,
    Regardless of his soul:
    The burthen and the task of prayer
    He may on others cast,
    And left to damnable despair
    Die in his sins at last. (pp. 152–3)

Ac. 8:25, *And they, when they had testified and preached the word of the Lord, returned to Jerusalem, &c.*

1. Who can the joy express
    That swells a pastor's heart,
    Whene'er the God of grace
    Hath sent him to impart
    The welcome news of sin forgiven,
    And seal'd his word with signs from heaven?

2. Our ministry we prove
    On unbelievers poor,
    And tell them of his love
    Who did the cross endure,
    Laid down his life for sin t'atone,
    And make their dearer souls his own.

3.   Our Peacemaker, & Peace,
            That did for sinners die,
        'Tis all our happiness
            Of him to testify,
        And see the world in Jesus' blood
        Implung'd, & all brought home to God. (p. 153)

Ac. 8:26, *The angel of the Lord spake unto Philip, saying,*
Arise, and go toward the south, &c.

        Not by voice Angelic taught,
            Yet, Lord, we plainly know
        Whither, & to whom we ought
            At thy command to go:
        Each evangelist pursues
        His heavenly Providential Guide,
        Runs to spread the joyful news
            Of Jesus crucified. (p. 154)

Ac. 8:29, *Then the Spirit said unto Philip, Go near, & join*
thyself to this chariot.

        When the Spirit and the word
            Conspire in part to show
        The good pleasure of our Lord,
            We with his message go;
        Ready to perform his will,
        Ourselves we to the chariot join,
        Still intent, & waiting still
            To know his whole design. (p. 155)

Ac. 8:31, *And he said, How can I, except some man should guide*
me?

        God by the ministry of man
            Hath oft on man his light bestow'd,
        But ah, the teacher's toil is vain
            Except himself be taught of God:
        Yet if the Lord his Guide appear,
            A wise instructor of the blind,
        He preaches Christ: his voice we hear,
            And God & Heaven in Jesus find. (pp. 155–6)

Ac. 8:32, *He was led as a sheep to the slaughter, and like a lamb dumb before his shearers, so he opened not his mouth.*

Lamb of God, I would like Thee
 Quiet to the slaughter go,
Silent, meek humility
 Toward my cruel murtherers show;
Never murmur, or complain;
 Crush'd by persecuting power,
Suffer all the wrongs of man,
 God in humble peace adore. (p. 156)

Ac. 8:36, *See, here is water; what doth hinder me to be baptized?*

Can I be near the mingled pool
 That flow'd from Jesus' side,
And not desire to plunge my soul
 Into the sacred tide?
Impatient of the least delay,
 This moment, Lord, I would
Enter, and wash my sins away
 In thine atoning blood. (p. 159)

Ac. 8:39, *And when they were come up out of the water, the Spirit of the Lord caught away Philip.*

A minister of grace,
 Soon as his work is done,
Should quickly vanish from the place,
 Amusements vain to shun;
Should hastily retire,
 From human converse flee,
Nor stay to hear the croud admire
 His prosperous[23] ministry. (p. 161)

23. [Above "prosperous" Wesley wrote "powerful" as an alternative.]

Ac. 9:4, *And he fell to the earth, & heard a voice, saying, etc.*

> In sin we rush impetuous on,
> Till grace arrests & casts us down,
>   Alarm'd with sacred fear,
> Till Christ with sudden light surround,
> And then, as groveling on the ground
>   The voice of God we hear. (p. 165)

Ac. 9:5, *And he said, Who art thou, Lord? And the Lord said, I am Jesus whom thou persecutest, etc.*

> 1. Conversion is by just degrees:
>   The light divine a sinner sees,
>   And stops his ears no more,
>   But listning now, while conscience calls,
>   And struck with dread of judgment, falls
>   Before Almighty Power.

> 2. Trembling he doth his sin confess,
>   Convinc'd th'outragious wickedness
>   Against the Lord was done;
>   Grace unexperienc'd he desires,
>   And feebly after Christ inquires,
>   His Advocate unknown. (p. 166)

Ac. 9:6, *Lord, what wilt Thou have me to do?*

> 1. When the celestial light appears,
>   O'rewhelm'd with huge, increasing fears,
>   The sinful soul astonish'd lies,
>   Afraid to lift his guilty eyes:
>   Rul'd by the Saviour's will alone,
>   He would, he would renounce his own,
>   And waits, as unopposing clay,
>   Till Jesus gives the power t'obey.

2. Mine eyes are ever unto Thee,
    Till open'd by thy love they see:
    Yet still Thou must thy counsel shew,
    For still I know not what to do:
    I would not see, but in thy light;
    I would not walk, but by thy might;
    Or work a work, or speak a word,
    Or think a thought, without my Lord. (pp. 166–7)[24]

Ac. 9:6, *The Lord said unto him, Arise, and go into the city, & it shall be told thee what thou must do.*

1. What but th'omnipotence of grace
    Can a poor prostrate sinner raise?
    Whate'er of good on earth is done,
    Is wrought by God, & God alone:
    Yet still He strangely condescends
    By man to serve his gracious ends;
    And listning, we our pardon hear
    Pronounc'd by Jesus' minister.

2. If Thou their ministry ordain
    And man employ t'inlighten man,
    I dare not, Lord, the means despise,
    Appointed to unseal my eyes:
    I wait th'atoning blood to feel;
    The counsels of thy grace reveal,
    And tell my heart, by whom Thou wilt,
    Thy death hath cancel'd all my guilt. (pp. 167–8)

Ac. 9:8–9, *And Saul arose from the earth; and when his eyes were opened, he saw no man: but they led him, etc.*

1. A conscious unbeliever see!
        His blindness spiritual he knows,
    Shut up in sin & misery,
        In darkness palpable he goes,
    As a blind child, by others led,
    And quite forgets to eat his bread.

24. [Verse 2 appears in *Poet. Works*, XII, p. 235.]

2. Jesus in wisdom and in love
   Unsav'd a while the sinner leaves,
To feel his help is from above,
   And God alone salvation gives;
He speaks the word, Let there be light,
And bids the soul receive its sight. (p. 168)

Ac. 9:10–11, *The Lord said to him in a vision, Ananias, And he said, Behold, I am here, Lord, &c.*[25]

Lord, if Thou call me by my name
   Thy grace to testify,
Made ready by thy grace I am,
   And answer, Here am I!
Thou knowst the souls convinc'd of sin;
   Send forth thy messenger
To find, & bring the wanderers in,
   Who seek Thee now in prayer. (p. 169)

Ac. 9:16, *I will shew him how great things he must, &c.*

1. A mission to the ministry
   Is but a call to pain,
To bleed with Jesus on the tree,
   That we with Him may reign:
Us, Lord, with views of grief, & shame,
   And death, Thou dost allure
To preach salvation in thy name;
   And thus our own secure.

2. Great things ordain'd for Thee to do,
   Thou dost our souls prepare
By labouring strength, and patience too
   Great things for Thee to bear;
Afflictions with Thy grace abound,
   And make Thy favourites known,
And those who suffer most are found
   The nearest to Thy throne. (p. 172)[26]

25. [The AV reads: "To him said the Lord in a vision." Here again Charles used his brother's translation in *Notes*.]
26. [Verse 2 appears in *Poet. Works*, XII, p. 238.]

Ac. 9:17–18, *And he received sight forthwith, and arose,* &c.

[I]

1.   A faithful brother now,
The persecuting Saul,
Doth to the cross of Jesus bow,
And at his footstool fall:
He first obtains his sight,
And then his pardon seal'd,
Wash'd in the pure baptismal rite,
With Jesus' Spirit fill'd.

2.   His sight he first receives:
And thus the Will Divine
Sometimes to humbled sinners gives
The grace without the sign:
Baptiz'd, he then obeys,
And shows it right and fit
That all who have obtain'd the grace
Should to the sign submit. (pp. 172–3)[27]

II

1.   Jesus, today appear,
As yesterday the same,
And put thine enemies in fear
Who persecute thy name;
Convince them from above
Who fiercely now pursue
With Jewish hate the God of love,
But know not what they do.

2.   Give them on Thee to call
Inquiring who Thou art,
And O, command the scales to fall
From every faithless heart;

27. [Verse 2 appears in *Poet. Works*, XII, p. 238.]

Then, then thy wounds display!
And by thy cross subdued
They rise, and wash their sins away
In thine all-cleansing blood. (pp. 173–4)

Ac. 9:20, *Straightway he preached Christ in the, &c.*

1.   In the Spirit of holiness,
      And grateful, fervent zeal,
    Spirit of ministerial grace
      His office to fulfil,
    Lo, the new Apostle flies
Upborne on wings of faith & prayer,
    Jesus' name and sacrifice
      Throughout the world to bear.

2.   Eager to repair the wrong
      He to the church had done,
    Christ he spreads before the throng
      And makes his Saviour known;
    Jesus' love his heart constrains,
And all who know the precious grace
    Spend their utmost strength and pains
      To save the sinful race.

3.   Jesus' love I cannot feel
      And hide it in my heart;
    No: I must the secret tell,
      I must to all impart,
    Publish God's eternal Son —
Sinner, He bought us on the tree,
    Tasted death for every one,
      And offers life to Thee! (pp. 174–5)[28]

28. [Verses 2–3 appear in *Poet. Works*, XII, pp. 238–9.]

Ac. 9:21, *But all that heard him were amazed, and said, Is not this he that destroyed them which called, etc.*

1. Thee if thy foes confess,
    And Pharisees adore,
    Thy clemency I praise,
    But wonder, Lord, no more,
    Who know the power of grace Divine
    Which chang'd so hard an heart as mine.

2. A persecutor I,
    A murtherer of my God,
    The virtue testify
    Of that victorious blood:
    It ransom'd me from every sin,
    It made the foulest sinner clean.

3. Ye need not now despair
    Whose souls are black as hell,
    Who Jesus' purchase are
    His sprinkled blood may feel;
    If mercy is for me and Saul,
    Our Lord abounds in grace to all! (p. 175)

Ac. 9:22, *But Saul increased the more in strength.*

1. Who Jesus to the world confess
    And preach before His foes,
    Our labour doth our strength increase,
    Our grace by using grows;
    Our talents more and more abound,
    Who Christ proclaim abroad,
    And prove (his haters to confound)
    This is th'eternal God.

2. With every gospel-minister
    Still, Lord, vouchsafe to be,
    And help us boldly to declare
    Thy sovereign Deity,

Proofs incontestible to bring
From thy own Spirit's power
That Thee our Prophet, Priest, & King
Both earth & heaven adore. (pp. 175–6)[29]

Ac. 9:23, *The Jews took counsel to kill him.*

Jesus, who now thy cause maintain,
No mercy we expect from men,
But mortal enmity;
Yet lo, by danger & distress
Imbolden'd, we thy name confess,
And closer cleave to Thee. (p. 176)

Ac. 9:26, *He assayed to join himself to the disciples, but they were all afraid of him, &c.*

When Jesus knows it good for me,
Let brethren fly my company,
And all the church disown:
Happy, if so detach'd I can
Withdraw my confidence in man
And cleave to God alone! (p. 177)

Ac. 9:29, *And he spake boldly in the name of the Lord Jesus.*

1. The valiant in his valour trusts,
   But Christians in the Lord of hosts,
   When blackest storms impend;
   And who his sure protection claim,
   The bold defenders of his name
   He will himself defend.

2. What can the friend of Jesus dread,
   Who toils his Saviour's name to spread,
   Who in his person speaks!
   Speaks, as the Spirit utterance gives,
   To serve his Saviour's cause he lives,
   And Jesus' glory seeks!

29. [Verse 1 appears in *Poet. Works*, XII, p. 239.]

3. Jesus, this feeble heart of mine
    Inspire with confidence divine
        And teach me what to say;
    So shall I fearlessly go on,
    And make thy name, thy nature known
        Though death obstruct the way. (p. 178)

Ac. 9:29, *He disputed against the Grecians: but they went about to slay him.*

1. Sound words the world can never bear,
    And thus unwittingly declare,
        That speaking in his name,
    And treated like our Lord below,
    The truth we by his Spirit show,
        We preach with Christ the same.

2. Who still of Jesus testify
    Though perils, pains, and death are nigh,
        We must the truth maintain:
    Their threats with unconcern we view;
    But more than all their rage can do,
        We dread the smiles of man. (p. 179)

Ac. 9:30, *Which when the brethren knew, they brought him to Cesarea.*

When Jesus' prosperous messenger
Thinks not himself of danger near,
    More anxious for their guide,
The flock should send him far away,
Till Christ his sovereign power display
    And turn the storm aside. (p. 179)

Ac. 9:34, *Peter said unto him, Eneas, Jesus Christ maketh thee whole; arise, and make thy bed, etc.*

Whate'er the instrument or means
'Tis Jesus makes the sinner whole;
    He only saves us from our sins,
    And cures the palsy of the soul:

The virtue which his grace supplies
Transmitted by the gospel-word,
Strengthens my impotence to rise,
And others turns to serve my Lord. (pp. 180–1)

Ac. 9:36, *This woman was full of good works, and almsdeeds which she did.*

1. A widow on the poor bestow'd,
   Full of good works, divinely good,
   (Works in the Spirit of Jesus done,
   In faith & love to Christ alone)
   Who not on them, but Christ, relies,
   She lays up treasure in the skies.

2. Who thus to God devotes her days
   In works of genuine righteousness,
   How shall her life the world condemn
   Whose life is but an idle dream,
   A useless tale, an empty void,
   Or all for hell, not heaven, employ'd! (pp. 181–2)

Ac. 9:37, *It came to pass in those days, that she was sick, and died.*

Happy the soul, whom death shall find
Possest of the Redeemer's mind,
Rich not in gold, or knowledge vain,
But faith & love to God & man,
Rich in the works which Christ will own,
And the great Judge pronounce "Well done!" (p. 182)

Ac. 9:40, *But Peter put them all forth, and kneeled down, and turning him to the body, said, Tabitha, arise.*

The rest must all give place,
When Peter bows the knee
In wrestling prayer to seek his face
Who doth in secret see;

By violent faith to take
A saint from paradise,
Bring her departed spirit back
And bid her body rise.
The poor afflicted saints
Their common loss bemoan,
And God regards in their complaints
The Spirit of His Son:
Who gave the Son of man,
He lets the servant go
Out of His arms to earth again
And tend His church below. (p. 182)[30]

Ac. 9:41-2, *He presented her alive. And it was known throughout all Joppa; & many believed in the Lord.*

1. God hearkens, and hears
   His sorrowful saints
   Replies to their tears,
   And troubles, & wants;
   His only good-pleasure
   Doth freely restore
   An heavenly treasure,
   A friend to the poor.

2. One woman of grace
   To life is restor'd
   That many may praise
   And turn to the Lord;
   A single believer
   From death they receive,
   That thousands forever
   With Jesus may live. (p. 184)

30. [The second half of the verse appears in *Poet. Works*, XII, p. 242, as the opening verse of a poem continuing with the next poem in MS Acts.]

Ac. 9:43, *He tarried many days in Joppa with one Simon a tanner.*

1. The rich who delicately live
    Are not worthy to receive
    An Apostolic guest;
    Nor will he seek a calm retreat,
    In the proud mansions of the great,
    Or share a glutton's feast.

2. The fisher chuses to remain
    With an upright heart & plain,
    The tanner's house prefers,
    And palaces, & thrones, & stalls,
    Leaves to the men whom Babel calls
    His lawful successors. (p. 185)

Ac. 10:1, *There was a certain man in Cesarea, called Cornelius, a centurion.*[31]

The God of universal grace,
    The Father of mankind,
Doth worshippers in every place
    And all conditions find:
With blind idolaters they live,
    Preserv'd from outward blame
Till a seal'd pardon they receive
    Thro' faith in Jesus' name. (p. 186)

Ac. 10:3, *He saw in a vision an angel of God coming up to him, and saying to him, Cornelius.*

God knows his own, wheree'er[32] they are
    And answers their request,
When by some chosen messenger
    He draws them to his breast;

31. [Above this poem in Wesley's shorthand is written: "Jan. 4" (1765).]
32. [Wesley usually wrote "where'er."]

The ministerial spirits above
Salvation's heirs attend,
And Christ shall soon with all his love
Into their hearts descend. (pp. 186–7)

Ac. 10:4, *Thy prayers and thine alms are come up for a memorial before God.*

1. Were his alms & ceaseless prayers
   Splendid sins in God's esteem?
   No; the Lord himself declares
   Both acceptable to Him;
   Graceful both as incense rise,
   Bring an angel from the skies.

2. Prayers & alms to heaven ascend;
   But they first from heaven come down:
   Man to help if man intend,
   Good design'd is not his own:
   If to God his heart aspire,
   God infus'd the chast desire.

3. Offer'd by an heart sincere
   Prayers & alms the Lord receives
   From an upright worshipper;
   While, whate'er he prays, or gives,
   Thro' his Advocate unknown
   Finds a passage to the throne. (p. 187)[33]

Ac. 10:6, *He lodgeth with one Simon a tanner.*

1. Not with the doctors of the law,
   The learn'd, the noble, or the great,
   Did Jesus' minister withdraw,
   To find a sanctified retreat,
   But long abode with Simon made,
   And taught his host an heavenly trade.

33. [Verses 1 and 2 appear in *Poet. Works*, XII, pp. 243–4.]

2. The tanner to a merchant wise
   Was turn'd, & goodly jewels sought,
   And finding one of countless price,
   Sold all, the pearl of pardon bought,
   Laid up his heart & wealth above,
   And liv'd upon his Saviour's love. (p. 188)

Ac. 10:9, *Peter went up upon the housetop to pray about the sixth hour.*

Still at the stated hours of prayer
   We hold communion with our God,
Who then doth his designs declare,
   And sheds his richest love abroad:
Detatch'd, upborn from things below
   We comprehend our Saviour's mind,
And feel, when Him we fully know,
   Our hearts inlarg'd to all mankind. (pp. 189–90)

Ac. 10:12, *Wherein were all manner of four-footed beasts of the earth, &c.*

An emblem of the Gentiles see!
   Men without law, & void of grace,
Abandon'd to brutality,
   Prone to the earth in all their ways,
As serpents vile the dust they lick,
   As ravenous birds their prey devour,
And here their base delights they seek
   Like beasts that die to live no more! (pp. 190–1)

Ac. 10:16, *The Vessel was received up again into heaven.*

Of heavenly origin divine
   Of water and the Spirit born,
We shall our spotless souls resign
   And to our native place return.

Expecting our immense reward
   On earth we a few moments live,
And when He hath his bride prepar'd
   The Lord shall to himself receive. (pp. 191–2)

Ac. 10:21, *Then Peter went down to the men, and said, Behold, I am he whom ye seek: what is the cause, etc.*

Lord, Thou see'st my heart's desire,
Still I of Thyself inquire,
Ask, & long thy will to know,
In the knowing grace to grow;
Step by step my Guide pursue,
More & more thy pleasure do,
Do with love's alacrity
All the works prepar'd for me. (p. 193)

Ac. 10:29, *I came as soon as I was sent for: I ask therefore for what cause ye have sent for me.*[34]

A faithful minister
Will not discourse in vain,
A moment longer, or defer
Attending souls to gain:
Soon as his work he sees,
He to his work applies,
And preaches Christ, the sinner's Peace,
And draws us to the skies. (p. 195)

Ac. 10:31, *Cornelius, thy prayer is heard, & thine alms are had in remembrance in the sight of God.*

The man who God devoutly fear'd,
But had not Jesus known,
His prayer for farther light was heard
At the eternal throne:
His faith that work'd by love sincere
Acceptance found in heaven:
And then the Saviour's messenger
Proclaim'd his sins forgiven. (p. 195)

34. [Both the AV and *Notes* read "intent," not "cause."]

Ac. 10:32, *When he cometh, he shall speak unto thee, &c.*

> The God of love our souls prepares
> All his commands t'embrace,
> And then, in season due confers
> The dear Redeemer's grace:
> A general willingness he gives;
> And then the suppliant poor
> The gospel-happiness receives,
> And knows his pardon sure. (pp. 195–6)

Ac. 10:36, *The word which God sent unto the children of Israel preaching peace by Jesus Christ (he is Lord of all).*

> 1. The word of reconciling grace
> The Father's will made known,
> Who sent to all our fallen race
> Salvation in his Son:
> Jesus internally reveals
> The peace 'twixt man & God,
> The pardon by his Spirit He seals
> Who bought it with his blood.

> 2. The peace mysterious he bestows,
> When he himself imparts;
> River of life, it then o'reflows
> Our pure believing hearts;
> We know him then the Lord most-high
> Who hath the earnest given,
> And taste the joys that cannot die,
> The ripest joys of heaven. (p. 198)

Ac. 10:38, *God anointed Jesus of Nazareth, &c.*

> 1. By Love Divine bestow'd,
> Thee, Jesus, we receive,
> Thee, the eternal God
> With all our heart believe,
> Anointed by the Spirit of power
> Thee Prophet, Priest, & King adore.

2.   Thine Unction we partake,
        Thy threefold office share,
        Our souls to God give back
        In sacrificial prayer,
    Make known thy Father's will to man,
    And sufferers in thy kingdom reign. (p. 199)

Ac. 10:38, *Who went about doing good, & healing all that were oppressed of the devil: for God was with him.*

1.   The same in every place,
        Thou dost thy love reveal,
        The virtue of thy grace,
        Distemper'd souls to heal
    By Satan's iron yoke opprest
    Who sigh for liberty and rest.

2.   "Jesus of Nazareth,
        (Thou hearst the prisoner cry)
        Redeem my soul from death
        Or Satan's slave I die:
    In proof that God supreme Thou art,
    Expel the fiend, & fill my heart." (p. 199)

Ac. 10:42, *He commanded us to testify that it is He which was ordained of God to be the Judge, etc.*

1.   Sinners, the day is near,
        Prepare your doom to meet,
    Ye all must suddenly appear
        Before the judgment seat;
        Your everlasting state
        Doth on the Man depend,
    The God, whom ye by nature hate
    And every hour offend.

2.   The Father doth intrust
        All judgment to his Son,
    To whom your every deed unjust
    And word & thought is known:

How will ye stand the test,
Or lift your guilty eyes,
When all the hell in every breast
Without a covering lies! (pp. 200–1)

Ac. 10:43, *To him give all the prophets witness that through his name whosoever believeth in him, etc.*

1. What help alas, or hope
    For sinners lost like you?
    Condemn yourselves, to Christ look up,
    Your Judge & Saviour too:
    Your Advocate & Friend
    The Prophets all proclaim,
    Who saves the souls that dare depend
    For pardon on his name.

2. Whoe'er in Him believes
    Of all the ransom'd race
    A pardon absolute receives
    Thro' his redeeming grace.
    I take him at his word,
    On Jesus' name rely,
    And witness, that my pardning Lord
    Doth freely justify! (p. 201)

Ac. 10:46, *For they heard them speak with tongues, and magnify God.*

1. The wonders they claim
    Are wonders of grace,
    And sav'd by his name
    They publish his praise:
    Rejoicing & blessing
    Their Lord from above,
    Their faith they express in
    The language of love:

340

2. A language unknown
    Till Him they receive
    Whose Spirit alone
    Doth utterance give:
    But blest with his favor
    Thro' life they commend
    Their merciful Saviour,
    And world without end. (p. 203)

Ac. 11:1, *The brethren heard that the Gentiles also had received the word of God.*

1. What numbers now are found
    Who call the Saviour Lord,
    Yet never heard the joyful sound,
    The reconciling word!
    The Christian name they take,
    Nor see the way to heaven,
    Or know that God for Jesus' sake
    Hath all their sins forgiven.

2. O might they now receive
    The word of pardning grace!
    Gentiles baptiz'd, in Christ believe,
    The world's Desire embrace,
    By faith rejoice to know
    The truth of Jesus' love,
    And gladden all his saints below,
    And all his saints above. (p. 206)

Ac. 11:7, *Arise, Peter, slay & eat.*

1. 'Tis slaughter in the outward sign;
    In the reality
    An holy sacrifice Divine
    Of sinful souls we see,
    When by the Spirit's two-edg'd sword
    The beast in man is slain,
    That sinners thro' the gospel-word
    May reason's life regain.

2. Sinners by the commandment kill'd,
   And sav'd by Jesus' grace
Experience in themselves reveal'd
   The vital holiness:
With Peter thus we kill & eat,
   The heavenly charge fulfil,
Our soul's repast, our pleasant meat
   To do our Father's will. (p. 209)

Ac. 11:8, *Not so, Lord: for nothing common or unclean hath at any time entred into my mouth.*

I want the gospel-purity,
   Th'implanted righteousness of God:
Jesus, reveal thyself to me,
   And wash me in thy hallowing blood;
Enter thyself & cast out sin,
   Thy nature spread thro' every part,
And nothing common or unclean
   Shall ever more pollute my heart. (p. 210)

Ac. 11:9, *What God hath cleansed, that call not thou common.*

Jesus expiring on the tree
   Hath purg'd the universal sin,
Redeem'd from all iniquity,
   And made a world of sinners clean:
Yes; the whole earth is wash'd in blood,
   And every soul beneath the skies
May now be offer'd up to God
   A pure, accepted sacrifice. (p. 210)

Ac. 11:10, *And this was done three times; & all were drawn up again into heaven.*

The thrice-repeated vision seals
   The truth inviolably sure;
Drawn up again to heaven, it tells
   That all in that bright place are pure:

Nothing unclean can enter there;
But whom the Lord hath sanctified
Shall mount, & meet him in the air
And shine forever at his side. (pp. 210–11)

Ac. 11:12, *Moreover these six brethren accompanied me, &c.*

1. The church's servant should be wise,
   Appearances of evil shun,
   Walk in the light, abhor disguise,
   And nothing act unseen, alone,
   But vouchers for his conduct take
   For Jesus' and the gospel's sake.

2. Bold the attested truth to tell,
   He should in Jesus' footsteps tread,
   And simply to the word appeal,
   In secret have I nothing said,
   In secret have I nothing done,
   But all my life to all is known. (p. 211)[35]

Ac. 11:14, *He shall tell thee words, whereby thou and all thy house shall be saved.*

1. Happy the man divinely led
   A minister of grace to find,
   A preacher of good news indeed,
   Of Christ, the Saviour of mankind!
   Happy the man, who truly poor
   The words of life eternal hears:
   By faith he knows his pardon sure,
   When Jesus to his heart appears.

2. Teaching his house to serve the Lord,
   On them he brings the blessing down,
   And listening to the gospel-word
   They feel their joy on earth begun;

35. [Verse 1 appears in *Poet. Works*, XII, p. 255.]

Salvation now they all receive,
Th'experience of their sins forgiven,
The blameless life of Jesus live
And then his endless life in heaven. (p. 212)

Ac. 11:17, *Forasmuch then as God gave them the like gift as he did
unto us, what was I, that I could withstand God?*

1. And what are we, who still withstand
   Our God, & thwart his Spirit's design,
   Impose the yoke of man's command
   On souls that know the grace Divine?
   Whom God receives we oft reject,
   Part of the church invisible
   We force into a separate sect,
   And dare exclude them from our pale.

2. New terms of fellowship we frame,
   And modes & forms, & orders new,
   And absolute obedience claim
   To rules the Scriptures never knew:
   More we invent; th'important stress
   On buttons,[a] caps,[b] and ruffles[c] lay,[36]
   As they of our religion's dress
   Were surely sav'd, & only They.

3. Thus let us God withstand no more,
   No more usurp the Saviour's right,
   But bow to true religion's power,
   And honour all the sons of light,
   Into our hearts and church receive
   As saints begotten from above
   Whoe'er in our dear Lord believe,
   And live by faith, which works by love. (pp. 213–14)

36. (a) the F. [i.e., Friends], (b) the B. [i. e. , the Moravians], (c) the M. [i.e. , Methodists. Wesley mistakenly wrote (3) for (c) in the MS. Also (a) is written above the line *preceding* the word "buttons"in the MS.]

Ac. 11:20, *Some of them were men of Cyprus and Cyrene, which when they were come to Antioch, spake, etc.*

1. God employs whome'er he will
    To spread the joyful sound,
    Fills some private men with zeal
    An infant church to found:
    Outcasts, his Apostles rise,
    And vagrants poor, by all abhor'd,
    Fools, they proselyte the wise
    By preaching Christ the Lord.

2. Jesus, still with favor see
    The meanest of the croud,
    Scorn'd by man, but sent by Thee
    To preach thy saving blood:
    Let the faithless world disown,
    So Thou thy pardning grace reveal,
    Make by us salvation known,
    And thus our mission seal. (pp. 216–17)

Ac. 11:23, *He exhorted them all that with purpose of heart they would cleave unto the Lord.*

1. O that we all who now believe
    Might to our dear Redeemer cleave,
        Firmly resolv'd in heart
    To hold, & never let him go,
    Till from himself, we surely know
        He will not let us part.

2. Saviour, in whom by faith we live,
    Grace upon grace persist to give;
        Thy church shall then abide
    In thee, & patient to the end
    And faithful unto death, ascend,
        Thy own unspotted bride. (p. 218)

Ac. 11:24, *He was a good man, and full of the Holy Ghost, and of faith.*

> Faith & the Holy Ghost bestow'd
> On man, can make the evil good:
> And such who form'd them by his grace,
> God only knows his saints to praise:
> And saints all other praise disown
> But that which comes from God alone. (p. 219)

Ac. 11:26, *A whole year they assembled themselves with the church, and taught much people.*

1.　　Surely the worldly god
　　　　Was by a Stronger bound,
　　When the loud cry of blood
　　　　Did thro' the city sound,
　　The place, where Satan reign'd alone
　　Till Jesus preach'd o'return'd his throne.

2.　　The same Almighty Hand
　　　　Doth now restrain the foe,
　　While at our Lord's command
　　　　His bleeding cross we show,
　　Assembled with his people meet,
　　And teach, where Satan keeps his seat.

3.　　Thus may we still improve
　　　　The precious time of rest,
　　And preach the Saviour's love
　　　　That all with pardon blest
　　May know, & imitate the Lamb
　　And truly bear the Christian Name. (p. 221)

Ac. 11:30, *Which also they did, and sent it to the elders, by the hands of Barnabas & Saul.*

1. The sacrifice of Christian love
    For Apostolic hands is meet;
 Alms which acceptance find above
    Remembred at the mercy-seat,
 The priests should to their brethren bear,
 And make the poor their choicest care.

2. The sacred charge they undertook
    They to their successors commend,
 That each after the poor may look,
    Their guide, their father, & their friend,
 That each into his heart may take
 And serve & feed for Jesus' sake. (p. 222)

Ac. 12:1, *Now about that time, Herod the king stretched out his hands to vex certain of the church.*

The power he had from God receiv'd
 He impiously employ'd
 Against that God whose Spirit he griev'd,
    Whose servants he destroy'd;
 Stretch'd out his cruel hands, to tear
    And slay them with the sword,
 Nor fear'd the vengeful wrath to dare
    Of their Almighty Lord. (p. 223)

Ac. 12:17, *But he beckning unto them with the hand to hold their peace, declared unto them how the Lord, etc.*

1. Should we not hold our peace
    When God hath heard our prayer,
 And Jesus' witnesses
    His mighty works declare,
 Who hath the strange deliverance wrought,
 And spirits out of prison brought.

2.   When Him alone they praise
        With meek & lowly fear,
      Let us partake the grace
        In fixt attention hear,
      Admire his mercy, truth, & power,
      And Christ with silent awe adore.

3.   Then let our Jesus' fame
        Throughout the church resound,
      Publish his saving Name
        To earth's remotest bound,
      Whose only love a way could find
      To loose the souls of all mankind. (pp. 232–3)

Ac. 12:18, *There was no small stir among the soldiers, what was become of Peter.*

1.   The troubled sea can never rest;
      The storm they carry in their breast,
        When gusts of passion rise:
      Pride, malice, wrath, & every sin
      Keep up the hurricane within,
        And mingle earth & skies.

2.   But most disturb'd the wicked are,
      If Christ their lawful captive bear
        Beyond the reach of hell,
      Of Satan ready to devour,
      And save a soul from all their power,
        And in Himself conceal. (pp. 233–4)

Ac. 12:22, *The people gave a shout saying, It is the voice of a god, & not of a man.*

1.   A prince who bears the Christian name
        Should flattery with abhorrence shun,
      But praises above all disclaim
        And honours due to God alone,
      Nor dare to rival the Most-High,
      Or the great King of kings defy.

2. The sole immortal Potentate,
   His dread prerogative maintains,
   Inthron'd in everlasting state
   And jealous of his glory reigns
   While monarchs mingle with the rest,
   And make the worms a royal feast. (pp. 235–6)

Ac. 12:24, *But the word of God grew & multiplied.*

1. If Thou the word bestow,
   If Thou the preachers bless,
   Thy church will always grow,
   Thy witnesses increase,
   And help'd by every obstacle
   Thy gospel over all prevail.

2. Didst Thou not give the seed
   We in thy name have sown,
   And send us forth indeed,
   To make thy goodness known?
   Give then the multiplied success,
   And let the world our Lord confess. (p. 237)

Ac. 13:2, *As they ministred to the Lord, and fasted, the Holy Ghost said, &c.* [37]

Who minister the gospel-word,
And truly fast unto the Lord,
   And seek his face in prayer,
To them He doth unfold his mind,
(Whate'er he hath for each design'd),
   And all his will declare. (p. 238)

37. [Above Ac. 13:1 in Wesley's shorthand is written: "J. 21" (January 21).]

Ac. 13:3, *And when they had fasted, & prayed, and laid their hands on them, they sent them away.*

1. The days of abstinence were come,
   The Bridegroom now was taken home
       To highest heaven restor'd;
   The Master's mind his servants knew,
   Who oft in prayer & fastings too
       Obey'd his parting word.

2. But chiefly when their Lord's intent
   Call'd forth some chosen instrument,
       Fasting to prayer they join'd,
   Till Christ in his appointed ways
   Reveal'd the counsels of his grace,
       And shew'd them all his mind.

3. Jesus from them we learn to' obey
   With sacred abstinence to pray,
       That God his church would bless
   With chosen, Apostolic men,
   And preachers by his Spirit ordain,
       And give their word success. (pp. 239–40)

Ac. 13:6, *And when they had gone through the isle unto Paphos, they found a certain sorcerer.*

But now (if we believe the fiend)
His magical illusions end:
We Vote, Resolve, Enact, Decree
"There's no such thing as sorcery!
"It might be once at Paphos found;
"But Britain's isle is holy ground:
"And if he here dispute our power,
"The devil himself shall be no more!" (p. 241)

Ac. 13:7, *The deputy . . . who desired to hear the word of God.*

1. Not by the crafty wizard sway'd
      The prudent man his judgment show'd,
    Not of the slander'd truth afraid,
      But listening to the word of God,
    For God infus'd the good desire
    And stirr'd a sinner up t'inquire.

2. The work of grace is then begun,
      When first a soul inclines his ear,
    Willing to find the God unknown
      Proclaim'd by Jesus' messenger,
    Ready the doctrine to receive
    That Christ can still on earth forgive. (p. 241)[38]

Ac. 13:9, *Then Saul (who is also*[39] *called Paul) filled with the Holy Ghost, set his eyes on him, and said.*

1.   Ye that all your powers exert
        The gospel to gainsay,
      Jesus' doctrine to pervert,
        And mock his perfect way:
      Ye that seek our faith t'o'rethrow,
      Who in his blood redemption feel,
        Leagued with our malicious foe,
        Ye serve the cause of hell.

2.   Full of Satan's subtlety
        Ye all his arts employ,
      With the felon old agree
        Who would our souls destroy:
      Children of that Wicked one
      Your father's deeds ye gladly do,
        Slander whom ye have not known,
        And lie, and murther too.

38. [Verse 1 appears in *Poet. Works*, XII, pp. 274–5.]
39. [Wesley followed *Notes*. The AV reads: "also is."]

3.   Haters of all righteousness
        Haters of Christ, ye are:
   Judgments on your souls shall seize,
      If still his wrath ye dare;
  God shall strike your spirits blind,
And leave in nature's penal chains,
    Earnest of the wrath behind,
      And hell's eternal pains.

4.   Turn, while grace may yet be found,
      Accept a Guide from heaven,
  Grace doth more than sin abound,
     To every sinner given:
  Seek, thou infidel, and find,
The glorious Sun in Jesus see,
    Him who shines on all mankind
     And offers faith to thee. (pp. 242–3)

Ac. 13:17, *The God of this people chose our fathers, & exalted the people, when they dwelt as strangers in the land, etc.*

1.   The Lord our fathers chose,
      And ransom'd from their foes;
  Slaves they long in Egypt dwelt,
    Subject to the world's command,
All the power of sin they felt,
    All the weight of Satan's hand.

2.   But God was pleas'd to raise
      A people to his praise,
  Strangers to themselves & Him,
    Groaning in captivity,
Jesus mighty to redeem
    Bared his arm, & set them free.

3.   Thro' grace the threefold yoke
      Off from their souls he broke,
  Brought them thro' the parted tide,
    Children of a pardning God,
By his merits justified,
    Sav'd by his redeeming blood.

4.   Who didst deliver them,
          Us, Lord, ev'n us redeem;
      Arm of God, thy strength put on,
      Wake as in the antient days,
      Make thy great salvation known,
      Now reveal the gospel-grace! (p. 247)

Ac. 13:24, *When John had first preached before his coming the baptism of repentance to all the people of Israel.*

1. Repentance sincere
       Is preach'd unto all,
    But few that appear
       And answer the call
    The true preparation
       From Jesus receive
    And then by his passion
       In paradise live.

2. Repentance alone
       Makes ready his way
    Who sets up his throne
       In them that obey:
    To feel our condition
       The grace He imparts,
    And breaks by contrition,
       And enters our hearts.

3. Now, Lord, (if we know
       Thy work is before)
    The pardon bestow,
       The kingdom restore;
    From all condemnation
       Thy mourners set free,
    And bring thy salvation
       With heaven — to me! (pp. 251–2)

Ac. 13:26, *Men & brethren, children of the stock of Abraham, and whosoever among you feareth God, to you is the word, etc.*

Brethren, the gospel hear,
Ye all are Abraham's line,
Ye all the righteous God may fear,
And taste the love divine,
The promis'd Seed embrace,
Your father's steps pursue;
The word of truth and saving grace
Is surely sent to you:
The soul-converting word
To sinners we proclaim,
Redemption in a dying Lord,
And peace by Jesus' name:
And while our God imparts
The Comforter from heaven,
The word is sent into your hearts,
And seals your sins forgiven. (pp. 252–3)

Ac. 13:27, *Because they knew him not, nor yet the voices of the prophets, which are read every sabbath-day, etc.*

While, as a Jew, thy word I read,
The veil over my heart is spread;
The veil of unbelief remove,
And shew me, Lord, thy pardning love,
That when *my* Lord I know, & see,
No longer by rejecting Thee,
But by obedience to thy will
I may the prophecies fulfil. (p. 253)

Ac. 13:28, *They found no cause of death in him.*

No cause of death, no slightest blame
In Christ the human judge could find,
But God in that unblemish'd Lamb
Beheld the sins of all mankind! (p. 253)[40]

40. [*Rep. Verse*, No. 192, p. 228.]

Ac. 13:31, *He was seen of them — who are his witnesses unto the people.*

> Jesus risen from the dead
>   We truly testify,
> By the Spirit of our Head
>   Translated to the sky;
> Dead to all the things below
> We set our hearts on joys above,
>   Joys which from his presence flow,
>   And make the heaven of love. (p. 254)

Ac. 13:32-3, *And we declare unto you glad tidings, how that the promise which was made unto the fathers, etc.*

1.   Let all mankind give ear
          To God's authentick word,
      The joyful tidings hear
          Of Christ to life restor'd;
      The precious promises are seal'd
      Are all in Jesus' rise fulfill'd!

2.   The God of truth & grace
          Hath glorified his Son,
      That our devoted race
          Might live thro' Him alone,
      That all might after Him arise,
      And share his kingdom in the skies. (p. 254)

Ac. 13:33, *Thou art my son, this day have I begotten thee.*

> God who bad the grave restore
>   His well-beloved Son,
> Made by his almighty power
>   The Filial Godhead known,
> First-begotten from the dead
> He rais'd him up, our souls to bless,
>   Sent him, that our quickned Head
>   Might all his members raise. (pp. 254-5)

Ac. 13:34, *And because he raised him from the dead, no more to return to corruption, he spake thus, I will give, etc.*[41]

1. Father of our glorious Lord,
       Thee we praise & magnify:
    Thou hast verified thy word
       Rais'd him up, no more to die:
    Thus thou dost the blessings give
       Certain, solid, firm, and sure,
    Which the faithful all receive,
       Which from age to age endure.

2. By his rising from the dead
       We the life of grace obtain,
    From our heart-corruptions freed,
       New-begot, & born again:
    Thou from sin hast lifted up,
       Hast our trespasses forgiven,
    Fill'd us with a living hope,
       Earnest sure of all our heaven. (p. 255)

Ac. 13:35, *Thou shalt not suffer thy Holy one to see corruption.*

Essence of Holiness Divine,
   Thou couldst not, Lord, corruption see:
Thy flesh, to all of Adam's line
   The seed of immortality,
Doth now to all thy saints impart
A taste of glory in their heart. (pp. 255–6)

Ac. 13:38–9, *Be it known unto you, men & brethren, that through this man is preached unto you the forgiveness of sins: etc.*

1. Be it to Adam's offspring known!
    Redeem'd thro' Jesus Christ alone
       Ye all may boldly claim
    A pardon purchas'd with his blood,
    By his authority bestow'd
       And offer'd in his name.

41. [Wesley quoted *Notes* and not the AV.]

356

2. By Him ye all are justified,
   Thro' his atoning blood applied
       The benefit receive;
   The Holy Ghost his peace imparts,
   And writes forgiveness on your hearts
       The moment ye believe. (pp. 256–7)

Ac. 13:39, *And by him all that believe are justified from all things, from which ye could not be justified, etc.*

1. The blood of goats & bullocks slain
   Could not efface your guilty stain;
       By moral rectitude,
   By works, & partial righteousness
   Ye never could the wrath appease,
       Or buy the grace of God.

2. But if on Christ ye dare rely,
   Your sins & crimes of deepest die
       Are purg'd & done away,
   And blest with absolution here,
   Ye shall with confidence appear,
       And triumph in that day! (p. 257)

Ac. 13:42, *The Gentiles besought that these words might be preached to them the next sabbath.*

1. When we long the word to hear,
   To salvation we draw near:
   But we should not idly stay
   (Once directed in the way),
   Stop in good desires, or rest
   Short of our Redeemer's breast.

2. Lord, the love of truth impart,
   Bless me with a docile heart,
   With a full, effectual will
   All thy pleasure to fulfil,
   Constant in the cause Divine,
   Thine to live, entirely thine. (p. 259)

THE UNPUBLISHED POETRY OF CHARLES WESLEY

Ac. 13:43, *They persuaded them to continue in the grace of God.*

> When sinners have the call obey'd,
>   The grace of Jesus known,
> We still incourage & persuade
>   The converts to go on,
> With constant faith to persevere
>   In their Redeemer's love,
> And look for all his blessings here,
>   And all his joys above. (p. 259)

Ac. 13:45, *But when the Jews saw the multitudes, they were filled with envy, & spake against those things, &c.*

> 1. Who now themselves the church profess,
>   Of outward priviledges proud,
>   Intrusted with the words of grace,
>   The lively oracles of God,
>   They dare oppose & vilify,
>   And every gospel-truth deny.

> 2. With envious indignation fill'd,
>   They now the flocking people see,
>   Afraid, lest all that hear should yield,
>   And give their hearts, O Lord, to Thee,
>   Lest the whole frantic multitude
>   Should feel redemption in thy blood. (pp. 260–1)

Ac. 13:49, *And the word of the Lord was published throughout all the region.*

> 1. When Jesus imparts
>   His pardon and peace,
>   The faith of our hearts
>   Our mouth must confess,
>   Throughout the whole region
>   We publish the word,
>   The life of religion,
>   The love of our Lord.

2. Wherever we go,
   The tidings we spread
   That sinners may know
   Him risen indeed,
   Who hath by his passion
   Redeem'd us from thrall,
   And purchas'd salvation
   And heaven for all. (p. 264)

Ac. 14:1, *In Iconium, they went both together into the synagogue.*[42]

The martyrs' blood, the church's seed
Is by her banish'd servants spread,
   And scatter'd far & wide;
Where'er the confessors are driven,
They testify the world forgiven
   Thro' Jesus crucified. (p. 267)

Ac. 14:2, *The unbelieving Jews stirred up the Gentiles, and made their minds evil-affected against the brethren.*

1.   Who refuse the truth t'obey
        Would all its friends oppress,
     Others turn out of the way
        To life and happiness,
     Alienate th'unwary mind,
   Lest sinners should their Lord approve,
     Find what Jews disdain to find,
        And rest in Jesus' love.

2.   Outward Jews, who vainly still
        The Christian faith profess,
     Stir the heathens up & fill
        Their hearts with bitterness.
     Sinners they provoke to hate
   The followers of the bleeding Lamb,
     Harden in their lost estate,
        And keep in Satan's name. (p. 268)

42. [Above this verse in Wesley's shorthand is written: "J. 30" (January 30).]

Ac. 14:5, *And there was an assault made both of the Gentiles, and also of the Jews with their rulers, etc.*

1. Gentiles and Jews, by malice join'd,
   Professors formal, and profane,
   Too oft in strictest league we find
   The throne of Satan to maintain;
   And guardians of the public peace
   Assist the sons of wickedness.

2. Rulers themselves transgress the laws
   In outraging the church of God,
   Fierce champions for an hellish cause,
   Mixt with the furious multitude,
   T'assault the men by fiends abhor'd
   And stone the servants of the Lord. (p. 270)

Ac. 14:6, *They were ware of it, and fled unto Lystra, &c.*

1. The flight of those by Jesus sent
   That sinners may His grace obtain,
   To some a fearful punishment,
   To others is an heavenly gain;
   To every faithful soul that hears
   Christ in His exil'd messengers.

2. Instructed by his Spirit, we know
   Whene'er He wills us to retreat:
   And if he bids us face the foe,
   To every cruel wrong submit,
   We suffer on our Saviour's cross,
   As Martyrs in his blessed cause. (p. 271)[43]

Ac. 14:8, *There was a certain man at Lystra impotent, &c.*

While without strength we were,
   Unsav'd, unsanctified,
Our ruin'd nature to repair
   Jesus for sinners died:

---

43. [Verse 1 appears in *Poet. Works*, XII, p. 290.]

Our impotence of soul
He only can remove,
And make a world of cripples whole
Thro' his forgiving love. (p. 272)

Ac. 14:9, *The same heard Paul: who steadfastly beholding him, &*
perceiving that he had faith to be healed.

The Apostolic word
Ev'n now proclaim'd I hear,
But look for pardon from the Lord
And not the Messenger:
Saviour, Thou see'st my heart:
Faith to be heal'd I have:
Command my evil to depart,
My soul this moment save. (p. 272)

Ac. 14:10, *He said with a loud voice, Stand upright on thy feet.*
And he leaped, and walked.

Listening I wait to hear
The inward voice Divine,
Which doth the guilty conscience clear,
And whispers "Christ is mine;"
To feeble souls restores
The strength of active grace,
And bids me rise with all my powers
My pardning God to praise. (pp. 272–3)

Ac. 14:10, *And he leaped and walked.*

Jesus, thy kind command
My fallen soul shall feel,
With strength renew'd spring up, & stand
Prepar'd to do thy will;
The lame for joy shall leap
While faith the power supplies,
Thy steps pursue, thy statutes keep,
And run, & take the prize. (p. 273)

Ac. 14:11, *They lift up their voices saying, The gods are come down in the likeness of men.*

1.   God did indeed come down,
      In human likeness seen,
    He put our nature on,
      And dwelt with sinful men,
But few the heavenly Guest receiv'd
Or Christ th'eternal God believ'd.

2.   Unnumbred miracles
      Were wrought by Jesus' name;
    Who still his power reveals
      In every age the same,
And multitudes by grace restor'd
Confess the virtue of their Lord. (pp. 273–4)

Ac. 14:15, *We preach unto you, that ye should turn from these vanities unto the living God, which, etc.*

1. Sinners, your idols vain forego,
    The Source from whom your blessings flow
      With cordial love receive,
    Fountain of being & of power,
    The one eternal God adore,
      And to his glory live.

2. Who built this universal frame,
    Doth he not all your homage claim,
      So short of his desert?
    Whose Providence in earth & skies
    To man, his fav'rite creature, cries
      My son, give me thy heart! (p. 275)

Ac. 14:16, *Who in times past suffered all nations to walk in their own ways.*

1. Turn then to Him, ye heathens turn,
   Who hath with much long-suffering borne
      Your past idolatries,
   And left you each in his own way
   Far from the living God to stray,
      Far from the paths of peace.

2. Heathens baptiz'd, who never knew
   The pardning God, He suffer'd you,
      Idolators profane,
   Lovers of earth, yourselves to please
   With empty forms of godliness,
      And take his Name in vain. (p. 275)

Ac. 14:17, *Nevertheless he left not himself without witness, in that he did good, &c.*

1. Yet did he not his offspring leave,
   But frequent proofs vouchsafe to give
      Of his Paternal love,
   With fruitful showers of timely rain
   With bread that chears the heart of man
      He bless'd us from above.

2. Whate'er we have 'twas God bestow'd,
   The power to taste our pleasant food
      His bounteous mercy gave;
   We all injoy thro' Him alone,
   Who gave at last his only Son
      Our sinful souls to save. (p. 276)

Ac. 14:22, *Confirming the souls of the disciples, and, &c.*

1. Saviour, thy preaching servants bless,
      When most we suffer in thy cause
   Our labours crown with full success,
      And spread the doctrine of thy cross;

As vessels of confirming grace
Give us to build thy people up,
To root and ground the pardon'd race
In loving faith, and patient hope.

2. O may we still the truth declare
Which flesh and blood cannot receive,
Our brethren for the lot prepare
Of all resolv'd in Thee to live;
Teach us their calling here to show
Which ascertains the glittering prize,
The narrow path of sacred woe
That leads thy followers to the skies.

3. Arm'd with thy mind and doubly blest
With stedfast faith & patience too,
We shrink not from the fiery test,
But Thee to Calvary pursue;
In trouble's fiercest furnace tried
Experiencing thy perfect power,
The great distress we long abide,
And bear it to our latest hour.

4. This is the consecrated way,
The true and royal way to God!
Here will we with our Captain stay,
And strive, resisting unto blood:
The suffering and reward are sure;
And who thy daily cross sustain,
And faithful unto death endure,
We, only we, thy crown shall gain. (pp. 278–9)[44]

Ac. 14:23, *They commended them to the Lord, on whom, &c.*

1. May we not trust our flock to Him,
To Him our children leave,
Who did their precious souls redeem,
Who did their pardon give?

44. [Verses 1, 2, and 4 appear in *Poet. Works*, XII, p. 293.]

Jesus the saving grace bestow'd,
   And will His saints defend,
Who hang on their redeeming God,
   Till faith in vision end.

2. Wherefore in sure & stedfast hope,
    Into those hands Divine
My charge I joyfully give up,
    Whom Thou hast mark'd for thine:
My ministry they cannot need
    Who trust their Saviour's love,
Their heart is fixt, their life is hid,
    Their souls are safe above. (p. 280)[45]

Ac. 15:3, *They passed through Phenice, and Samaria, declaring the conversion of the Gentiles; and they caused, etc.*

1. Wherever we go
    Who Jesus proclaim
The wonders we show
    Perform'd by his name,
The fruits of his passion
    Which sinners receive,
The present salvation
    Of all that believe.

2. Poor heathens confess
    The power of his word,
The doctrine of grace,
    And turn to their Lord:
In sin the most harden'd
    By love are subdued,
And multitudes pardon'd
    Thro' Jesus's blood.

3. His church will approve
    The work He hath done,
Rejoice in his love
    To sinners made known;

45. [Verse 1 appears in *Poet. Works*, XII, p. 294.]

Praise, honour, & blessing
To Jesus we owe
For daily increasing
His household below.

4. Fresh matter of joy
Is multiplied grace;
It bids us employ
Our lives to his praise:
For every believer
His grace we adore,
And triumph forever
When time is no more. (p. 284)

Ac. 15:5, *Saying, that it was needful to circumcise them, &c.*

Burthens which ourselves did bear
We would on others lay
Till He all the truth declare,
And bring the perfect day:
Sun of righteousness, appear,
And light we in thy light shall see,
See, our whole of duty here,
Our heaven — is Love to thee. (p. 286)

Ac. 15:8–9, *And God, [. . .] gave them the Holy Ghost, [. . .]
purifying their hearts by faith.*

1. Holy Ghost, my heart inspire,
And by thy breath remove
Every vain and base desire
That fights against thy love;
Purge the sins which I confess,
Thro' Jesus' hallowing blood applied,
All this fleshly filthiness,
And all this hell of pride.

2. Spirit of faith in Jesus' blood,
Who dost my pardon seal,
Depths of an expiring God
With Christ my Lord reveal,

Witnessing that Christ is mine,
Essential holiness impart,
Perfect charity divine,
And purity of heart. (p. 554)

Ac. 15:9, *He put no difference between us and them.*

When first I feel thy blood applied,
And know that mine Thou art,
Lord, I am fully justified,
And pure my sprinkled heart;
I am redeem'd for thy dear sake
From all iniquity,
And God doth no distinction make
Betwixt a saint & me. (p. 288)

Ac. 15:11, *We shall be saved, even as they.*

1. The worst, the foulest slaves of sin
   May this salvation know,
   Thro' faith in Jesus' blood made clean
   And wash'd as white as snow:
   Heathens, whene'er to Him they turn,
   He takes their sins away,
   Equall'd with us who long have borne
   The burthen of the day.

2. One only way for both remains;
   The fountain open'd wide:
   And lo, we lose our inbred stains
   In our Redeemer's side;
   Thro' his almighty grace alone
   Redeem'd we both remove
   To cast our crowns before his throne,
   And sing his praise above. (p. 292)

Ac. 15:14, *God at the first did visit the Gentiles, to take out of them a people for his name.*

1.   Our all-redeeming Lord
In honour of his word,
Hath in every age and place
    Pour'd the Spirit from above,
Visited the sinful race,
    Sav'd us by his pardning love,

2.   From earth & sin set free,
Jesus, we worship Thee:
Therefore hast Thou brought us forth,
    That we may thy grace proclaim,
Testify thy saving worth,
    Spread the wonders of thy Name.

3.   O might we truly bear
The Christian character!
Be indeed what we profess,
    Glory to our Saviour give,
All thy holy mind express,
    Partners of thy nature live! (pp. 293–4)

Ac. 15:19, *My sentence is, that we trouble not them which from among the Gentiles are turned to God.*

Should we not young beginners spare
The burthens which they cannot bear,
    The legal yoke remove?
The Sovereign Unity Divine
No other worship doth enjoin
    Than pure & simple love. (p. 295)

Ac. 15:22, *Then pleased it the Apostles & elders to send chosen men to Antioch, &c.*

1. Such wisdom, watchfulness and love
    Ye Apostolic Fathers show,
And thus your heavenly mission prove,
    Who rule the Saviour's church below:

The church he purchas'd with his blood
Cherish, & guard with kindest care,
Instructed by the Shepherd good
The weakest in your arms to bear.

2. Jesus, that precious grace of thine
To thy assembled church impart,
And fill with charity Divine
And reign in every pastor's heart:
Thy zeal for God in them be shewn,
Thy love for souls in them appear,
And all who see their lives shall own
Th'Apostles' successors are here! (p. 296)

Ac. 15:33–4, *They were let go in peace: notwithstanding, &c.*

1.   God to Apostolic men
An holy freedom leaves,
By some secret way unseen
The true direction gives:
Oft His servant's heart inclines
To that or this distinguish'd place,
Answers thus His own designs,
And manifests His grace.

2.   By the Spirit's instinct led,
And not by flesh & blood,
Let the minister proceed
As call'd & sent of God:
God who joins his witnesses,
Doth each from each far off remove:
All things work t'ensure the peace
Of those that Jesus love. (p. 301)[46]

46. [Verse 1 appears in *Poet. Works*, XII, p. 309.]

Ac. 15:35, *Paul & Barnabas continued in Antioch, preaching the word of the Lord.*

1. The word whose energy we feel,
   Which in our hearts doth richly dwell
     We constantly declare:
   The fire shut up fatigues our breast;
   We must speak on, forbid to rest,
     And never can forbear.

2. To all the gospel we proclaim,
   The word of peace thro' Jesus' Name,
     Of righteousness and love,
   Which saves & wholly sanctifies,
   Assures us of our calling's prize,
     And crowns with life above. (pp. 301–2)

Ac. 16:1, *Behold, a certain disciple was there, the son of a certain woman which was a Jewess, and believed.*

Who wisely for her offspring cares,
May find the answer of her prayers
  And tears before the throne,
Anticipate her full reward,
A zealous servant of the Lord
  Beholding in her son. (p. 306)

Ac. 16:2, *Which was well reported of by the brethren.*

Christians, who know the price of grace,
May virtue in another praise,
  The gift of Jesus own;
Love, only love, from envy free
His neighbour's excellence can see
  Admiring God alone. (p. 306)

Ac. 16:5, *So were the churches established in the faith, and increased in number daily.*

1.   Lord, into thy harvest send
The men foreknown by thee,
Men who may thy word commend
In true simplicity,
All thy written counsel tell,
As taught by wisdom from above,
Fill'd with Apostolic zeal,
With meek & lowly love.

2.   Then thy watred church below
Shall flourish & increase,
More & more in numbers grow,
In faith and holiness;
Millions added to thy fold
Shall do whate'er thy laws require,
Live in Thee, like those of old,
Like those in Thee expire.[47] (p. 308)

Ac. 16:7, *They assayed to go into Bithynia, but the Spirit suffered them not.*

1. Supremely wise, supremely kind
God doth not act by fancy blind
And most[48] refuse to call:
The reasons of his choice are known
To his omniscient Spirit alone
Who loving is to all.

2. But men are blind, presumptuous men
Who would th'Unsearchable explain
And prove his mercy free;
In vain they cloak their partial pride,
And forge, (their ignorance to hide)
The *horrible decree.*

47. [The last line of this poem is crossed out, but no substitute is made.]
48. [In the MS "some" is written in the margin as an alternative to "most."]

3. The friends whom most we wish to save
   No power to serve their souls we have,
        Nor know the reason why;
   But know the reason cannot be
   That God from all eternity
        Had sentenc'd them to die.

4. Here then we humbly, Lord, confess
   Our folly and shortsightedness,
        For resignation pray;
   Suffice it now, that Thou art Love,
   And wilt, O God, the veil remove
        In that decisive day. (pp. 309–10)

Ac. 16:9, *Come over to Macedonia, and help us.*

1. Thee I cannot seek in vain
        With resign'd simplicity:
   Thou hast various ways t'explain
        What thy love designs for me:
   Patient if I wait to know,
        Thou thy purpose shalt reveal,
   Teach me when and where to go,
        Manifest thy perfect will.

2. If Thou thwart my best design,
        My submission, Lord, approve;
   Then by clearest light divine
        Shew th'intention of thy love,
   Then the gospel-door display,
        Fill'd with active knowing zeal
   Send me all thy words t'obey,
        All thy counsels to fulfil. (p. 310)

Ac. 16:10, *Immediately we endeavoured to go into Macedonia,
assuredly gathering that the Lord, etc.*

When we have the Master's mind
        Plainly in our hearts made known,
Then we cast the world behind,
        Swift with Jesus' message run,

Dare not lose a moment's space,
In his name on sinners call,
Spread the news of pardning grace,
Preach the Lamb that died for all. (pp. 310–11)

Ac. 16:15, *She constrained us.*

A worthy labourer of the Lord
Never of his own accord
Desires our guest to be:
Nor will to invitation yield,
Till by the violence compel'd
Of fervent charity. (pp. 314–15)

Ac. 16:18, *Paul being grieved, turned & said to the spirit, &c.*

Servants of Christ the witness vain
Reject, the praise that comes from man:
And will their Apostolic zeal
Accept the praise that comes from hell? (p. 316)

[Ac. 16:30], *What must I do to be saved?*

1. O Thou who dost not put to pain
    The creatures of thy will,
    Why am I thus, a wretched man,
    An helpless sinner still?
    For ever strugling to get free,
    Why am I yet a slave,
    If saved indeed I fain woud be,
    And Thou art near to save?

2. Out of the deep of inbred woe
    To Thee, my God, I cry,
    And ask the hindring thing to know,
    And urge thee to reply:
    Able if now to make me clean,
    If willing now Thou art,
    Why am I unredeem'd from sin,
    And unrenew'd in heart?

3. Dost Thou with-hold thy pardning love,
    Thy sanctifying grace,
    My old backslidings to reprove,
    My past unfaithfulness?
    My hasty, vehement spirit to break
    Dost Thou thy help defer,
    And leave me thus to knock, and seek,
    And ask in fruitless prayer?

4. Is there some cursed thing unknown
    From which I will not part,
    A bar which nature fears to own,
    An idol in my heart?
    Some base reserve, some bosom-lust
    Thou knowst if yet I have,
    Which makes me secretly mistrust
    Thy readiness to save.

5. Surely I woud in Thee believe,
    I own Thee good and true
    Thou art almighty to forgive
    Almighty to renew;
    Thou canst into my soul derive [49]
    Such purity and power,
    That I with sin no more shall strive,
    Shall yield to sin no more.

49. [The use of the verb "derive" in the sense of "to cause to come, to bring down" was already obsolete in Wesley's day. The *Oxford English Dictionary* notes that John Fletcher (1772) speaks of "those who derive putrefaction *into* their bones."]

6. Thou canst my inbred foe expel,
    Its last remains erase,
   Hallow my sinless soul, and seal
    With persevering grace:
   Thou canst my sinless soul assure
    That I shall ne'er remove
   But faithful unto death endure,
    And reign with Thee above.

7. And can I doubt thy gracious will
    To save and sanctify,
   My every soul-disease to heal,
    My every want supply?
   Thou waitest now to show thy grace,
    My burthen to remove,
   For all thy mind is tenderness,
    And all thy heart is love.

8. What hinders then, I still inquire,
    And in thy name believe:
   The thing I ask, expect, desire,
    Why do I not receive?
   I hunger after righteousness,
    I gasp for purity,
   Yet, O my God, I must confess
    The bar is all in me.

9. Confounded and condemn'd I am,
    I sink despairing down,
   In darkness, ignorance, and shame
    Before the God unknown:
   The thing which keeps me dark and blind,
    And void of holy love,
   I cannot by my wisdom find
    Or by my strength remove.

10. But O whate'er obstructs thy will,
    Whate'er thy work delays,
  Almighty God of Love, reveal,
    And scatter by thy grace;
  Work in me both to will and do
    According to thy word,
  In perfect holiness renew,
    And make me as my Lord.

11. Till Thou create me pure within,
    Assist me, Lord, to pray;
  The guilt, the power, the root of sin
    Destroy, and take away:
  The cause of my salvation find
    Hidden, O God, in Thee,
  And as thy loving heart's inclin'd,
    For ever deal with me. [50]

Ac. 16:33, *He was baptized, he and all his, straightway.*

  Surely their redeeming God
    Wrought his sudden work of grace,
  Precious faith on all bestow'd,
    Cloath'd them in his righteousness:
  All who wash'd their sins away
    In that pure, baptismal stream,
  Teach us, that a single day
    Is a thousand years to Him. (p. 325)

Ac. 16:34, *And having brought them up into his house, he set a table before them.* (Gr.)[51]

1. For him they first a table spread,
   His soul with hidden manna fed,
     Meat to the world unknown;
   We only taste the pardning God
   Who eat the flesh, & drink the blood
     Of his beloved Son.

50. [MS Misc. Hymns, pp. 37–40. The poem is not included in MS Acts.]
51. [The English translation of the Greek is taken from *Notes.*]

2. We up into his house are brought,
   Sinners who sold ourselves for nought,
     By causeless grace forgiven,
   With pardon & salvation blest,
   On Him we in his kingdom feast,
     And eat the Bread of heaven. (pp. 325–6)

Ac. 16:38, *They feared, when they heard that they were Romans.*

1. Who beat thy confessors & wound
     With wanton cruelty & scorn,
   Saviour, Thou canst alarm, confound,
     Their fierceness to thy glory turn,
   Or by the servile fear of man
   Our most outragious foes restrain.

2. With that infernal murther fill'd,
     The men who now thy people see
   As sheep appointed to be kill'd,
     Damp'd by a secret look from Thee
   Shall dread the sovereign ruler's frown,
   And lay their slaughtering-weapons down. (p. 328)

Ac. 16:39, *They came and besought them, and brought them out,*
and desired them to depart out of the city,&c.

Easy to be intreated, mild
  And gentle toward his fiercest foes,
Placable as a little child,
  A Christian no resentment knows;
He cannot injuries retain,
  As one of a vindictive mind,
But loves the authors of his pain,
  And meekly yields to all mankind. (pp. 328–9)

377

Ac. 17:2–3, *He reasoned with them out of the scriptures, &c.* [52]

1. Reason he did not cast aside
    As a vain gift on men bestow'd,
   Nor deem'd it a sufficient guide
    T'interpret all the mind of God,
   But rightly used its glimmering ray
   Which shew'd the need of brighter day.

2. Discoursing from the written word,
    Strong arguments of Christ he gave,
   Dead, and again to life restor'd,
    By both a sinful world to save:
   He died for all your sins t'atone,
   And rais'd, He draws you to His throne.

3. Preachers of Christ, His death we prove
    Th'accomplishment of His decree:
   That strange necessity of love
    Humbled, and nail'd Him to the tree:
   Yet urge, evince, and testify
   That God, or all mankind, must die.

4. His death the prophecies fulfill'd,
    And laid the general ransom down;
   The promises His rising seal'd,
    Insuring man's immortal crown:
   And Jesus whom we preach, is He
   The Christ that died and rose — for thee.

52. [Above Acts 17:1 Charles Wesley has written: "F. 18" (i. e., February 18).]

5. For us, for all He died and rose;
    The scandal of his cross we own,
    The truth which earth & hell oppose,
    The basis sure, it stands alone:
    And all who in his death abide
    Shall reign with Jesus glorified. (pp. 330–1)[53]

Ac. 17:7, *These all do contrary to the decrees of Cesar.*

Still the world misrepresent
    Us who on our Saviour wait,
"Dangerous to government
    Men whom all should dread & hate:"
Rulers thus they put in fear,
    Rouse the jealousy of power,
"Rebels are in Christians near,
    "Lambs will all the wolves devour!" (pp. 334–5)

Ac. 17:18, *Others said, He seemeth to be a setter forth of strange Gods: because he preached unto them, etc.*

1.   Strange indeed He is to you,
            The God whom we proclaim:
        Sensual, proud, ye never knew
            The virtue of his Name:
        Jesus, Saviour of mankind,
        The dying Man, the living God,
            Beasts, and fiends, receive, and find
                Redemption in his blood.

2.   Man & God for sinners slain,
            We offer Him to all:
        Crucified, He rose again
            To raise you from your fall:
        Jesus' preaching witnesses,
        His resurrection's power we show:
            O might all his life of grace,
                His life of glory know! (p. 343)

53. [Verses 1–4 appear in *Poet. Works*, XII, pp. 327–8.]

Ac. 17:30, *The times of this ignorance God winked at, but now commandeth all men everywhere to repent.*

1. The times of ignorance are still,
       If idols ye fall down before,
   And blindly follow your own will,
       And gold, or precious stones adore;
   Your happiness in riches place,
   In power, in pleasure, or in praise.

2. But God his messengers hath sent
       That all may from their idols turn,
   May now, commanded to repent,
       Accept from Him the grace to mourn,
   The objects visible despise,
   And seek their bliss beyond the skies.

3. Sinners, this instant day & hour,
       Yourselves renounce, your sins forsake:
   The word Divine conveys the power;
       The proffer'd power this moment take
   (Warn'd by th'ambassadors of heaven)
   And fall condemn'd & rise forgiven.

4. The word which cries to all, Repent,
       The universal guilt declares,
   And proves our God's sincere intent
       That all should be his sons & heirs,
   Should turn, thro' Jesus' grace, & live,
   And heaven into their hearts receive. (pp. 350–1)

Ac. 17:32, *When they heard of the resurrection of the, &c.*

1. Proud sinners, who in learning trust,
       Learning unsanctified,
   The hope and wisdom of the just
       They always will deride;
   The gospel-truth they laugh to scorn,
       That man on earth forgiven
   By Jesus' rise again is born,
       And lives the life of heaven.

2. They mock his resurrection's power
    Our fallen souls to save,
  Our moulder'd bodies to restore,
    And ransom from the grave:
  The power of faith and godliness,
    The preachers they condemn;
  And our true glory, we confess,
    Is to be hiss'd by them. (pp. 352–3)[54]

Ac. 17:34, *Howbeit, certain men clave unto him, and believed; among whom was Dionysius the Areopagite, etc.*

  But one for Jesus gain'd we see,
  But one of all th'Academy:
  So learn'd, so curious, and so wise,
  The rest a babling Paul despise:
  And should he now on earth appear,
  Might we not reasonably fear,
  He would not meet with more success
  In both our—U[niversitie]s. (pp. 354–5)

Ac. 18:1, *Paul departed from Athens, and came to Corinth.*

    Athens indolent and vain
      He quits as barren ground,
    Fruit in other parts to gain,
      And spread the gospel sound;
    Carries Christ, where'er he goes,
    The ministerial pattern gives:
    Every soul that Jesus knows,
      To Jesus' glory lives. (p. 356)

54. [The first half of verse 1 and the second half of verse 2 are combined to make one verse in *Poet. Works*, XII, p. 344.]

Ac. 18:3, *Because he was of the same craft, he abode with them, and wrought.*

1. Where are the venerable men
    Who Paul for an ensample take,
    Their living by their labour gain,
    Of none expence the gospel make,
    Their uncontested right forego,
    And freely ministring the word
    Nothing desire, or seek below
    But souls converted to their Lord!

2. Worthy of double honour they
    Who dare with sweating brows appear,
    Walk in the Apostolic way,
    Nor shame, nor degradation fear!
    Gladly their all to Christ they give;
    And when He in the clouds comes down
    Shall surely in his smiles receive
    A larger joy, a brighter crown. (pp. 356–7)[55]

Ac. 18:4, *And he reasoned in the synagogues every sabbath and persuaded the Jews and Greeks.*

1. With generous industry he strove
    To propagate the faith & love
    Of his redeeming Lord;
    Servant of all, he labour'd on,
    Fixt to receive from Christ alone
    His infinite reward.

55. [Verse 1 appears in *Poet. Works*, XII, pp. 346–7.]

2. How shall his zeal in judgment rise
   'Gainst those who only riches prize,
   And mock the Spirit's call!
   Right-reverend thieves & robbers they,
   Who eagerly accept the pay,
   But never work at all! (p. 357)

Ac. 18:5, *When Silas and Timotheus were come, Paul was pressed in spirit, &c.*[56]

When many in the service join,
   They urge their way with vigour new,
Bound in the bond of love divine
   True yokefellows their work pursue,
More zealous, more laborious prove,
And wider spread their Saviour's love. (pp. 357–8)

Ac. 18:6, *When they opposed themselves, and, &c.*

1. Who dares the gospel-truth blaspheme,
   Self-harden'd in his lost estate,
   What hope, alas, remains for him,
   A seal'd, abandon'd reprobate!
   Who mock th'inspiring Spirit's grace,
   Deride the sense of pardon'd sin,
   They challenge hell as their own place,
   They force the pit to take them in.

2. Jesus persisting to deny
   While all his doctrines they gainsay,
   Them, only them he passes by,
   And takes his slighted word away;
   His pearls we then no more expose
   To swine, who tread them in the mire,
   But turning from our Saviour's foes,
   We leave them in their sins t'expire. (pp. 358–9)[57]

56. [Wesley followed *Notes.* AV editions vary at this verse. Some read: "in the Spirit."]
57. [Verse 1 appears in *Poet. Works,* XII, p. 347.]

Ac. 18:9, *Then spake the Lord to Paul in a vision, Be not afraid, but speak, and hold not thy peace.*

1. Thou seest, Omniscient as Thou art,
    The ground of every human heart,
    Continually prepar'd to grant
    The comfort which thy servants want:
    Who on thy truth & love rely,
    In dangers we perceive Thee nigh;
    We see th'Invisible appear,
    And in thy sight disdain to fear.

2. While labouring in thy church below
    Thee, only Thee we vow to know;
    Thou hast a thousand secret ways
    To chear us with the life of grace.
    Inspir'd, & strengthen'd from above,
    Assur'd of thy protecting love,
    We wait the promis'd fruit to see,
    And give up all our lives to Thee. (p. 360)

Ac. 18:10, *For I am with thee, and no man shall set, &c.*

1. Jesus, Thou tak'st Thy servant's part,
    Present with us Thou always art,
    Who Thee proclaim the Christ of God,
    Who publish pardon in Thy blood:
    The threatening world assault in vain,
    If Thou their violent rage restrain,
    If Thou thy messengers defend,
    And hide our life, till time shall end.

2. By all their power unterrified,
    Their wealth, their learning, & their pride,
    We speak, & cannot hold our peace,
    We speak, secure of full success;

Thy voice prophetical we hear,
"To harvest white the fields appear,"
And thousands hungring for the word
Are ready to receive their Lord. (pp. 360–1)[58]

Ac. 18:12, *The Jews made insurrection with one accord against Paul.*

Multitudes cannot distress
A gospel-minister:
Still th'Invisible he sees,
Th'Almighty Jesus near;
Trusting in his Saviour's aid,
Against a world of worms combin'd,
Single, firm, and undismay'd,
He faces all mankind. (pp. 361–2)

Ac. 18:12, *They brought him to the judgment-seat.*

With infernal malice fraught,
The guiltless criminal
To the judgment-seat they brought,
And loud for justice call;
Christ himself his servant led,
To let the furious zealots know,
"Hitherto ye may proceed,
"But can no farther go." (p. 362)

Ac. 18:19, *He himself entred into the synagogue, and reasoned with the Jews.*

1. Not for some condemning all,
Turning from th'impenitent,
Sinners deaf to mercy's call,
Still to other Jews he went;
Jews he could not overlook,
Sent salvation to proclaim,
First in synagogues he spoke,
Christ he offer'd first to them.

---

58. [The first six lines of verse 1 appear in *Poet. Works*, XII, p. 348.]

2. Ye that now dispense the word,
   Jesus' name to heathens bear,
   Keep the beaten track; your Lord
   First within the walls declare:
   If they cast the word behind,
   Will not hear of sin forgiven,
   Preach — & save, where'er ye find,
   Every creature — under heaven! (p. 366)

Ac. 18:20, *When they desired him to tarry longer, &c.*

1. Long, undesir'd, with foes he stay'd,
   Yet could his friends' request withstand,
   By no inferior motives sway'd,
   A servant at his Lord's command
   With messages to sinners sent,
   Only where Jesus will'd, he went.

2. Above our civil forms & ways
   The preachers' motives lie conceal'd:
   The counsels of Almighty grace
   Thro' them are by their God fulfil'd,
   Who secretly their heart inclines
   To serve his own unseen designs. (pp. 366–7)[59]

Ac. 18:21, *I will return again unto you, if God will.*

1. 'Tis not in foolish man
   To order his own way;
   And hence, till Jesus make it plain,
   We for direction stay,
   Patient on Him attend;
   And undetermin'd still,
   We nothing promise, who depend
   On our great Master's will:

2. Where He appoints, & when,
   With readiness we go,
   And leave the rest to Him, & then
   Rejoice no more to know,

59. [Verse 1 appears in *Poet. Works*, XII, p. 352.]

> As instruments divine,
> As servants in the word,
> Our only business & design
> To please our heavenly Lord. (p. 367)

Ac. 18:23, *He . . . went over all the country of Galatia, &c.*

1. An apostolic minister
   His pastoral, unwearied care
       By restless labours shows,
   Travels, and flies from place to place,
   And precious souls in Jesus' grace
       Confirms, where'er he goes.

2. To each he severally applies,
   In strengthening all his children, tries
       Each moment to redeem,
   Till life's last hour he labours on,
   And grieves that he hath nothing done
       For One who died for him!

3. Thus may I in my measure strive,
   For Jesus & his people live
       Hard-toiling all my days
   To see his kingdom here restor'd,
   To spread the Evangelic word,
       And minister the grace.

4. Saviour, on me thy mind bestow,
   And in thy servant's steps I go,
       Myself the meanest see,
   The least of saints, the sinners' chief;
   And find my comfort & relief,
       My hope & heaven in Thee. (pp. 368–70)[60]

---

60. [Verses 1–2 appear in *Poet. Works*, XII, p. 353.]

Ac. 18:28, *He mightily convinced the Jews, and that publickly, shewing by the Scriptures, that Jesus was the Christ.*[61]

1.   The omnipotent God
    Thro' his love shed abroad
Doth extraordinary messengers send,
    And He arms us with grace,
    Whom he pleases to raise
Against error & sin to contend.

2.   The Jews we convince,
    Who are proud of their sins
Which they virtue & righteousness call:
    By the Spiritual sword,
    By the power of the word
We confound them, in presence of all.

3.   In Jesus his name
    We forgiveness proclaim;
And his witnessing Spirit He gives:
    From the Scriptures we show,
    He who suffer'd below
Is the God that eternally lives.

4.   The Anointed of God,
    The great Prophet bestow'd
On a wilfully ignorant race,
    True faith He imparts,
    And instructs our dull hearts
By the light & the unction of grace.

5.   Our Priest we declare,
    Thro' whose blood & whose prayer
We are pardon'd, & perfect in one;
    Our King we extol,
    Who presides over all,
And vouchsafes us a share of his throne.

61. [Wesley followed *Notes*. The AV reads: "was Christ."]

6.   Priest, Prophet, and King,
    He his kingdom doth bring,
    With his Wisdom & Peace from above;
    And who Jesus receive,
    Priests, & prophets we live,
    And we reign in the Spirit of love! (pp. 374–5)

Ac. 19:2, *Have ye received the Holy Ghost, since ye believed?*[62]

    I who long have call'd him Lord,
    And Jesus mine believ'd,
    Have I prov'd the Saviour's word,
    The Comforter receiv'd?
    Him do I my Leader know,
    His power throughout my life express,
    All the fruits, the tempers show,
    The works of righteousness? (p. 376)

Ac. 19:3, *Unto what then were ye baptized?*

1.   Baptiz'd into the name of God,
    The Father, Son, & Holy Ghost,
    That inward grace was then bestow'd,
    If now ye have the Spirit lost;
    He makes, to every sinner given,
    The child of God, the heir of heaven.

2.   Renouncing your baptismal right,
    Whoe'er the Holy Ghost disclaim,
    Ye do the gracious Spirit despite,
    Falsely usurp the Christian name,
    And tell the Lord, ye are not his,
    And spurn the hope of heavenly bliss. (pp. 377–8)

Ac. 19:5, *They were baptized in the name of the Lord Jesus.*

    Truly baptiz'd into the Name
    Of Jesus I have been,
    Who partner of his nature am,
    And sav'd indeed from sin:

62. [Above Ac. 19:1 in Wesley's shorthand is written: "March 1."]

Thy nature, Lord, thro' faith I feel,
Thy love reveal'd in me;
In me, my full Salvation, dwell
To all eternity. (p. 379)

Ac. 19:7, *And all the men were about twelve.*

Twelve inspir'd Apostles new
Are in a moment made!
Jesus, merciful & true,
On Thee our souls are stay'd:
Us Thou canst inspire, and fill:
And lo, we at thy feet appear,
Trust thy sanctifying will
For all thy fulness here. (p. 380)

Ac. 19:8, *He went into the synagogues,*[63] *and spake boldly, disputing*
& persuading the things concerning the kingdom of God.

1. The joyful news of pardon'd sin
   Did at Jerusalem begin;
   And Paul the rule Divine pursues,
   And offers first the grace to Jews,
   The kingdom of celestial peace,
   And joy, and endless righteousness.

2. Jesus, with his undaunted zeal
   If Thou thy weakest servant fill,
   I shall th'experienc'd truth maintain,
   Like him, nor fear the face of man,
   But fully my commission prove,
   Nor ever doubt thy faithful love.

63. [The plural "synagogues" is probably a slip on Wesley's part. The AV and *Notes* read: "synagogue."]

3.   What can resist thy powerful word,
    Or stand against thy Spirit's sword?
    With this I combat every foe,
    And conquering, on to conquer go,
    Convince, persuade them to believe,
    And Thee into their hearts receive. (pp. 380–1)

Ac. 19:10, *This continued by the space of two years; so that all they which dwelt in Asia heard, etc.*

1.   Who might not hear the word before,
      Their time is come, their gracious day,
    And Asia's sons may all adore
      The Lamb that bears their sins away;
    They all the healing[64] doctrine hear
      Which God by signs & wonders seals,
    And Christ's acknowledg'd messenger
      His prosperous ministry fulfils.

2.   The mouth which our Almighty Lord
      Hath made & open'd, who can close?
    We preach, intrusted with his word,
      Fearless, tho' earth & hell oppose:
    The fire breaks out, in vain represt;
      Constrain'd to speak, we must speak on,
    And never pause, & never rest,
      Till all our work with life is done. (p. 383)

Ac. 19:11–12, *God wrought special miracles by the hands, &c.*

1.   "Greater miracles than these
      Shall My disciples do;"
    Lord, we at Thy feet confess
      The Prophecy is true:
    Yet Thine only power we own
    Who didst by Paul the fiends expel;
      Virtue flows from thee alone,
      Body and soul to heal.

64. [In the MS "heavenly" is written in the margin as an alternative.]

2.   Still the promise is fulfill'd
To them that trust in Thee;
Thine almighty arm reveal'd
With awe we daily see;
Outward signs but shadows were
Of greater miracles within,
Fiends expel'd the soul by prayer,
And sinners sav'd from sin.

3.   One diseas'd, tormented soul,
Redeem'd & dispossest,
By a gracious touch made whole
With faith & pardon blest,
Speaks thy gracious promise seal'd,
Thy power, & truth, & goodness join'd,
More than all the bodies heal'd
Of all our dying kind. (pp. 383–4)[65]

Ac. 19:16, *The man in whom the evil spirit was, leapt on them, &*
overcame them, & prevailed, etc.

1. Ye, who the name of Jesus take,
But will not all your sins forsake,
May well the rage of Satan fear,
And fly from the old murtherer:
The tempter first by guile prevails,
With terror then his slaves assails:
And if your souls in hell he tear,
Ye never can escape him there.

2. Naked of Christ ye now are found,
And bleeding with your desperate wound;
But turn to Him who pardon gives,
And naked, wounded souls receives;
Then, when He doth the grace bestow,
With stedfast faith resist the foe,
On Jesus' powerful Name rely,
And see the prince of darkness fly! (pp. 386–7)

65. [Verses 1–2 appear in *Poet. Works*, XII, p. 360.]

Ac. 19:17, *This was known to all; & fear fell on them all, and the name of the Lord Jesus was magnified.*

1. Infidels, if God compel,
   And devils themselves shall join
   His o're-ruling power to tell,
   And further his design:
   While of Satan's rage they hear,
   Which Sceva's scatter'd sons proclaim,
   Heathens struck with sacred fear
   Bow down to Jesus' name.

2. Above every name ador'd
   Most holy & most high,
   Heaven & earth's Almighty Lord
   With them we magnify:
   Jesus, manifest below,
   More fully still thy name declare,
   Till we all thy nature know,
   And all thine impress bear. (p. 387)

Ac. 19:18, *And many that believed, came, and confessed, and shewed their deeds.*

1. Wounded by the Spirit's sword,
   Which joints & marrow parts,
   Jesus' efficacious word,
   They own, has reach'd their hearts,
   Laid the depths of Satan bare,
   The soul's most intimate recess:
   Now they all their deeds declare,
   And all their sins confess.

2. O that we who have believ'd
   May thus our fall bemoan,
   Self-condemn'd, & deeply griev'd
   For faith & mercy groan,
   (Vilest we of all mankind
   To trample on his pardning love)
   Restless, till again we find
   Our Advocate above! (pp. 387–8)

Ac. 19:19, *Many also of them which used curious arts, brought their books, &c.*

Satan the title soft imparts,
And Magic calls his curious arts,
Worthy their own infernal name,
And black as hell from whence they came!
Ah, no; his advocates reply;
"The harmless fiend no more bely:
"He sleeps secured by our *repeal*,
"And witchcraft is — Impossible!" (p. 388)

Ac. 19:22, *He sent into Macedonia Timothy*[66] *and Erastus; but he himself stayed in Asia for a season.*

Attentive to his people's needs,
A pastor tarries, or proceeds;
    His journeys or abode
He regulates in every place,
As best may minister the grace
    And feed the flock of God. (p. 390)

Ac. 19:23, *And the same time there arose no small stir about that way.*

Peace with the world, how short its stay!
While each pursues his sinful way,
    The restless sons of night
Must still the Saviour's way abhor,
Infesting with perpetual war
    The children of the light. (pp. 390–1)

---

66. [Both the AV and *Notes* read: "Timotheus."]

Ac. 19:25, *Sirs, ye know that by this craft we have our wealth.*

1. The love which worldly men pretend
   To things divine, will always end
      Where it at first begun:
   Gain is their only godliness,
   In all their actions they confess
      They love themselves alone.

2. The hellish tyrant of mankind
   Doth sinners by their passions bind,
      And thus his sway maintains;
   But chiefly thro' the lust of gold
   He rules his slaves, to avarice sold,
      The worldling's god he reigns. (p. 391)[67]

Ac. 19:26, *Throughout all Asia this Paul hath persuaded, and turned away much people, saying, etc.*

      The world may well complain
      Of endless mischief done
   By these ungovernable men
      Who o're the kingdom run;
      Much people they pervert,
         That throng'd the downward road,
   From idols turn away their heart
         To serve the living God:
      The works by sinners wrought
         They scorn & vilify,
   And set the craft of priests at nought,
         And all their gods deny;
      Honour, & wealth & power
         They daringly tread down,
   And teach the multitude t'adore
         Th'Incarnate God alone. (pp. 391–2)

67. [Verse 1 appears in *Poet. Works,* XII, p. 362.]

Ac. 19:28, *When they had heard these sayings, they were full of wrath, and cried out saying, Great is Diana, etc.* [68]

> Interest and superstition join'd
>   Will never fail the world to raise,
> And stir up all the passions blind
>   Of those that hate the sons of grace,
> The great Diana to defend,
> And furiously for Self contend. (p. 393)

Ac. 19:29, *The whole city was filled with confusion: and having caught Gaius & Aristarchus, &c.*

> Destroyers of the public peace,
>   The city they with tumult fill,
> The Christians as seditious seize,
>   As Authors vile of every ill,
> As pests, & poisoners of the air,
> As Atheists they in pieces tear! (p. 393)

Ac. 19:30, *When Paul would have entred in unto the people, the disciples suffered him not.*

> By their Saviour's Spirit led
>   And fill'd with faith unfeign'd,
> Saints themselves sometimes may need
>   To be by man restrain'd:
> Pastors who their lives expose
> Thro' hasty zeal, the flock should hold,
> Screen from their outragious foes,
>   And hide them in the fold. (p. 393)

---

68. [The AV reads: "when they heard."]

Ac. 19:32, *Some cried one thing, and some another: for the assembly was confused, &c.*

> Passions, though nicely varnish'd ore,
> Themselves by their effects bewray,
> Infernal strife and wild uproar
> Expose the fiend to open day;
> Howe'er themselves the craftsmen blind,
> In rage, revenge, & anarchy,
> The ground of all their zeal we find,
> And by the fruit discern the tree. (p. 394)

Ac. 19:34, *All with one voice about the space of two hours cried out, Great is Diana of the Ephesians!*

> 1. When reason is by wrath supprest,
>   And frantic Superstition reigns,
>   Hark, how the many-headed beast
>   The great Diana's cause maintains,
>   And Legions fierce with all his powers
>   The church, the church, incessant roars!

> 2. "High is the Church, whoe'er oppose,
>   "Whoe'er attempt to pull her down!
>   "High is the Church! 'gainst all her foes,
>   "The drunken sons of Babylon,
>   "*Reeling* — we stand — in Order's aid —
>   "And *swear* — t'uphold the Craftsmen's trade!"
>   (pp. 394–5)

Ac. 19:36, *Ye ought to be quiet, and to do nothing rashly.*

> 1. The universal fault
>   O how shall I eschew?
>   Precipitate in thought,
>   In word and action too,
>   My nature's turbulence I own,
>   And look for help in Christ alone.

2.　　My hastiness is stay'd
　　　Thro' faith's o're-ruling power,
　　　By Jesus' Spirit led,
　　　　I hurry on no more,
　　　But subjected to his command,
　　　I join the quiet in the land. (pp. 395–6)[69]

Ac. 19:38, *The law is open: let them implead one another.*

1.　Conscious the laws are on our side
　　　(Not for the just but lawless made)
　　Our foes refuse the test t'abide,
　　　Or sue for Magisterial aid,
　　While us they violently oppress
　　With an high hand of wickedness.

2.　The legal way they wisely shun,
　　　Which would our innocence display,
　　Make their unrighteous dealings known
　　　Who hate the children of the day,
　　And break, to compass their design,
　　All statutes, human and Divine. (p. 397)

Ac. 20:1, *Paul . . . departed for to go into Macedonia.* [70]

1.　Beyond his persecutors' sight
　　　Th'apostle prudently withdraws,
　　Not by an hasty shameful flight
　　　Deserting his Redeemer's cause,
　　But sent on other souls to call
　　And Christ proclaim the Lord of all.

69. [Verse 1 appears in *Poet. Works*, XII, p. 364.]
70. [At the top in Wesley's shorthand is written: "March 6."]

2. Ye men sent forth in Jesus' name,
    The storm, when He appoints, decline,
    Follow th'Apostles of the Lamb,
    Fulfil your gracious Lord's design,
    O're earth as lawless outcasts driven,
    T'increase th'inhabitants of heaven. (p. 398)[71]

Ac. 20:3, *The Jews laid wait for him.*

1. Could God's peculiar people fight
    Against his kingdom here,
    And seek with rancorous despite
    To slay his messenger;
    Rulers and magistrates engage,
    Stir up the furious croud
    And watch with unrelenting rage
    To shed the martyrs' blood?

2. If envy and self-interest rule
    And pride their zeal inflame,
    The world of the same spirit full
    Will always do the same:
    And Christians in profession, still
    Accomplishing his word,
    Would every real Christian kill,
    And drive us to our Lord. (p. 399)

Ac. 20:4, *There accompanied him into Asia, Sopater, Aristarchus, and Secundus; Gaius & Timotheus, etc.*

1.   Labourers dreadful to the fiend,
        Men of one mind & heart,
        Still, O Christ, vouchsafe to send
        The heathen to convert,
        (Heathen who usurp thy Name)
        And fill with Apostolic zeal
        Brands to pluck out of the flame
        And rescue souls from hell.

71. [Verse 1 appears in *Poet. Works*, XII, p. 365.]

2.   Who an army can withstand,
        When Thou art at their head?
Lead us forth, throughout the land
        Thy dying love to spread:
While thy bloody cross we show,
      Victorious in the sacred sign,
      Satan's kingdom we o'rethrow,
        And plant, & stablish thine. (p. 400)

Ac. 20:9, *As Paul was long preaching, Eutychus sunk down with sleep, and fell down from the third loft, etc.*

1.   The Lord, the sovereign Lord
      To every careless heart
Preaches himself that awful word,
      "Be ready to depart!"
He bids us all give heed,
      Nor seem to hear in vain;
He calls a preacher from the dead
      To caution mortal man.

2.   Sinner, the warning take,
      With meek and lowly fear,
The slumber from the spirit shake,
      For death is always near:
Thy gracious season know,
      And carefully attend:
Thy life, and trial here below
      May with this moment end. (p. 403)

Ac. 20:10, *And Paul went down, & fell on him, & embracing him, said, &c.*

1. A minister of Jesus
      Doth pitying zeal express
When doubly dead he sees us
      In sins and trespasses;
Himself to the salvation
      Of pretious souls applies,
With earnest supplication
      For our recovery cries.

2. With diligence attending,
    As born for this alone,
And kindly condescending
    He makes our case his own,
With tenderest love embraces,
    And offers us his aid:
But only Jesus raises
    A sinner from the dead. (pp. 403–4)

Ac. 20:13, *We . . . sailed unto Assos, there intending to take, &c.*

1. Fresh fatigue for Jesus' sake
    Is an apostle's rest;
Happy who his zeal partake,
    His successors confess'd!
They with joy renounce their ease,
Themselves in everything deny,
Sinners for their Lord to seize,
    And Jesus glorify.

2. Pomp & equipage & state
    To preachers are unknown,
Men who on their Master wait
    And with his message run:
Run, or walk, or ride, or sail,
And fully thus their mission prove,
Thus to every creature tell
    Their dear Redeemer's love. (p. 405)[72]

Ac. 20:25, *I know that ye all, among whom I have gone preaching the kingdom of God, shall see my face no more.*

An angel of the church below
    May leave us here forlorn,
And by the Spirit's presage know
    He never shall return:
But after him we soon remove,
    The first-born church to join,
And with our minister above
    Behold the face Divine. (p. 413)

72. [Verse 1 appears in *Poet. Works*, XII, p. 369.]

Ac. 20:29, *I know this, that after my departing shall grievous wolves enter in among you, etc.*

1. With grief a father must foresee
       The havock of his children nigh:
    But Jesus suffers it to be,
       And kindly turns his servant's eye
    From gazing on his own success,
    To future scenes of sad distress.

2. Ev'n now, in deep prophetic woe
       The prosper'd ministry may say,
    After my death too well I know
       The grievous wolves expect their prey:
    The grievous wolves will entrance find,
    And rend the flock I leave behind. (p. 416)

Ac. 20:30, *Also of your own selves shall men arise, speaking perverse things, to draw away, etc.*

1. Already ye the men behold,
       Who from among yourselves arise,
    Loquacious, turbulent, and bold
       Far above all in their own eyes,
    They proudly take the highest place,
    And witness their own perfect grace.

2. Perverters of the sacred word
       Th'apostles false their teacher show,
    The sons of Nicholas[73] abhor'd
       They scatter death where'er they go,
    The flock determin'd not to spare,
    But into sects & parties tear.

---

73. [In *Notes* John Wesley commented on this verse as follows: "Such were the Nicolaitans, of whom Christ complains, Rev. 2:6;" and on that verse he says: "Probably so-called from Nicholas, one of the seven deacons, (Acts 6:5). Their doctrines and their lives were equally corrupt," etc.]

3. The church they labour to divide,
   That each the largest share may seize,
   May draw disciples to his side,
   Challenge the separatists for his,
   By error multiply his gain,
   And Satan's great vice-gerent reign. (pp. 416–17)

Ac. 20:33, *I have coveted no man's silver, or gold, or apparel.*

The servant of a Master poor,
Possest of treasures that endure,
Can no terrestrial good desire,
Silver, or gold, or gay attire;
Nor will he judge who riches have,
Limit th'Almighty's power to save,
Or lump them with invidious zeal,
And rashly send them all to hell. (p. 419)

Ac. 20:35, *I have shewed you all things, how that so labouring ye ought to support the weak; and to remember the words of the Lord Jesus, how he said, It is more blessed to give than to receive.*

1. Your duty let th'Apostle show:
   Ye ought, Ye ought to labour so,
      In Jesus' cause employ'd,
   Your calling's works at times pursue,
   And keep the Tent-maker in view,
      And use your hands for God.

2. Work for the weak, & sick, & poor,
   Raiment & food for them procure,
      And mindful of his word,
   Enjoy the blessedness to give,
   Lay out your gettings, to relieve
      The members of your Lord.

3. Your labour which proceeds from love,
Jesus shall graciously approve,
With full felicity,
With brightest crowns your loan repay,
And tell you in that joyful day
"Ye did it unto Me."

Ac. 20:36, *When he had thus spoken.*

The poor, as Jesus' bosom-friends,
The poor he makes his latest care,
To all his successors commends,
And wills us on our hands to bear:
The poor our dearest care we make,
Aspiring to superior bliss,
And cherish for their Saviour's sake,
And love them with a love like his. (p. 421)

Ac. 20:36, *When he had thus spoken, he kneeled down, and prayed with them all.*

Worthy the great Apostle's zeal,
The solemn Valediction shows
A pastor how to bid farewell,
When from his weeping flock he goes:
O might I thus my love declare,
My pious friends, like Paul, resign,
Commend to Christ in faithful prayer,
And leave them in the hands Divine! (p. 421)

Ac. 21:1, *And when we were torn away from them. . . .*[74]

1. Saints in Jesus' Spirit one
(Union to the world unknown),
Torn as from each other's heart,
Friends in Christ are loth to part;
Thus the power of friendship prove,
Thus evince their mutual love.

74. [Wesley quoted the text of *Notes*: "When we were torn away. " The AV reads: "After we were gotten from them."]

2. Yet commanded to divide,
   When his will is signified,
   Separating without delay,
   They their dearest Lord obey,
   Freely all for Jesus leave,
   Closer to their Saviour cleave. (p. 424)

Ac. 21:26, *Then Paul took the men, and the next day purifying himself with them, entred into the temple.*

His meek humility
(If others err'd) we see:
He yields without reply,
His love to testify
Takes on himself the legal yoke,
That theirs might from his foes be broke. (p. 434)

Ac. 21:27, *The Jews of Asia, when they saw him in the temple, stirred up all the people, &c.*

Even love cannot repress
Malicious stubbornness,
Conquer the factious zeal
Of Jews implacable,
Or furious superstition tame,
While Satan blows th'infernal flame. (pp. 434–5)

Ac. 21:27, *They stirred up all the people, and laid hands on him.*

1. The man by passion sway'd,
   By prepossession led,
   The croud of reason void,
   In Satan's cause employ'd,
   As fittest instruments he sends
   Against the truth & all its friends.

2.   The messenger of peace
With wicked hands they seize,
In furious haste to kill,
And murtherers in will
His blood they shed, to please the skies,
And mix it with his sacrifice. (p. 435)

Ac. 21:28, *Crying out, Men of Israel, help: this is the man that teacheth all men everywhere against the people, etc.*

Hark, how the rabble roar
In every age the same,
The wolves collected to devour
A follower of the Lamb!
For help the ruffians cry
A desperate sheep to seize,
A man who dares their lair defy
And break their hellish peace:
Custom & rule he slights,
And rambling up & down,
Like Ishmael, with sinners fights
And mercy shews to none;
To leave the world so good
On all he loudly calls,
Against the church — of stone & wood,
Against the *sacred* walls! (pp. 435–6)

Ac. 21:31, *As they went about to kill him, tidings came to the chief captain, &c.*

His hour of suffering is not yet,
His toilsom course is not compleat,
   And Legion roars in vain:
Tho' all in his destruction join,
Till Paul fulfils his Lord's design,
   He never can be slain. (p. 437)

Ac. 21:34, *He could not know the certainty for the tumult.*

Questioning a clam'rous croud,
   Wild, absurd, injurious men,
Men as Babel's builders loud,
   Must we not inquire in vain?
Boistrous as the winds and sea,
   While they all at once exclaim,
Can we know the certainty,
   Can we learn the truth from them? (p. 438)

Ac. 21:38, *Art not thou that Egyptian who*[75] *madest an uproar, &*
leddest out, &c.

And let the world for Jesus' sake
   His confessors oppress,
For vile, seditious ruffians take,
   And foes to public peace:
Not of the dark Egyptian race,
   But Israelites indeed,
We still the great Apostle trace,
   As he pursued our Head. (p. 439)

Ac. 21:39, *Suffer me to speak unto the people.*

A servant of th'incarnate God
   Cannot faint beneath his load,
      Or sink, howe'er opprest,
The Spirit of faith, & hope, & love
   Will bear him to the throne above,
      And hide in Jesus' breast. (p. 440)

Ac. 21:40, *And when he had given him license, Paul stood, &c.*

1. Who take the name of Christ in vain,
       Justice we cannot obtain
          Or leave to speak, from them:
    Impatient of the least delay
    Our brethren hurry us away,
       Our countrymen condemn.

75. [Wesley followed *Notes*. The AV reads: "which."]

2. But heathens will their prisoners hear,
  Suffering us ourselves to clear,
    They still the zealots' cry;
  And then we make our bold defence,
  And then with humble confidence
    Our Lord we testify. (p. 440)

Ac. 22:7, *Saul, Saul, why persecutest thou Me?*

Zealots the Church of Christ oppose,
  Fierce champions for a God unknown,
And think they persecute his foes,
  When most they persecute his Son. (p. 444)

Ac. 22:8, *I answered, Who art Thou, Lord?*

A conscious unbeliever, I
  Perceive my blindness now,
And at the feet of Jesus lie
  Inquiring, Who art Thou?
Thy sin-convincing voice I hear;
  But tell me Who Thou art,
And now, my Lord, & God, appear,
  In mercy, to my heart. (p. 444)

Ac. 22:10, *And I said, What shall I do?*

For farther light I then shall sue,
  Master, what woudst Thou have me do?
    Make all thy counsel known:
  By faith I now my Lord receive,
  And from this happy moment live
    To serve thy will alone. (p. 446)

Ac. 22:10, *Arise, & go into Damascus, and there it shall be told thee of all things which are appointed for thee to do.*

1. By whom Thou wilt thy pleasure show
    Where'er Thou sendest me, I go,
        After my Leader move:
    Alone, my way I would not find,
    But walk in all the works design'd
        To exercise my love.

2. Made free, & willing to obey
    Wilt Thou not, gracious Lord, display
        Thy whole design to me?
    Thy mind immediately reveal,
    Or by thy chosen servants tell,
        I gladly follow Thee. (p. 446)

Ac. 22:13, *Ananias came & said, Brother Saul, receive thy sight.*

1. When the great God intends
        A sinner to restore,
    Some messenger he sends
        To exercise his power,
    To make his pardning mercy known;
    Yet Jesus doth the work alone.

2. The word of righteousness
        And truth Himself applies,
    He opens by his grace
        The unbeliever's eyes,
    His Spirit bids the heart believe,
    And then our souls their sight receive. (p. 447)

Ac. 22:15, *For thou shalt be his witness unto all men, of what thou hast seen & heard.*

For thy truth & mercy sake
    To my drooping soul appear,
Me thy faithful witness make
    Of the things I see & hear;

Then I shall thy love confess,
Conscious of my Saviour's mind,
Bold proclaim the general peace,
Peace in Christ for all mankind! (p. 448)

Ac. 22:16, *Arise, . . . and wash away thy sins.*

1.   Call'd from above, I rise
And wash away my sin,
The stream, to which my spirit flies,
Can make the foulest clean:
It runs divinely clear,
A fountain deep and wide;
'Twas open'd by the soldier's spear
In my Redeemer's side!

2.   Believing in thy name,
Jesus, the peace I gain,
And wash'd I every moment am,
And still the grace retain;
In ceaseless prayer to Thee
The life of faith I prove,
And cleans'd from all iniquity
Continue in thy love. (p. 449)[76]

Ac. 22:17–18, *While I was praying*[77] *in the temple, I was in a trance, &c.*

1.   He that in the temple prays,
Seeking at th'appointed place,
There the God of truth shall find,
There be taught his Saviour's mind;
Christ will his disciples shew
Where to go, & what to do.

---

76. [Verse 1 appears in *Poet. Works*, XII, p. 397.]
77. [Wesley followed *Notes*. The AV reads: "While I prayed."]

2. Lo, I in thy house attend:
   Where thou wilt, thy servant send;
   Send; but O, prepare my way,
   Teach me everywhere to pray,
   Everywhere to preach thy word,
   Everywhere to meet my Lord. (pp. 449–50)

Ac. 22:21, *And he said unto me, Depart; for I will send thee far hence unto the Gentiles.*

Jesus, evermore the same,
   We on thy word rely,
Still thy promis'd presence claim,
   And still perceive Thee nigh:
Yes, thy faithful love we know,
Where'er Thou dost thy servants send,
   With us Thou thyself wilt go,
Our Guide till time shall end. (p. 451)

Ac. 22:25, *Is it lawful for you to scourge a man that is a Roman, and uncondemned?*

1. Of civil priviledges here
      A Christian may himself avail,
   And put his heathen foes in fear
      Of breaking thro' the legal pale,
   His heathen foes who God disown
   But tremble at a mortal's frown.

2. While Thee we own in all our ways,
      To us Thou wilt thy counsel show,
   And led by thine unerring grace
      We shall in every trial know
   When the affliction to decline,
   And when accept the Gift Divine. (pp. 453–4)

Ac. 23:1, *Men and brethren, I have lived in all good conscience before God, until this day.* [78]

1.   Since he had the Saviour known
And felt the sprinkled blood,
Paul had blamelessly went[79] on,
In presence of his God:
Ev'ry happy, pardon'd man
May thus continue in his sight,
Faith & innocence maintain,
And walk with Christ in white.

2.   Help me, Saviour, *from* this day
To keep a conscience pure,
Lead me in the perfect way,
And make my footsteps sure:
When my heart doth not condemn,
To stand before my foes I dare,
Bold to meet the Judge supreme,
And face them at thy bar. (p. 455)

Ac. 23:3, *God shall smite thee, thou whited wall, &c.*

1.   Transported by Prophetic zeal,
Constrain'd the judgment to foretell,
He speaks divinely right;
The threaten'd woe belongs to all,
And God shall every whited wall
With sure destruction smite.

2.   Hear this, who now abuse your power
And treat as criminals, before
The innocent ye hear,
Who break the laws ye should maintain,
And rouse the rage of riotous men
'Gainst Jesus' messenger!

78. [At the top in Wesley's shorthand is written: "M. 26" (March 26).]
79. [This is an unusual use of "went" as a past participle. The only example of this usage in the eigtheenth century in the *Oxford English Dictionary* is from Lavington's *Enthusiasm of Methodists and Papists compar'd* (1749).]

3. By pomp ye charm the people's sight,
   Your monumental wall is white
       And beautified by art;
   With goodly forms ye hide your sin,
   The rubbish, dirt, & trash within
       A worldly, rotten heart.

4. But cast in this your gracious day
   The world with all your sins away,
       The true repentance feel,
   Or God shall make your evil known,
   Your daub'd, untemper'd wall throw down,
       And smite you into hell. (pp. 456–7)[80]

Ac. 23:6, *When Paul perceived that the one part were Sadducees and the other Pharisees, he cried out, etc.*

Not meerly human policy,
    But the true wisdom from above
Taught him to use the real plea
    And mix the serpent with the dove,
Willing to die, yet still to shun
The death, till all his work were done. (p. 458)

Ac. 23:6, *Men & brethren, I am a Pharisee, and the son of a Pharisee: of the hope & resurrection, etc.*

1. His foes by lawful means he tries
       By dis-uniting to confound,
   Midst infidels' & zealots' cries
       In doctrines & opinions sound,
   A zealot, & a zealot's son
   And question'd for the truth alone.

---

80. [Verse 1 appears in *Poet. Works*, XII, p. 401.]

2. A prisoner for the gospel-hope,
   And still in this a Pharisee,
   Jesus he preach'd who lifts us up
   To glorious immortality,
   Who rose that all his saints may rise,
   The grave exchanging for the skies. (pp. 458–9)

Ac. 23:11, *And the night following, the Lord stood by him, & said,*
Be of good chear, Paul: etc.

1. O Jesus, in Thee
   My salvation I see,
   Thy presence confess
   Most near to assist in my greatest distress;
   In the gloomiest hour
   Sustain'd by thy power,
   And reviv'd by thy word
   I acknowledge the voice of my heavenly Lord.

2. I both see Thee & hear
   Inexpressibly near
   To deliver thine own,
   And to comfort my heart in a manner unknown:
   But believers can tell
   What an heaven I feel,
   When Thou bidst me pursue,
   And accomplish the work Thou hast sent me to do.

3. Thy messenger, I
   On the promise rely
   Of thy presence below,
   To uphold me & guide wheresoever I go:
   And I only would live
   My whole witness to give,
   And in every place
   Spread abroad thy unsearchable riches of grace.
                                        (pp. 461–2)

Ac. 23:15, *Now therefore ye with the council, signify to the chief captain, &c.*

"Ye must applaud our act so good
"Who shed a vile deceiver's blood,
"Who for the *old religion* fight,
"Furious in *holy church's* right:
"Partners with us, our crown ye share
"Worthy to sit in Peter's chair,
"The glorious zeal of Phineas show,
"And God ye serve, who slay his foe." (p. 464)

Ac. 23:17, *Then Paul called one of the centurions unto him, & said, Bring this young man, etc.*

The promise of preserving grace
   He knows divinely sure,
Yet uses properest means & ways
   His safety to secure:
Thro' these the Lord deliverance gives,
   But bids his servant own
The help which he by man receives
   Descends from God alone. (p. 464)

Ac. 23:29, *Whom I perceived to have nothing laid to his charge worthy of death or of bonds.*

With ease a wise, unbiass'd man
   May innocence perceive,
And should against its foes maintain,
   And full assistance give;
But guiltier far than all the rest
   The friend of equity,
Unless he rescue the opprest,
   And set the captive free. (p. 466)

Ac. 23:33, *They presented Paul before the Governor.*

> Bound by the prophetic word,
>   And before rulers brought,
> Paul must manifest his Lord
>   Who Jews & Heathens bought;
> Preach redemption in his blood,
> And spread the tidings far & wide,
>   Witness for a dying God,
>   A Saviour crucified. (pp. 467–8)

Ac. 24:4, *Notwithstanding, that I be not farther tedious unto thee, I pray thee that thou wouldst hear us, etc.* [81]

> Lame preface, lame transition too,
>   Conclusion lame let all admire!
> As eloquent, as just & true,
>   The pleader well deserves his hire:
> Still ready to harangue — for pay, —
> Against the vagrants — of our day! (p. 470)

Ac. 24:6, *Who hath also gone about to profane the temple.*

> "Himself the standard bears,
>   "The giddy vulgar leads:
> "For sacred forms he nothing cares,
>   "Or heaven-deserving deeds:
> "He calls our virtue vice,
>   "Our rules he tramples down,
> "And impiously the church denies,
>   "The church of brick & stone!
> "So evident the case
>   "The court may take my word,
> "The judge a righteous sentence pass,
>   "And use the civil sword;
> "The horrid wretch profane
>   "May up to justice give,
> "Unfit with Christians to remain,
>   "Or on the earth to live." (pp. 471–2)

81. [Above Ac. 24:1 in Wesley's shorthand is written: "M. 29" (March 29).]

Ac. 24:9, *And the Jews also assented, saying, that these things were*
so.

1. 'Tis thus, when Satan's instrument
   Blackens the followers of the Lamb,
   Our grave self-righteous foes assent,
       By words, not facts, confirm the same,
   With confidence our crimes assert,
   And take the old Accuser's part.

2. As pestilent, seditious men,
       As factious schismaticks, they brand
   The followers of the Nazarene,
       Who stir up strife throughout the land,
   Throughout the world as madmen run,
   And turn their kingdom upside down.

3. Our sacrilegious wickedness
       The Jews & all their elders know,
   Profaners of the holy place,
       The church, the church we mean t'o'rethrow,
   Foes to the church they us declare,
   And what they cannot prove — they swear. (pp. 472–3)

Ac. 24:12, *They neither found me in the temple disputing with any*
man, neither raising up the people.

No; the servants of the Lord
    Cannot, as zealots, strive,
Wrangling is by all abhor'd
    Who one with Jesus live;
Peacemakers, where'er we go,
Factions we cause & wars to cease,
    Love diffuse, & concord sow,
        And true eternal peace. (p. 474)

Ac. 24:13, *Neither can they prove the things whereof they now accuse me.*

> Who the truth and us oppose,
>   Its blacken'd witnesses,
> Once confronted with our foes
>   We easily repress;
> When their slanders most abound,
> Superior in the strength of love,
>   All our haters we confound
>   By calling them to prove. (pp. 474–5)

Ac. 24:20–1, *Or else let these same here say, if they have found any evil doing in me, etc.*

1.   Ye men of Jewish zeal,
          Who Christian truth oppress,
      We make our bold appeal
          To your own consciences,
      What fault or evil have ye found
      In those that spread the gospel-sound?

2.   Ye prudently forbear
          Before the judge to cite
      The witnesses who dare
          With sin & error fight,
      Who testify th'atoning God,
      And grace & glory thro' his blood.

3.   This only have we done,
          And still we persevere
      To make his passion known
          Who bought our pardon here,
      And rose to prove our sin forgiven,
      And seal it with the peace from heaven.

4.   His resurrection's power
          To sinners we declare:
      Faith antedates that hour,
          And sets us at the bar;
      By faith we live, & rise, & fly
      And reign with Christ above the sky.

5.   With all his members one
        He now himself imparts,
      And form'd by faith alone
        We find him in our hearts,
      The present Resurrection know,
      The life of heaven reveal'd below.

6.   This is our only crime,
        And this we dare avow,
      Eternity in time,
        The Resurrection now,
      The bliss Supreme believers prove,
      Th'indwelling God of glorious love. (pp. 478–9)

Ac. 24:23, *He commanded a centurion to keep Paul, & to let him have liberty, & that he should hinder, etc.* [82]

1.   Prisoner at large, by Jesus' will,
        His friend's assistance he receives,
      Servant of all with active zeal
        Help to imprison'd spirits gives,
      Who triumph in redemption found,
      And feel, his gospel is not bound.

2.   His friends the happy prisoner see,
        And daily hear his welcome voice,
      Witness of inward liberty,
        Of peace divine, & heavenly joys,
      Which those that can the body slay,
      Can neither give, nor take away. (p. 480)

Ac. 25:2, *Then the high priest, and the chief of the Jews informed him against Paul.*

      Restless, malicious hate,
      Revenge implacable,
      Will not permit its slaves to wait,
      Or slack their furious zeal;

---

82. [Wesley followed the text of *Notes* using "hinder." The AV reads: "forbid."]

A day they cannot lose
Who blood & threatnings breathe,
Eager, impatient to accuse,
And hunt a saint to death. (p. 484)

Ac. 25:5, *Go down with me, & accuse this man, if there be any wickedness in him.*

The heathen judge will not condemn
Before the cause he hears,
But innocent th'accus'd esteem,
Till prov'd his guilt appears:
Yet Christian priests, by envy mov'd,
Their character fulfil,
And when our innocence is prov'd,
Suppose us guilty still. (p. 485)

Ac. 25:7, *The Jews laid many & grievous complaints against Paul, which they could not prove.*

Modern, as ancient priests, presume
To load the odious Heretick,
Adopt the politicks of Rome,
"Throw dirt enough, & some will stick:"
In transport of religious zeal,
Pestilent Lollards they pursue,
With countless crimes th'indictment swell,
When not one single charge is true. (p. 486)

Ac. 25:9, *Festus willing to do the Jews a pleasure, &c.*

Worldly men thro' worldly views
Betray the public trust,
Odious innocence abuse,
And sacrifice the just:
Sordid slaves of earthly hope,
A fortune great intent to raise,
Readily, like Festus, stoop,
To all unrighteousness. (p. 487)

Ac. 25:10, *I stand at Cesar's judgment-seat, where I ought to be judged.*

> Subject to the laws of man
> Who Christ have truly known
> Cesar's rights we all maintain,
> And Jurisdiction own;
> Teachers no exemption plead,
> But while the King of kings we fear,
> Honour, and obey, and dread
> His great Vice-gerent here. (p. 488)

Ac. 25:10, *To the Jews have I done no wrong, as thou very well knowest.*

> 1.   Against the good & just
>   If men false witness bear,
>   They may, and, called upon, they *must*
>   Their innocence declare:
>   The debt themselves they owe;
>   And must maintain their plea,
>   And urge, in sight of every foe,
>   Their own integrity.

> 2.   A servant of the Lord
>   Insists with righteous zeal
>   Ye know, by publishing the word
>   That I have done no ill;
>   The messenger who hate
>   They hate me without cause;
>   I have not injur'd church or state,
>   I have not broke the laws. (pp. 488–9)

Ac. 25:11, *But if there be none of these things, whereof these accuse me, no man can*[83] *deliver, etc.*

> But if the clam'rous tribe
> Can nothing fairly prove,
> Nor fear nor hope, nor threat nor bribe
> Th'impartial judge should move:
> No upright ruler can
> By violence oppress,
> Or sacrifice an harmless man
> Malicious priests to please. (pp. 489–90)

Ac. 25:11, *I appeal unto Cesar.*

> 1. Prisoner of Christ, to death pursued
>   By priestly hate implacable,
>   From those who thirsted for his blood
>   He doth to Nero's self appeal,
>   More just than those who saints traduce,
>   More merciful than canker'd Jews.

> 2. Far better 'tis that righteous men
>   Into the heathen's hands should fall,
>   Than theirs, who holy things profane,
>   Themselves the Christian temple call,
>   And dare as all their own to claim
>   The church's venerable name.

> 3. The men who God profess to know,
>   But basely ministring for hire,
>   Their faith by persecution show,
>   By casting saints into the fire,
>   Their sacred power, their bitter zeal,
>   Their whole religion is from hell.

83. [Wesley followed *Notes*. The AV reads: "may."]

4. Hear this, ye Jewish elders, hear,
   And know your dreary hour is past:
   Your thunders we no longer fear,
   Judg'd by the civil Powers at last,
   The ministers to us for good,
   Th'avengers sure of guiltless blood.

5. Your courts unspiritual, unjust,
   No more shall the relapses try;
   Ye cannot into dungeons thrust,
   Or doom the innocent to die;
   Cesar receives the poor's appeal,
   And rescues us from Satan's will. (pp. 490–1)[84]

Ac. 25:[16], *It is not the manner of the Romans to deliver any man to die, before that he which is accused, &c.*

1. But you, who modern Rome foreswear,
   And for a purer faith contend,
   Is it your equitable care
   Prejudging censures to suspend?
   Can ye forbear the just to blame
   When branded with an odious name?

2. From every secret bias free
   Have ye the truth sincerely sought,
   Unmov'd by popular calumny
   Us & our foes together brought,
   Produc'd the foul-mouth'd witnesses,
   And heard us pleading face to face?

3. Your conscious hearts the answer give:
   And if our Lord we truly know,
   Godly in Him resolve to live,
   And daily in his footsteps go,
   We look not at your hands to find
   The justice due to all mankind. (pp. 492–3)

84. [Verses 1–2 appear in *Poet. Works*, XII, p. 418.]

Ac. 25:18–19, *Against whom when the accusers stood up, they brought none accusation of such things, etc.*

1. Who listen to our clam'rous foes
     Against the servants of our Lord,
   Vilest of men they must suppose
     The men by all revil'd, abhor'd;
   The croud lift up their voice so high,
     With furious, fierce, fanatic zeal,
   So loud the reverend Elders cry
     "Away with hereticks to hell!"

2. But let the witnesses stand forth,
     And all our crimes in one declare,
   We preach a Saviour's dying worth,
     The vouchers of his rise we are!
   Jesus, the Lamb for sinners slain,
     He did the general ransom give,
   He once was dead, but lives again,
     That every soul thro' Him may live. (pp. 493–4)

Ac. 25:25, *I found that he had committed nothing worthy of death.*

1. His innocence to all appears;
   The Roman Judge in public clears
     Before his fiercest foe,
   But bound himself by fear of man,
   He dares not loose the prisoner's chain,
     Or let th'Apostle go.

2. 'Tis thus, convinc'd in their own heart,
   Our judges shrink to take the part
     Of men whom all condemn:
   They must the people gratify;
   For, if they favour us, the cry
     Will then be turn'd on them. (pp. 495–6)

Ac. 26:3, *Wherefore I beseech thee to hear me patiently.*[85]

When Christ we preach the sinner's Friend,
Should they not patiently attend,
    Our testimony weigh,
And while the truth its power exerts,
Believe in Him with all their hearts,
    And then with joy obey? (p. 500)

Ac. 26:6, *And now I am judged for the hope of the promise made of God unto our fathers.*

1. Be this our only crime, To trust
    In Christ the Lord, the promis'd Seed,
Who rose to animate our dust,
    (But first to raise our spirits dead)
By Love divine on all bestow'd,
That all may live, enthron'd with God.

2. The promise to our fathers made,
    Is to their faithful offspring sure;
On this our stedfast hope is stay'd,
    And all that to the end endure
Suffering with Christ, with Christ shall rise
And grasp thro' death th'immortal prize. (p. 501)

Ac. 26:7, *Unto which promise our twelve tribes, instantly serving God day & night, hope to come; etc.*

1. True Israelites, we now believe
    The promises of God to man,
His plenitude of grace receive,
    His life reveal'd with Jesus gain,
And when our faithful Head comes down,
Inherit an eternal crown.

---

85. [Above Ac. 26:1 in Wesley's shorthand is written: "Ap. 7" (April 7).]

2. Nothing on earth but Christ we know,
   Nothing we seek but Christ alone,
And while we live his life below,
   The world accuse, condemn, disown,
And as out-landish monsters chase
The pilgrims to their heavenly place. (pp. 501–2)

Ac. 26:10, *Which thing I also did: and many of the saints did I shut up in prison; and when, etc.*

1. Blind in our natural estate,
   Of forms & notions proud,
Born of the flesh, we scorn & hate
   The sacred sons of God;
The men who trust in Jesus' death
   As hereticks we doom,
And unreform'd, the spirit breathe
   Of persecuting Rome.

2. Bishops by superstition steel'd
   Have drawn the slaughtring sword,
Bishops have oft their dungeons fill'd
   With servants of the Lord,
Cast out the saints of the Most-high
   As execrable names,
Adjudg'd the wretches vile to die,
   And drag'd them to the flames. (pp. 503–4)

Ac. 26:11, *I persecuted them even unto strange cities.*

1. Mad-men, who us for madmen take,
   But wise yourselves esteem,
Madmen in God's account, awake
   Out of your frantick dream;
Ye persecutors fierce, suspect
   Your own religious rage,
Who ravage, as an impious sect,
   God's chosen heritage.

2. Error, ye Pharisees sincere,
   Ye mean t'exterminate,
   Nor know, who hate his members here,
   That Christ himself ye hate;
   Exposing us to pain and shame,
   While in his steps we move,
   Ye act against the Saviour's name,
   Ye grieve[86] the God of love. (pp. 504–5)[87]

Ac. 26:13, *I saw a Light from heaven, above the brightness of the sun.*

Shining in his strength & height
   With full meridian glare,
With the uncreated Light
   This sun cannot compare;
True, essential Light we see,
Th'eternal Sun of righteousness,
Brightness of the Deity
   In Jesus' open face. (p. 505)

Ac. 26:13, *And them which journeyed with me, &c.*

The light reflected from his face,
   Not Jesus in the light they view'd:
The inward evidence of grace,
   This only can our fears exclude,
And raise our souls out of the dust,
And shew the God in whom we trust. (p. 505)

86. [The MS has "hate" written in the margin as an alternative to "grieve."]
87. [Verse 2 appears in *Poet. Works*, XII, p. 425.]

Ac. 26:15, *Who art thou, Lord?*

1. Prostrate in the dust, and crying
   After Thee,
   Mercy, see,
   See my soul a-dying.
   Save the conscious unbeliever,
   Save, or I
   Faint, & die,
   Die, undone forever.

2. In my last distress relieve me:
   God unknown,
   Thou alone
   Canst, & wilt forgive me;
   By thy Spirit's inspiration
   Faith impart,
   Tell my heart
   I am thy Salvation. (p. 507)

Ac. 26:26, *I am persuaded that none of these things are hidden from him: for this thing was not done in a corner.*

1. No secret practices that shun
   The day, doth true religion own,
   To mysteries of night:
   A city on an hill you see,
   A Christian man's simplicity
   Is open as the light.

2. But chiefly he, whose single aim
   And call, is, Jesus to proclaim
   And testify his grace,
   No screen, or subterfuge he seeks,
   But bold avows, whate'er he speaks,
   To all the ransom'd race. (p. 513)

Ac. 26:31, *They talked between themselves, saying, This man doth nothing worthy of death or of bonds.*

1. The man that had no evil done,
    Is in their consciences made known,
        Who yet will not receive
    The truth from Jesus' messenger,
    Embrace the free salvation here
        Or by his gospel live.

2. Still, when they hear his pardning word,
    The great ones of the earth their Lord
        With unconcern pass by;
    Content the preacher to approve,
    They will retain the sins they love
        Till unrenew'd they die. (p. 516)

Ac. 26:32, *Then said Agrippa unto Festus, This man might have been set at liberty, if he had not, etc.*

1. Guiltless the saint by all declar'd;
    But short & useless their regard,
        Their testimony vain;
    Their favor is a broken reed,
    And tells us, at our greatest need
        There is no help in man.

2. Ye sufferers who your Lord confess,
    The world perhaps in your distress
        Your innocence may own;
    But let your mind on Christ be stay'd,
    And hope for no effectual aid
        Except from Christ alone. (p. 517)

Ac. 27:29, *Fearing lest they should have fallen upon rocks, they cast four anchors out of the stern, etc.*

    Ye followers of the Lord,
    Who serve with heart sincere,
    And humbly tremble at his word,
        While sin & death are near;

Without that heavenly light
Alas, what can ye do,
Who dare not in the shades of night
Your doubtful course pursue?
Your stedfast anchor cast,
And languish for the morn;
The heavy night will soon be past,
The joyful day return:
And lo, to end your fears
And all your sins remove,
The Sun of righteousness appears,
Th'Almighty God of love. (p. 528)

Ac. 27:33, *While the day was coming on, Paul besought, &c.*

1. Who would not his advice pursue,
   He ceases not to give them new,
   He courts till he prevails:
   Love is the same, whoe'er oppose,
   Nor haughtiness nor anger knows,
   And never, never fails.

2. Their fainting souls with hope he feeds,
   And then to their frail bodies' needs
   His friendly care extends:
   A pastor will for both provide
   Till Christ rebukes the wind & tide,
   And full deliverance[88] sends. (p. 529)[89]

Ac. 27:39–40, *They discovered a creek with a shore into the which they were minded to thrust the ship, etc.*

Strugling long with wind & tide,
Should not a poor soul distrest
Labour for the port espied,
Quiet port of heavenly rest?

---

88. [The MS has "salvation" as an alternative to "deliverance."]
89. [Verse 1 appears in *Poet. Works*, XII, p. 442.]

From all earthly ties got free,
Sends he not his heart before,
Pants for full security,
Strives to make th'eternal shore? (p. 532)

Ac. 27:41, *They ran the ship aground; and the forepart, &c.*

1. The batter'd ship, by tempests tost,
    Had all the mighty shocks received,
  Clear of the rocks, and sands, and coast,
    Weather'd the storm and strangely lived;
  But when it to the land sticks fast
  In pieces dash'd, it sinks at last.

2. Thus if our hearts to earth adhere,
    Sad shipwreck of the faith we make:
  But while detach'd we persevere,
    Tho' all the storms of hell attack
  We mount above the world, we fly,
  And find our harbour in the sky. (p. 532)[90]

Ac. 28:5–6, *He shook off the beast into the fire, and felt no harm. Howbeit they looked when he, etc.*[91]

1. Our Christian savages expect
    That by the hellish viper stung,
  We soon shall feel the dire effect,
    The poison of a slanderous tongue,
  And gasp our last infected breath,
  And die the everlasting death.

2. But lo, the tooth of calumny
    Calm & unmov'd we still abide,
  From nature's fretful passion free,
    Hasty revenge & swelling pride;
  Men cannot their own spirit impart,
  Or taint a pure, believing heart.

90. [Verse 1 appears in *Poet. Works*, XII, p. 444.]
91. [Above Ac. 28:2 in Wesley's shorthand is written: "April 17."]

3. Ourselves with Jesus' mind we arm,
   And our invenom'd foes confound,
Defy their sharpest words to harm,
   Or once inflict the slightest wound,
While all the power of faith we prove
In meek invulnerable love.

4. Let Satan still their tongues employ;
   The vipers fasten'd on our fame,
The deadly things cannot annoy,
   Shook off at last into the flame:
But O, they never can expire,
The worms in that infernal fire! (pp. 536–7)[92]

Ac. 28:6, *They changed their mind, and said that he was a god.*

To opposite extreams so prone,
   The giddy, rash, misjudging croud
This moment think the saint unknown
   A murderer, and the next a god! (p. 537)[93]

Ac. 28:7, *In the same quarters were possessions of the chief man of the island, who received us, etc.*

Sent by our faithful Lord
   In every place we find
Strangers dispos'd to hear the word,
   And hospitably kind:
Our Lord their love repays,
   While of his love we tell,
And minister the balmy grace
   Their sinsick souls to heal. (p. 538)

92. [*Rep. Verse*, No. 194, pp. 229–30.]
93. [What is presumably the earlier form of this verse, in a different metre and much altered, appears in *Short Hymns*, II, p. 276, and in *Poet. Works*, XII, p. 447.]

Ac. 28:10, *Who also honoured us with many honours, &c.*

1.   Unspeakably blest
In a stranger distress'd,
Who Paul entertain,
Unawares they receive an angelical man:
Inrich'd by a wreck,
For his ministry's sake
They esteem and caress
The physician of souls, and the vessel of grace!

2.   Double honour they claim,
In Jesus his name
Who publish abroad
Salvation obtain'd by a crucified God!
When he gives them success,
We the instruments bless,
The messengers own,
But the glory ascribe to their Master alone. (pp. 539–40)

Ac. 28:11, *After three months we departed.*

1. Did not each soul throughout the isle
    (While Jesus' fervent messenger
Labour'd with unremitted toil)
    Glad tidings of his Saviour hear?
And might they not their Lord embrace,
And freely all be saved by grace?

2. The word of truth & grace & power
    Empty could not return or void;
And when his ministry was o're,
    And when, no more for Christ employ'd,
The parting saint his charge resign'd,
Surely he left his Lord behind. (p. 540)

Ac. 28:22, *But we desire to hear of thee what thou thinkest.*

1. The sentiments of those that know
    The Christian sect, are still the same:
   The faith of God reveal'd below,
    The men who truly bear his name,
   Expos'd to general enmity
   We were, and we shall always be.

2. Yet not a selfish party's cause,
    But Jesus' glory we maintain,
   Proclaim his purchase on the cross,
    His peace for every child of man,
   And still oppos'd by earth & hell
   In Jesus' strength o're all prevail. (p. 545)

Ac. 28:23, *To whom he expounded and testified the kingdom of God,
persuading them concerning Jesus, etc.*

If Christ the word bestow
 Which makes the minister,
We only live his grace to show,
 And spread his kingdom here;
Poor sinners to convince
 We labour night & day,
Persuading all to cast their sins
 And righteousness away:
We preach the righteousness
 Which Jesus shall restore,
The hidden joy, the heavenly peace,
 His kingdom, to the poor;
We faithfully impart
 Whate'er his word reveals;
And God on every contrite heart
 His genuine gospel seals. (p. 546)

At the conclusion of the manuscript are the following notes
by Charles Wesley:

Finished, April 24, 1765
The Revisal finished April 24, 1774
Another Revisal finished Jan. 28, 1779
A Third Revisal finished Febr. 29, 1780
A Fifth Revisal finished Aug. 6, 1783[94]
A Sixth finished Oct. 28, 1784
The Seventh, if not the last, finished Jan. 11, 1786
Gloria Tri-uni DEO!
The LAST finished May 11, 1787, Hallelujah. (p. 552)

94. [No fourth revisal is listed.]

OTHER SCRIPTURAL PASSAGES

OTHER SCRIPTURAL PASSAGES

Gen. 32:26, *I will not let thee go, except thou bless me.*

1. Now, in Jesu's name I pray,
   Father, take my sins away;
   Give me sight; I still am blind;
   Give me all my Saviour's mind:
   Let me enter into rest,
   Bless me,—for I will be blest.

2. Jesus is within the vail,
   Still his groans thine ears assail;
   Stronger pleadings have I none;
   Hear me, for his sake alone:
   Let me enter into rest,
   Bless me,—for I shall be blest.

3. My affections fix above,
   Rooted, grounded, in thy love
   Let me only Jesus see,
   Let me only dwell in thee;
   Let me enter into rest,
   Bless me,—for I will be blest.

4. Bruise, in me, thy hateful foe;
   Perfect me in love below;
   Let me Adam's loss regain;
   Wrestle, and the prize obtain:
   Let me enter into rest,
   Bless me,—for I will be blest.[1]

---

1. [*Arminian Magazine* (1793), p. 54.]

Exod. 33:19, *I will make all my goodness pass before thee.*

1. The God of awful power displays
   His Majesty in mercy's rays,
       Ineffably serene:
   He, that his creatures may not die,
   Th'insufferable blaze lays by;
       Thus, glorying to be seen!

2. O, gracious Father! why to man,
   So thankless, since the world began,
       Hast thou thy goodness shewn?
   Why dost thou help us to believe?
   Why dost thou bid us look, and live?
       The secret, now, make known!

3. Or, if thou wilt not yet reveal
   What only thy great self canst tell,
       Still, let us here abide!
   Let us thy goodness keep in view,
   And let thy goodness keep us true,
       Lest from thy ways we slide.[2]

Exod. 33:22, *I will cover thee with my hand while I pass by.*

While shelter'd by my Saviour's hand,
Justice, on me, has no demand;
    With boldness may I cry,
God justifies, and who condemns?
Where is the foe that harshly blames?
    Jesus himself is nigh.[3]

---

2. [*Arminian Magazine* (1793), p. 54.]
3. [*Arminian Magazine* (1793), p. 56.]

Psalm 21 Verse 13, [*Be thou exalted, Lord, in thine own strength: so will we sing and praise thy power.*]

1. Help us, Lord, shew forth thy Power;
   Now arise, Bow the Skies,
   Bring the welcom Hour.

2. Power supreme to Thee is given,
   Every Knee Bows to Thee
   Hell, and Earth, and Heaven.

3. Fiends, and Men, and Sins oppress us:
   Us redeem Thro' thy Name,
   O Almighty Jesus.

4. Thine eternal Power and Glory
   Now display, That we may
   Joyfully adore Thee.

5. Sav'd from Sin and Condemnation
   We shall sing Thee our King,
   Thee our strong Salvation.

6. Thee Almighty to deliver
   We shall praise, Sav'd by Grace,
   Sanctified for ever.[4]

Psalm 23d. (as a prayer)

1. O gentle Shepherd, hear my cry,
   And hearken as thou passest by
   To a poor wand'ring sheep;
   Relieve me with thy tender care,
   Behold my want of help; draw near
   And save me from the deep.

---

4. [MS Psalms, p. 40.]

2. Come, lead me forth to pastures green,
   To fertile meads, where all serene
     Invites to peace & rest;
   Near the still waters let me lie,
   To view them gently murmur by,
     Then bless the Ever-blest.

3. O God, thy promis'd aid impart,
   Convert my soul & change my heart,
     And make my nature pure;
   Come, change my nature into thine;
   Still lead me in the path divine,
     And make my footsteps sure.

4. When thro' the gloomy shade I roam,
   Pale death's dark vale, to endless home,
     O save me then from fear;
   Vouchsafe with love my soul to fill,
   That I in death may fear no ill,
     And only praise declare.

5. Tho' foes surround, before their face
   Prepare a table deck'd with grace,
     Thy food, O Lord, impart;
   With sacred oil anoint my head,
   And let thy mighty love o'erspread
     With joy my willing heart.

6. A pilgrim whilst on earth I rove,
   O let me all thy goodness prove;
     Let mercy end my days;
   Admit, at last, my wand'ring feet
   Thy courts to enter, Thee to greet
     With everlasting praise.[5]

5. [MS CW IV, 92, pp. 6–7.]

Ps. 45:10–11, *Hearken, O daughter, and consider, and incline thine ear; forget also thine own people, and thy father's house; so shall the king greatly desire thy beauty.*

1. Shapen in guilt, conceiv'd in sin,
   My father Adam's house, unclean,
       I now would freely leave;
   But who can wash the Ethiop white?
   'Tis thine own work, thou God of might,
       I hearken, let me live!

2. I[f] thou, indeed, desir'st this heart,
   If I would never from thee part,
       Why am I not restor'd?
   O, beautify me with thy mind!
   Lord, let my pray'r acceptance find!
       And realize thy word.[6]

Ps. 69:15, *Let not the pit shut her mouth upon me.*

1. Tophet its mouth hath open'd wide,
       To swallow up my soul;
   And still I on the brink abide
       Of the sulphureous pool.
   O let thy mercy interpose,
       While on the brink I stay;
   And suffer not the pit to close
       Its mouth upon its prey.

2. The inextinguishable fire
       Kindled in me I feel;
   And never was a sinner nigher,
       Yet not shut up in hell.
   As scorch'd I call on Jesu's name,
       Thou dying Lamb of God;
   No water can assuage the flame, —
       O quench it in thy blood!

---

6. [*Arminian Magazine* (1793), p. 56.]

3. Thou hast, if to thy wounds we look,
     For fiends incarnate died;
    The brand out of the burning took
     Extinguish in thy side:
    Thy death if Thou remembrest yet,
     Pronounce my sins forgiven,
    And raise me from the hellish pit,
     To praise thy love in heaven.[7]

Ps. 73:25, *Whom have I in heaven but thee? And there is none upon earth I desire in comparison of thee.*[8]

1. Ever nigh to those who call,
    Jesus, thou art all in all;
    Righteous Advocate of Love,
    Seated near the throne above;
    I to Salem's gates draw near,
    Fearless, when thy voice I hear.

2. Whom have I but thee to plead?
    'Twas thyself alone that bled!
    Who but thee could e'er prevail?
    Legions of archangels fail!
    Only thou to us art given,
    Only thou,—the king of heaven!

3. Whom on earth but thee have I?
    Who but thee for me would die?
    Who can ev'ry care relieve?
    Who can ev'ry blessing give?
    Who can ev'ry sickness heal?
    Who can mysteries reveal?

7. [MS Scriptural Hymns, p. 55. Verses 1 and 2 of the above poem appear in *Poet. Works*, IX, p. 306. Both the Old and New Testament sections of this MS are dated "May 11, 1783." After p. 139 in Charles Wesley's handwriting is written: "Finished May 26 1783." On p. 1 of the New Testament section is a further note: "Begun May 18 1783."]
   8. [Wesley quoted the Psalter of *The Book of Common Prayer*.]

4. When impending storms appear,
   Who can save, or who can cheer?
   Who can re-create the heart?
   Who can life and bliss impart?
   Only thou, my gracious Lord,
   Thou alone can'st all afford!

5. Let me not from thee e'er swerve,
   Only thee I'll love and serve;
   Only thou shalt be my theme,
   Only thou, resolv'd I am!
   Whom have I in heaven but thee?
   Who on earth compar'd can be.[9]

Psalm [77:1], *I will cry unto GOD with my voice even unto, &c.*

1. To the Lord in deep distress
      Cries my soul a bitter cry,
   Neither day nor night I cease,
      Till he answer from the sky,
   Eager to indulge my grief,
   Scorning all but his relief.

2. No relief on earth is found
      Still I groan beneath the load,
   Still incurable my wound,
      Till I know the pardning GOD,
   Let me then to him complain,
   Tell my Saviour all my pain.

3. By thy heaviest wrath opprest
      To thy smiting hand I turn,
   Stranger to a moment's rest,
      Stript of all my power I mourn,
   Lift mine eyes, & pine away,
   Look for help, but cannot pray.

---

9. [*Arminian Magazine* (1793), p. 55.]

4. Musing on the ancient days
    Now I weep my comforts gone
    [   ] lays
    Make my melancholy moan.[10]

Psalm LXXX (Adapted to the Church of England).

[PART I]

1. Shepherd of Souls, *the Great, the Good,*
    Who leadest *Israel* like a Sheep,
    Present to guard, and give them Food,
    And kindly in thy Bosom keep;

2. Hear thy afflicted People's Prayer,
    Arise out of thy holy Place,
    Stir up thy Strength, thine Arm make bare,
    And vindicate thy chosen Race.

3. Haste to our Help, thou GOD of love,
    Supreme Almighty King of Kings,
    Descend all-glorious from above,
    Come flying on the Cherubs' Wings.

4. Turn us again, thou GOD of Might,
    The Brightness of thy Face display,
    So shall we walk with Thee in Light,
    As Children of the Perfect Day.

5. We all shall be thro' Faith made whole,
    If Thou the Healing Grace impart,
    Thy Love shall hallow every Soul,
    And take up every sinless Heart.

6. O Lord of Hosts, O GOD of Grace,
    How long shall thy fierce Anger burn
    Against Thine own peculiar Race
    Who ever pray Thee to return!

---

10. [MS Richmond, p. 118. The poem is incomplete and the next page of the MS is blank.]

7. Thou giv'st us plenteous Draughts of Tears,
    With Tears Thou dost thy People feed,
    We sorrow, till thy Face appears,
    Affliction is our daily Bread.

8. A Strife we are to All around,
    By vile intestine Vipers torn,
    Our bitter Hous[e]hold Foes abound,
    And laugh our Fallen Church to scorn.

9. Turn us again, O GOD, and shew
    The Brightness of thy lovely Face,
    So shall we all be Saints below,
    And sav'd, and perfected in Grace.

PART II

10. Surely, O Lord, we once were Thine,
    (Thou hast for Us thy Wonders wrought)
    A generous and right noble Vine,
    When newly out of *Egypt* brought.

11. Thou didst the Heathen Stock expel,
    And chase them from their quiet Home,
    Druids, and all the Brood of *Hell*,
    And Monks of anti-Christian *Rome*.

12. Planted by thine Almighty Hand,
    Watred with Blood, the Vine took Root,
    And spread throughout the happy Land,
    And fill'd the Earth with golden Fruit.

13. The Hills were cover'd with her Shade,
    Her branchy Arms extending wide
    Their fair luxuriant Honours spread,
    And flourish'd as the Cedar's Pride.

14. Her Boughs she stretch'd from Sea to Sea,
    And reach'd to frozen *Scotia*'s Shore,
    (They once rever'd the Hierarchy,
    And bless'd the Mitre's Sacred Power).

15. Why then hast Thou abhor'd Thine own,
    And cast thy pleasant Plant away:
    Broke down her Hedge, her Fence o'er thrown,
    And left her to the Beasts of Prey?

16. All that go by pluck off her Grapes,
    Our *Sion* of her Children spoil,
    And Error in ten thousand Shapes
    Would every gracious Soul beguile.

17. The Boar out of the *German* Wood
    Tears up her Roots with baleful Power;
    The Lion roaring for his Food,
    And all the Forest Beasts, devour.

18. Deists, and Sectaries agree,
    And *Calvin* and *Socinus* join
    To spoil the Apostolic Tree
    And Root and Branch destroy the Vine.

19. Turn Thee again, O Lord our God,
    Look down with Pity from above,
    O lay aside thy vengeful Rod,
    And visit us in pard'ning Love.

PART III

20. The Vineyard which thine own right Hand
    Hath planted in these Nations see;
    The Branch that rose at thy Command
    And yielded Gracious Fruit to Thee:

21. 'Tis now cut down, and burnt with Fire,
    Arm of the Lord, awake, awake,
    Visit thy Foes in righteous Ire,
    Vengeance on all thy Haters take.

22. Look on them with thy flaming Eyes,
    The sin-consuming Virtue dart;
    And bid our fallen Church arise,
    And make us after thy own Heart.

23. To us our Nursing-Fathers raise,
    Thy Grace be on the Great bestow'd,
And let the King shew forth thy praise,
    And rise to build the House of GOD.

24. Thou hast ordain'd the Powers that be:
    Strengthen thy Delegate below;
He bears the Rule deriv'd from Thee,
    O let him All thine Image shew.

25. Support him with thy guardian Hand,
    Thy royal Grace be seen in Him,
King of a re-converted Land
    In Goodness as in Power supreme.

26. So will we not from thee go back,
    If Thou our ruin'd Church restore,
No, never more will we forsake,
    No, never will we grieve thee more.

27. Revive, O GOD of Power, revive
    Thy Work in our degenerate Days,
O let us by thy Mercy live,
    And all our Lives shall speak thy Praise.

28. Turn us again, O Lord, and shew
    The Brightness of thy lovely Face,
So shall we all be Saints below,
    And sav'd, and perfected in Grace.[11]

Psalm CXIII

1. Ye Saints and Servants of the Lord,
    The triumphs of his Name record,
        His sacred Name for ever bless;
Where'er the circling Sun displays
    His rising Beams or setting Rays,
        Due Praise to his great Name address.

11. [MS Psalms pp. 129–30; MS Cheshunt pp. 72–5; MS Clarke pp. 80–4; *Poet. Works,*
VIII, pp. 161–5 (less three verses); *Rep. Verse,* No. 118, pp. 161–5. The various readings of
the verses are summarized in *Rep. Verse.*]

2. GOD thro' the World extends his Sway,
    The Regions of Eternal Day
        But Shadows of his Glory are:
    With Him, whose Majesty excells,
    Who made the Heaven in which He dwells,
        Let no created Power compare.

3. Tho' 'tis beneath his State to view
    In highest Heavens what Angels do,
        Yet He to Earth vouchsafes his Care:
    He takes the Needy from his Cell,
    Advancing him in Courts to dwell,
        Companion of the greatest there.

4. To Father, Son and Holy Ghost,
    The GOD, whom Heaven's triumphant Host
        And suffering Saints on Earth adore,
    Be Glory, as in Ages past,
    As now it is, and so shall last
        When Earth and Heaven shall be no more.[12]

Ps. 141:4, *Let not my heart be inclined to any evil thing.*[13]

1. Father, my wretched heart I find
    To every evil thing inclin'd:
    Yet shall it be inclin'd to none
    If Thou herein reveal thy Son.

2. Who made my peace, 'tis He, 'tis He
    Must make an end of sin in me,
    Finish th'original offence,
    And take the sinful nature hence.

3. But while it doth in me remain,
    Thy grace is able to restrain,
    To quench at once the kindling fire,
    And every spark of fond desire.

12. [MS Psalms, p. 185.]
13. [Psalter of *The Book of Common Prayer*.]

4. The moment I to sin incline,
Thou canst with Energy divine
Its strong propensity controul,
And crush the rebel in my soul.

5. Wherefore to Thee with faith I cleave,
My soul into thy keeping give,
Till Thou thy Spirit's sword employ
And Christ the carnal mind destroy.

6. Then Father, Son, & Holy Ghost,
I find in Thee what Adam lost,
The struggle's past, the Conflict o're,
And born of God, I sin no more.[14]

Isaiah 62

1. For Sion's sake I will not cease
   In Agony of Prayer to cry,
No, never will I hold my Peace,
   Till God proclaim Salvation nigh.

2. Worthy in her great Saviour's Worth,
   Till Sion doth illustrious shine,
And as a burning Lamp goes forth
   The Blaze of Righteousness Divine.

3. Thy Righteousness the World shall see,
   The Gentiles on thy Beauty gaze,
And all the Kings of Earth agree,
   In wondring at thy Glorious Grace.

4. Thy Glorious Grace what Tongue can tell?
   The Lord shall a New Name impart,
The'Unutterable Name reveal,
   And write it on his People's Heart.

14. [MS CW III(a), pp. 1–2.]

5. Sion, for Thee thy GOD shall care,
      And claim thee as His just Reward,
    Thee for His Çrown of Glory wear,
      The Royal Diadem of thy Lord.

6. Outcast of GOD & Man no more,
      No more forsaken & forlorn,
    The Desolate Estate is or'e,
      For GOD shall comfort all that mourn.

7. The Widow'd Church shall married be,
      And soon a Numer'ous[15] Offspring bear,
    Thy Every Son shall comfort Thee,
      And Cherish with an Husband's Care.

8. Thy duteous Sons to Thee shall cleave,
      (The Barren Woman that keeps house)
    Nor ever more the Bosom leave
      Of their dear Mother, & their Spouse.

9. The Lord Himself Thy Husband is;
      He bought, & claims Thee for His own,
    Thy GOD delights to call thee His,
      Flesh of His Flesh, Bone of His bone.

10. The Joy that swells a Bridegroom's Breast
      When glorying or'e his long-sought Bride,
    Shall swell thy GOD of thee possest,
      Of Thee for whom He liv'd & died.

11. Prophets to Thee thy Lord hath rais'd,
      O Holy City of our God,
    Hath on thy Walls His Watchmen plac'd,
      And with a Trumpet's Voice endued.

12. They cry, & never hold their Peace,
      His Promise Day & Ni[gh]t they plead,
    Till GOD from all thy Sins release,
      And make thee like thy Glorious Head.

15. [Probably Wesley wrote "Numer'ous" for "Num'rous" inadvertently.]

13. Call on Him Now, ye Watchmen, call,
    Cry, ye Remembrancers Divine,
    Give Him no Rest who died for All,
    Till All in His pure Worship join;

14. Till GOD appear, the Faithful GOD,
    And make Jerusalem a Praise;
    And spread thro' all the Earth abroad,
    And stablish her w[i]th perfect Grace.

15. The Lord by His Right-hand hath sworn,
    The Arm of His Almighty Power,
    No more shalt Thou to Sin return,
    Thine Enemies shall no more devour.

16. Satan, the World, & Sin too long
    Have robb'd the Children of their Bread;
    Poor lab'ring Souls, they Suffer'd Wrong,
    Nor saw their Legal Toil succeed.

17. They sow'd the Ground, & did not reap,
    Planted, & did not drink the Wine:
    But I will comfort all that weep,
    And fill the Poor with Food Divine.

18. No more shall strange Desires consume
    Their Holy, pure & constant Joy,
    The Waster Pride no more shall come
    Their Gifts & Graces to Destroy.

19. Surely the Faithful seed at last
    The Labour of their Hands shall eat,
    Shall praise the Lord, & more than taste
    The Heavenly Everlasting Meat.

20. They all shall sit beneath the Vine,
    In calm inviolable Peace,
    And drink within my Courts the Wine,
    My Courts of Perfect Holiness.

21. Go thro' the Gates ('tis GOD commands,
      Workers with GOD, the Charge obey)
    Remove whater'e his Word withstands,
      Prepare, prepare his People's Way.

22. Their even Course let Nothing stop,
      Cast up the Way, the Stones remove,
    The High & Holy Way cast up,
      The Gospel-Way of Perfect Love.

23. Lift up for All Mankind to see
      The Standard of their dying GOD,
    And point them to the Shameful Tree,
      The Cross all-stain'd with Hallow'd Blood.

24. The Lord hath Glorified his Grace,
      Throughout the Earth proclaim'd His Son;
    Say ye to All the Sinful Race,
      He died for All your Sins t'Atone.

25. Sion, thy Suffering GOD behold,
      Thy Saviour & Salvation too,
    He comes, He comes! (so long foretold)
      Cloth'd with a Vest of Bloody Hue.

26. Himself prepares His People's Hearts,
      Breaks, & binds up, & wounds & heals,
    A Mystic Death, & Life imparts,
      Empties the Full, the Emptied fills.

27. He fills whom first He hath prepar'd,
      With Him the Perfect Grace is given,
    Himself is here their Great Reward,
      Their future, & their Present Heaven.

28. They Now, the Holy People nam'd,
      Their glorious Title shall express,
    From All Iniquity redeem'd,
      Fill'd with the Lord their Righteousness.

29. A Chosen, Sav'd, Peculiar Race,
Sion with all thy Sons Thou art,
Elect thro' Sanctifying Grace,
Perfect in Love & pure in Heart.

30. A People glorious all within,
Now, only now, & not before
Born from above, Thou canst not Sin,
And GOD can never leave thee more.[16]

Jer. [4:14], *Wash thy heart, O Jerusalem, that thou mayst be
saved: how long shall thy vain thoughts lodge
within thee?*

1.   How shall I wash my heart
From every thought unclean?
I cannot from my nature part,
From my besetting sin:
The grief of threescore years
Will not efface the stain:
And rivers flow, & seas of tears,
But all alas, in vain!

2.   Impossible commands
Dost Thou, O God, injoin,
And mock the work of thy own hands,
This feeble soul of mine?
Thyself must wash my heart
From all impurity
Or never, Lord, shall I have part,
Or interest in Thee.

3.   Though filled the fountain was
To pay my actual sin,
Thy blood was shed upon the cross
To make my nature clean.[17]

16. [MS Cheshunt, pp. 168–71. Verses 1–29 appear in *Poet. Works*, IV, pp. 312–16.]
17. [MS CW IV, p. 77. The four lines of verse 3 are transcribed from shorthand but the verse is incomplete.]

Jer. 31:17, *There is hope in thine end.*

1. Hope in my end, my latest hour!
   Indulg'd with this, I ask no more,
      But hug my misery,
   But suffer out my evil days,
   Nor see the Saviour's smiling face
      Till I in glory see.

2. Dark as I am, bereav'd of sight,
   In the full blaze of gospel-light,
      No longer I complain,
   With death if my Redeemer come,
   To dissipate th'infernal gloom,
      And end my sin and pain.

3. Till then my punishment I bear,
   Shut up in temporal despair,
      Wretched, and unforgiven;
   A sinner against light and love,
   Far from the banks of peace I rove,
      As far as hell from heaven.

4. But let not those in darkness dwell,
   The dreary neighbourhood of hell,
      Till life's extremity,
   Who know not yet the Saviour's ways,
   But never forfeited his grace,
      Or quench'd his Spirit, like me.

5. They need not wait their Lord to know,
   But freely to the Fountain go:
      This is the gracious day,
   This the accepted time for Them:
   They now may plunge into the stream
      And wash their sin away.

6. They now may savingly believe,
And walk in Him whom they receive
And in his love abide,
Till Jesus crowns with perfect peace,
Fills up their faith and holiness,
And takes them to his side.[18]

Hosea 14:2, *Take away all iniquity, and give good.*[19]

[I]

Take this concupiscence away,
And while Thou dost the plague remove,
Saviour, into my heart convey
The chast desire, the heavenly love:
If Thou dost my salvation will,
If Thou hast bought me with thy blood,
My heart with pure affection fill,
And bring me back redeem'd to God.[20]

[Hosea 14:2.]

[II]

1. How long, how often shall I pray,
Take all iniquity away,
And the good things bestow?
Evil alas, I still remain,
Nor can the promis'd grace obtain,
Or my Redeemer know.

2. Yet will I, urging my request,
Pray on, pray always and not rest,
And never cease to cry,
Till Thou the Spirit of faith impart,
To sprinkle, and renew my heart,
And wholly sanctify.

18. [MS Scriptural Hymns, pp. 118–19.]
19. [Wesley supplied his own translation.]
20. [MS Misc. Hymns, p. 223.]

3. Thy Spirit alone can root out sin,
    Bring the celestial kingdom in,
        My Lord and God reveal,
    (While He is mine, and I am his)
    The earnest of eternal bliss,
        The Witness, and the Seal.

4. Here then a sinner at thy feet,
    Trembling I wait, my doom to meet,
        Thy sovereign will to prove
    Which leaves me in my sins to die,
    Or bids me live, to glorify
        Whom I intirely love.[21]

Rom. 12:3, *I say to every man, not to think of himself more highly
than he ought to think.*

[I]

1. To think more highly than you ought
        Of your own gifts or grace,
    Is it a crime, a real fault,
        Or perfect harmles[s]ness?
    "'Tis nature's innocent mistake,
        "Which God will ne'er reprove,
    "The chief of saints yourself to make,
        "And perfected in love.

2. "Yourself or good, or perfect call,
        "There's no offence in this:"
    Enthusiasts count the error small,
        You only think amiss:
    Call yourselves wholly sanctified,
        No evil still they see,
    No sin in what begins with pride,
        And ends in blasphemy.[22]

21. [MS Misc. Hymns, pp. 223–4.]
22. [MS Scriptural Hymns, p. 23.]

[Rom. 12:3.]

[II]

1.   When of themselves they thought
More highly than they ought,
Adam lost his paradise,
Lucifer as lightning fell,
Hurl'd by vengeance from the skies,
Plung'd in the profoundest hell.

2.   Thus in a gracious state
Whoe'er themselves or'erate,
Blinded with the proudest pride,
Altars to themselves they raise,
Lose the blessing magnified,
Forfeit all their boasted grace.

3.   And shall we scorn to fear
The dire delusion near?
In our own persuasion trust,
In our own conceit secure,
Suddenly compleatly just,
Pure at once, as God is pure!

4.   Can we in Satan's mind
No sin, or evil find?
Madness vindicates the fault,
Nature's arrogant offence,
"Vanity an harmless thought,
Pride is perfect innocence."

5.   But taught, O Lord, of Thee,
The dangerous rock I see,
Dare not trust my treacherous heart,
Whispering—"all the work is done:"
Thou my sole discerner art,
Thou art wise and good alone.

6.   Ah! leave me not to dream
        Myself whate'er I seem:
Every towering thought restrain,
    Lest I shine in my own eyes,
Lest my faith's minutest grain
    To a fancied mountain rise.

7.   My faith Thou dost bestow,
        Thou dost its measure know:
That I may the fulness find,
    Grace, and larger grace impart,
Bless me with a sober mind,
    Bless me with an humble heart.

8.   Rather, O God, than I
        My grace shou'd magnify,
Fall the tempter's wretched prey,
    Thou who dost my bliss desire,
Take me from the evil day,
    Let me at thy feet expire.[23]

I Cor. 2:12, *We have received the Spirit which is of God.* . . .

[I]

1. God hath on us his Spirit bestow'd,
    That we his other gifts may know,
A pardon bought with Jesu's blood,
    A taste of glorious bliss below:
The Spirit our conscience certifies
    That God to man hath freely given
Wine without money, without price,
    Forgiveness, holiness, and heaven.

2. The Comforter assures our hearts,
    Our Father, to his children dear;
Fresh strength continually imparts,
    To fight, o'ercome, and persevere.

23. [MS Scriptural Hymns, pp. 24–5.]

Our Father gave to Christ alone
Fulness of grace, and heavenly powers,
But hath on us conferr'd his Son,
And Christ, and all in Christ, is ours.

3. Yet God doth not his Spirit give
To nourish self-exalting pride,
That all, the moment they receive
His grace, may know his grace untried;
Nicely the Spirit's work explain,
Or boast their faith, before they prove,
Or counting every measur'd grain,
Tell all the world how much they love.[24]

[I Cor. 2:12.]

II

1. The Lord to us who now believe
Hath the revealing Spirit given,
That when the Witness we receive,
The Holy Ghost come down from heaven,
We may our Father's goodness know,
Who did on all his Son bestow.

2. Thou send'st his Spirit into my heart,
Of Christ the Lord to testify,
And conscious that my God Thou art,
I Father, Abba Father, cry;
Assur'd th'Eternal Life Divine,
And Christ, and all in Christ, is mine.

3. The things thy free unbounded love
Hath given our dearly-purchas'd race
Are, Christ the Saviour from above,
With all his plenitude of grace,
The gift which every gift implies,
Thy whole of good in earth and skies.

---

24. [MS Scriptural Hymns, pp. 30–1. Verses 1 and 2 appear in *Poet. Works*, XIII, pp. 24–5.]

4. Thy Spirit in my heart explains
 The heavenly Gift on me bestow'd,
He shows me what my Lord contains,
 The peace and portraiture[25] of God;
The prize for ransom'd sinners won,
The glorious joy, th'immortal crown.

5. The earnest when Thou dost bestow,
 I know the blessings I possess,
My faith's sincerity I know,
 But not its infinite degrees,
I know, the grace I feel is true,
But not that I have more than you.[26]

I Cor. 3:13–14, *Every man's work shall be made manifest, &c.*

1. Howe'er the labour'd Babels rise,
 With plausible appearance fair,
Perfect in the fond bigot's eyes;
 The day shall every work declare,
The great and final day unknown
Which brings our God to judgment down.

2. The process of that dreadful day,
 Discerning truth from specious lies,
Shall every principle display,
 Shall every doctrine scrutinise,
If one with the unerring word,
The standard of our heavenly Lord.

3. He comes triumphant from above,
 His lightnings set the world on fire;
The fire shall every fabric prove,
 And if, 'midst flaming worlds entire,
'Midst burning heat thy house remain,
Thou shalt a full reward obtain.

---

25. ["Portraiture" is perhaps a reference to the *Eikon Basilike*, i.e. the royal portraiture purported to have been written by Charles I.]
26. [MS Scriptural Hymns, pp. 31–2. Verses 1–4 appear in *Poet. Works*, XIII, pp. 25–6.]

4. But if the fire thy work consume,
   Thy labour's recompence is lost;
   Yet rescued from th'apostate's doom,
   Who feebly didst on Jesus trust,
   Thou shalt out of the burning fly,
   And scarcely sav'd, attain the sky.[27]

I Cor. 4:4, *I know nothing by myself, yet am I not hereby justified.*

1. Tho' nothing by myself I know
   Of outward, or of inward sin,
   But smoothly on in duties go,
   This does not prove my conscience clean.
   By this, without thy blood applied,
   Saviour, I am not justified.

2. Tho' in my sprinkled heart I feel
   Nothing but pure, o'reflowing love,
   I am not hence impeccable,
   Or sure I never can remove,
   Of finish'd holiness possest,
   Inthron'd in everlasting rest.

3. My thoughts, O God, are not as thine:
   My wounds I may have slightly heal'd,
   Beneath this flood of love divine
   The selfish root may lie conceal'd,
   And nature whisper from within,
   "I have all grace, I have no sin."[28]

27. [MS Scriptural Hymns, pp. 35–6. Verses 2–4 appear in *Poet. Works*, XIII, pp. 27–8 and are numbered 1–3.]
28. [MS Scriptural Hymns, p. 37.]

I Cor. 5:6, *Your glorying is not good; know ye not, etc.*

1. Who glory in your ripest grace,
       Your holiest, purest, perfect love,
   Yourselves ye ignorantly praise,
       Yourselves abundantly disprove,
   Nor can by folly's fig-leaves hide
   Your glaring nakedness of pride.

2. Impatient to be disbeliev'd,
       Is it for God alone ye speak?
   Self-confident, and self-deceiv'd,
       Your own applause ye blindly seek,
   When humble, not in heart, but word,
   Ye seem to glory in the Lord.

3. The smallest spark of self-respect,
       Of self-esteem, conceal'd within,
   Doth all your boasted gifts infect,
       And turns your graces into sin;
   Self-love and vanity the leaven
   Which lifts your swelling souls to heaven.

4. While there in fancied pomp ye reign
       Fond nature's pride in secret spreads,
   With visions turns your heated brain,
       With gilded rays adorns your heads,
   Till sunk at once ye lose your light,
   Ye lose your souls in endless night.[29]

I Cor. 12:3, *No man can say that Jesus is the Lord, but, &c.*

1. Unless thy Spirit the truth reveal
       That Thou the Lord Jehovah art,
   And give me faithfully to feel
       Thy Godhead streaming through my heart,
   Thee, Jesus, Thee I cannot know,
   God over all, made flesh below.

29. [MS Scriptural Hymns, pp. 38–9; *Rep. Verse*, No. 222, pp. 246–7.]

2. But Thou, expiring on the tree,
   As very man, as very God,
   Hast bought the Holy Ghost for me
   T'apply, and witness with the blood,
   And tell this bounding heart of mine
   The blood of sprinkling is Divine.

3. Fill'd with the Spirit of faith and love,
   The God supreme I Thee adore,
   The one true God who reigns above,
   (But stain'd the cross with heavenly gore)
   Who was from all eternity,
   Who lives, for ever lives, in me.[30]

I Cor. 16:22, *If any man love not the Lord Jesus Christ let him be Anathema Maranatha.*

1. O terrible, but just Decree!
   The Wretch that doth not love his Lord,
   Worthy of every Curse is He,
   Worthy to perish undeplor'd,
   His Punishment in Hell to bear,
   And howl eternal Ages there.

2. That lost unloving Wretch am I;
   My unbelieving Heart is Stone;
   Beneath my heavy Curse I cry,
   Beneath my Want of Love I groan,
   I cannot bear, nor hide my Shame,
   But damn'd, already damn'd I am.

3. Encompast by the Dogs of Hell,
   Horror, Astonishment, and Pain,
   The never-dying Worm I feel,
   And weep, & tear my Flesh in vain,
   A desp'rate Outcast from His Face,
   I go, I rush to my own Place.

30. [MS Scriptural Hymns, pp. 41–2. Verses 1 and 2 appear in *Poet. Works*, XIII, p. 36.]

4. How thick this Outward Darkness lies!
   In what a Depth of Sin I rowl!
Palpable Night hath seal'd mine Eyes,
   The Wrath is dropt into my Soul,
These Arrows of Almighty God —
They drink up all my poison'd Blood.

5. Then let me, while I breathe my last,
   In Jesus' Name on Sinners call,
Sinners, before your Day is past,
   Love Him who lov'd & died for All,
This only Word I leave behind,
He lov'd, & died for All Mankind.[31]

II Cor. 11:29, *Who is offended, and I burn not?*

1. The least of Jesus' little ones,
   Let him offended be,
And lo, my soul indignant groans
   Beneath the injury:
If worldlings, or enthusiasts turn
   The lame out of the road,
I strait with just resentment burn
   And bear the cause to God.

2. Now, O my God, the havock see
   Which wild delusion makes,
Implunging blind credulity
   In perilous mistakes;
Who boast their perfect holiness
   They stumble the sincere,
And grieve the hearts that know thy grace
   And pain the tingling ear;

3. Who of themselves too highly think
   As wholly sanctified,
Till instantaneously they sink
   Into the gulph of pride;

31. [MS Cheshunt, p. 209.]

OTHER SCRIPTURAL PASSAGES

Who to the ladder's topmost round
    By one short step ascend,
Their sober-minded brethren wound,
    And all thy church offend.

4. The dire contagion is begun,
    The mad, fanatic sect,
If Thou permit them to go on,
    Will all thy flock infect:
Come, Jesus, stand thyself between
    The living and the dead,
Rebuke the Luciferian sin
    And let the plague be stay'd.

5. The rock of error and offence
    By faith unfeign'd remove,
By deep, perpetual penitence,
    By pure, impartial love;
By true, substantial holiness
    Take all our pride away,
And then in thy unclouded face
    We see the perfect day.[32]

II Cor. 12:9, [*And he said unto me, My grace is sufficient for thee: for my strength is made perfect in weakness. Most gladly therefore will I rather glory in my infirmities, that the power of Christ may rest upon me.*]

1. Full oft have I besought Thee, Lord,
    To take this thorn away,
And still against my foe abhor'd
    In agony I pray;

2. Rebuking the malicious fiend,
    O bid his buffets cease,
The painful hour of darkness end,
    And give me back my peace.

32. [MS Scriptural Hymns, pp. 54–6.]

3. Again I ask, this torturing ill
     Command it to depart;
   I ask in vain: for yet I feel
     The mischief in my heart.

4. Thou dost not yet the plague remove,
     But stayst thyself with me,
   Thy all-sufficient grace to prove
     In my infirmity.

5. In wisest love Thou dost delay
     To answer my request,
   That, while I for deliverance stay,
     Thy power on me may rest:

6. While kept I every moment find
     Thy arms my sure defence,
   And glory in my weakness join'd
     To thy Omnipotence.[33]

Gal. 4:16, *Am I therefore become your enemy, etc.*

1. Because his self-deceit I show,
   Am I the self-deceiver's foe,
   When on the pinacle of pride
   He sits, as wholly sanctified?
   Or woud I rob him of his crown
   Who gently bring the boaster down?

2. Ye great and good in your own eyes,
   Who instantaneous saints arise,
   Without the Spirit's throes or groans
   Born babes, and full-grown men at once,
   To God's own oracles attend,
   The counsels of your heavenly Friend.

33. [MS Misc. Hymns, pp. 302-3.]

3. Deny yourselves, the cross embrace
   And walk in all his righteous ways,
   With lawful violence contend,
   Thro' all the means expect the end,
   From strength to strength go on to prove
   The truth of grace is humble love.[34]

Gal. 6:3, *If a man think himself to be something, etc.*

1. Who of himself as something thinks,
      Himself he doth not know,
   But from his lofty summit sinks
      Into the gulph below;
   A sinful nothing, he forgets
      His sin and nothingness,
   Himself by vain presumption cheats,
      And forfeits all his grace.

2. Woud Paul himself as quite secure,
      As crown'd already, say,
   "I, I am holy, perfect, pure,
      "And cannot err, or stray?"
   The holiest doth himself disclaim,
      The chief of sinners call,
   "Less than the least, I nothing am,
      "And Christ is all in all." [35]

I Tim. 1:15, *Of whom I am chief.*

   He will not speak a greater word:
   The aged follower of his Lord,
   Ready for Jesus' sake to die,
   Declares, "The chief of sinners I!"
   But now we hear a younkling say,
   "Pardon'd, and perfect in a day, [36]
   The instantaneous witness see,
   The chief of saints admire in me!"[37]

34. [MS Scriptural Hymns, pp. 62–3.]
35. [MS Scriptural Hymns, pp. 66–7.]
36. [Originally Wesley wrote "perfected today."]
37. [MS Scriptural Hymns, p. 82.]

Heb. 5:9, *He became the Author of eternal salvation unto all that obey him.*

> While I hang upon thy passion
>   Peace, and power in Thee I have,
> Author now of my salvation,
>   Thou shalt to the utmost save:
> Govern'd by the life of love,
> Freely in thy paths I move:
> Thus constrain'd, a true believer
> Must obey, and live for ever.[38]

Heb. 10:38, *The just shall live by faith.*

> O that I might the power receive
> The simple life of faith to live,
> A stranger by the world unknown,
> To live, shut up with Christ alone!
> Jesus, my real Life Thou art,
> Inspire Thyself into my heart,
> And fill'd with purity divine
> I live, thro' endless ages thine.[39]

James 1:20, *The wrath of man worketh not the righteousness of God.*

> 1.   The wrath of frantic man
>   Is impotent and vain,
>   Serves for no religious use,
>   Works no real righteousness;
>   Evil cannot good produce,
>   Cannot cause th'effects of grace.

38. [MS Scriptural Hymns, p. 96.]
39. [MS Scriptural Hymns, p. 101.]

2.   Then let me calmly flee,
Meek Lamb of God, to Thee:
From the rage of inbred pride
Thou my only refuge art;
Save me shelter'd in thy side,
In the centre of thy heart.

3.   There, there in patient peace
Let me my soul possess,
Hid from nature's furious zeal,
Buried in a sea of blood,
Fill'd with love unspeakable,
Arm'd with all the mind of God.[40]

James 5:13, *Is any merry? let him sing psalms.*

1. In the Belov'd accepted,
For Jesus' sake forgiven,
At the word of a King
We merrily sing
The Delight of earth and heaven.

2. Triumphant in his favor,
With joyful acclamation,
We thankfully raise
A full Anthem of praise
To the God of our Salvation.[41]

I Peter 3:18, *Christ suffered, that he might bring us to God.*

Jesus, purge our foul transgression
In the fountain of thy blood,
By thy powerful intercession
Bring me to my gracious God:
Sinners' Friend, I humbly claim
Pardon, glory in thy name,
Pardon now, thy passion's wages,
Glory thro' eternal ages.[42]

---

40. [MS Scriptural Hymns, p. 108. Verses 1 and 2 appear in *Poet. Works*, XIII, p. 166.]
41. [MS Scriptural Hymns, p. 109; *Rep. Verse*, No. 225, p. 249.]
42. [MS Scriptural Hymns, p. 110; *Rep. Verse*, No. 226, p. 249.]

I John 1:8, *If we say that we have no sin, etc.*

1. Before He purge my sin away
   And make me truly free,
   Is it a little thing to say,
   "I have no sin in me?"
   Is it no sin, to take my ease
   As wholly sanctified,
   And slightly heal the sore disease,
   The loathsom plague of pride?

2. Perfection if I boldly claim,
   My own fond heart believe,
   Myself (while full of sin I am)
   I fatally deceive:
   Howe'er I boastingly profess
   My spotless purity,
   Of real faith, and solid grace,
   There is no truth in me.

3. No true humility, and love,
   No true repentance I,
   No just, or holy tempers prove,
   But all I am's a lie:
   And if incorrigibly proud
   Myself I still miscall,
   I stand a witness false for God,
   Till into hell I fall.[43]

I John 3:5, *He was manifest to take away our sins.*

1. Eternal Son of God most high,
   Whose glory fills both earth and sky,
   Return, th'Incarnate Deity,
   And manifest thyself to me.

---

43. [MS Scriptural Hymns, pp. 120–1.]

2. Who didst for all mankind atone,
   Still make thy gracious purpose known,
   And answer on this soul of mine
   Thy sin-extirpating design.

3. My Saviour to the utmost here,
   Appear, that sin may disappear:
   It cannot in thy presence stay,
   But flies, and vanishes away.

4. Come, and thy precious Self reveal,
   Satan, with all his works t'expel,
   And more than conquering sin, remove,
   Destroy it, by thy perfect love.

5. Explain, great God, the mystery,
   Emptied thyself, to empty me,
   Made flesh, to finish inbred sin
   And endless righteousness bring in.

6. To crown these infinite desires
   Infinite Good my soul requires;
   Come then, and fill this boundless void,
   Fulness of Grace, of Love, of God![44]

I John 4:1, *Believe not every spirit.*

But is it possible to find
Such weakness in an human mind?
But is the blind credulity,
The dotage natural to me?
Yes; if Thou didst not stand between,
Good God, I coud believe the men,
Who, spite of all thy words, profess
Their instantaneous perfectness![45]

44. [MS CW III(a), p. 5; MS Misc. Hymns, p. 221. MS CW III(a) has a variant shorthand version.]
45. [MS Scriptural Hymns, p. 135.]

I John 5:6, *This is He that came by water & blood.*

> By water he came, and by blood
> My God who on Calvary died,
> A fountain of purity flow'd,
> A river of life from his side:
> The water it washes our hearts,
> The blood for our sins did atone,
> And when He his Spirit imparts
> We feel, the two currents are one.[46]

46. [MS Scriptural Hymns, p. 136.]

INDEX TO SECTION VI

OTHER SCRIPTURAL PASSAGES[1]

The scriptural passages for the books of Matthew, Mark, Luke, John, and Acts are arranged chronologically in Sections I–V respectively; therefore, they are not listed separately. There follows an index to Section VI.

1. For three fragmentary poems based on Hebrews 4:16, Philippians 2:6–7, and Revelation 3:19, see Section X (Fragments) in Volume III of *The Unpublished Poetry of Charles Wesley*.